WITHDRAWN BY THE
UNIVERSITY OF MICHIGAN

NATIONALISM IN INTERNATIONAL RELATIONS

Advances in Foreign Policy Analysis
Series Editor: Alex Mintz

Foreign policy analysis offers rich theoretical perspectives and diverse methodological approaches. Scholars specializing in foreign policy analysis produce a vast output of research. Yet, there were only very few specialized outlets for publishing work in the field. Addressing this need is the purpose of **Advances in Foreign Policy Analysis**. The series bridges the gap between academic and policy approaches to foreign policy analysis, integrates across levels of analysis, spans theoretical approaches to the field, and advances research utilizing decision theory, utility theory, and game theory.

Members of the Board of Advisors:

Allison Astorino-Courtois
Steve Chan
Margaret Hermann
Valerie Hudson
Patrick James
Jack Levy

Zeev Maoz
Bruce M. Russett
Donal Sylvan
Steve Walker
Dina A. Zinnes
Betty Hanson

Published by Palgrave Macmillan:

Integrating Cognitive and Rational Theories of Foreign Policy Decision Making
  Edited by Alex Mintz

Studies in International Mediation
  Edited by Jacob Bercovitch

Media, Bureaucracies, and Foreign Aid: A Comparative Analysis of United States, the United Kingdom, Canada, France, and Japan
  By Douglas A. Van Belle, Jean-Sébastien Rioux, and David M. Potter

Civil-Military Dynamics, Democracy, and International Conflict: A New Quest for International Peace
  By Seung-Whan Choi and Patrick James

Economic Sanctions and Presidential Decisions: Models of Political Rationality
  By A. Cooper Drury

Purpose and Policy in the Global Community
  By Bruce Russett

Modeling Bilateral International Relations: The Case of US-China Interactions
  By Xinsheng Liu

Beliefs and Leadership in World Politics: Methods and Applications of Operational Code Analysis
  Edited by Mark Schafer and Stephen G. Walker

Approaches, Levels and Methods of Analysis in International Politics
  Edited by Harvey Starr

The Bush Administrations and Saddam Hussein: Deciding on Conflict
  Alex Roberto Hybel and Justin Matthew Kaufman

Nationalism in International Relations: Norms, Foreign Policy, and Enmity
  By Douglas Woodwell

NATIONALISM IN INTERNATIONAL RELATIONS

NORMS, FOREIGN POLICY, AND ENMITY

Douglas Woodwell

NATIONALISM IN INTERNATIONAL RELATIONS
Copyright © Douglas Woodwell, 2007.

All rights reserved. No part of this book may be used or reproduced in any manner whatsoever without written permission except in the case of brief quotations embodied in critical articles or reviews.

First published in 2007 by
PALGRAVE MACMILLAN™
175 Fifth Avenue, New York, N.Y. 10010 and
Houndmills, Basingstoke, Hampshire, England RG21 6XS
Companies and representatives throughout the world.

PALGRAVE MACMILLAN is the global academic imprint of the Palgrave Macmillan division of St. Martin's Press, LLC and of Palgrave Macmillan Ltd. Macmillan® is a registered trademark in the United States, United Kingdom and other countries. Palgrave is a registered trademark in the European Union and other countries.

ISBN-13: 978–1–4039–8449–4
ISBN-10: 1–4039–8449–2

Library of Congress Cataloging-in-Publication Data is available from the Library of Congress.

A catalogue record for this book is available from the British Library.

Design by Newgen Imaging Systems (P) Ltd., Chennai, India.

First edition: September 2007

10 9 8 7 6 5 4 3 2 1

Printed in the United States of America.

CONTENTS

List of Figures   vii

List of Tables   ix

Acknowledgments   xi

1   Introduction   1

PART I

2   Nationality, Nation, and Ethnicity   13

3   Sovereignty and Self-Determination: Conflicting Norms as the Basis for International Conflict   25

4   The Determinants of Aggressive Behavior in Irredentist-Type Situations   41

5   Empirical Assessment   55

PART II   Introduction to Case Studies

6   Somalia, Ethiopia, and Kenya   99

7   India, Pakistan, and China   129

8   Greece and Turkey   157

9   Conclusions and Implications   187

Notes   201

Bibliography   211

Index   219

LIST OF FIGURES

1.1	Transborder Dyads in the International System	3
1.2	Theoretical Framework and Interrelation of Models	5
3.1	Causal Chain Linking Transborder Demographics to Bilateral Instability	27
3.2	Irredentist-type and Contending Government Systemic Interactions	35
4.1	Foreign Policy Formulation in Homeland States	42
6.1	Percentage of MID and Fatal MIDs per Dyad-years in Global Regions	100
6.2	GDP per capita (in Real 1996 U.S. Dollars)—Kenya and Somalia	121
6.3	Somalia GDP per capita (in Real 1996 U.S. Dollars) and MIDs Initiated	122
6.4	Somalia–Kenya–Ethiopia Capabilities	123
7.1	Pakistani GDP per capita (in Real 1996 U.S. Dollars)	146
7.2	Ratio of Indian to Pakistani Capabilities	147
7.3	Predicted Bilateral Dispute Probabilities and Actual Pakistani Dispute Initiation	148
8.1	Greco-Turkish Bilateral Relations during Different Eras	158
8.2	Capability Index Scores (pre-World War II)	182
8.3	Capability Index Scores, 1945–1991	182

LIST OF TABLES

1.1	Demographics and Associated Nationalism	2
1.2	Major Wars and Transborder Nationality (1946–1990)	8
3.1	International and Societal Norms, Predictive Relationships	28
3.2	Predicted Effect of Norms on State Behavior	29
5.1	Normative-Demographic Model Results	62
5.2	The Effect of Significant Systemic Variables on Bilateral MID and FATAL Probability	64
5.3	The Effect of Significant Systemic Variables on TERRMID, POLMID, and GOVMID Probability	65
5.4	Factors Affecting Bilateral MIDS during the Period 1992–2001 in Comparison with the Period 1951–1991	66
5.5	Domestic Foreign Policy Formulation Model Results (For Putatively Irredentist Homeland States)	68
5.6	Core Models—(Domestic Foreign Policy Model)	69
5.7	Domestic Foreign Policy Core Model—Baseline Probability Changes	70
5.8	Classification Tree Interactive Regression Results	72
5.9	Hypothesis Outcomes and Associated Variables	74
5.10	Factors Associated with Increased Dispute Initiation Solely within Irredentist-type Dyads and within Both Irredentist-type and "General" (Non-Transborder) Dyads	77
6.1	Predicted versus Actual MIDs and Fatal MIDs in Dyads	101
6.2	Somali Nationalism and Relations with Kenya	104
6.3	Somali Nationalism and Relations with Ethiopia	113
6.4	Somali Decision-making Factors and Fatal MID Initiation	119
7.1	Predicted versus Actual Bilateral MIDs and Fatal MIDs in Dyads	130
8.1	Military Interventions and subsequent Greek and Turkish Foreign Policies	179

ACKNOWLEDGMENTS

The involvement of many friends and colleagues made this work possible. First, I must thank Nicholas Sambanis and Bruce Russett for the many, many hours that they have spent reviewing my work and seeing me through this effort from start to finish.

I would also like to thank Sharon Goetz and Chinyelu Lee for their editorial assistance and suggestions as well as their support and friendship.

I am grateful to James Vreeland, John Lapinski, and Keith Darden, who took time off from their busy schedules to offer their input at different phases of the research and writing process.

I also extend my appreciation to the faculty of the Department of History and Political Science at the University of Indianapolis for offering me my current position (without which I may not have completed this project).

Last, but not least, I would like to thank my parents for their support and patience over the many years I spent as a "professional student."

CHAPTER 1

INTRODUCTION

Geopolitical struggles surrounding the competing ideologies of communism, capitalism, fascism, and democracy heavily influenced the course of events in twentieth century international relations. However, focusing on great powers, great wars, and great ideologies lends itself to the neglect of what has been the one consistent source of conflict throughout the century—the influence and destabilizing implications associated with the pursuit of nationalist objectives by revisionist states. From the Balkan Wars to the Gulf War and beyond, nationalist goals have led not simply to the fracturing of states and empires, but to conflict among preexisting states as well.

Transborder Nationalism and Transborder Nationalities

The term nationalism, as used in this work, and further explicated in the next chapter, refers to preferences stressing the rejection of excessive or illegitimate foreign influence and/or control over national populations or territory. This volume investigates the effect of nationalism on international relations by examining situations in which state boundaries divide national groups. I hypothesize that given the presence of demographic situations involving these *transborder nationalities*, interstate relations will systematically suffer in comparison to cases in which a transborder presence is absent. Nationalism arising from transborder situations spurs aggressive state policies that sow the seeds of regional suspicion, enmity, and instability.

Three broad demographic situations affect relationships between states by introducing the potential for nationalist preferences into the calculations of foreign policy decision makers. The three demographic situations are referred to as

1. *minority-majority* situations—the majority of one state is constituted by one national group whereas another state has a sizeable, or politically notable, minority population of the same group;
2. *majority-majority* situations—the majority of the population of two states is constituted by the same national group; and
3. *minority-minority* situations—two states each have a sizeable, or politically notable minority of the same national group.

Table 1.1 Demographics and Associated Nationalism

Demographic Situation	Associated Nationalism
Minority-Majority (MINMAJ)	Irredentist-type
Majority-Majority (MAJMAJ)	Contending Government
Minority-Minority (MINMIN)	Minority-Minority

Each of these demographic constellations is associated with a different type of potential transborder nationalism: irredentist-type, contending government, and minority-minority nationalism (see table 1.1). The three types of nationalism may breed instability and mutual suspicion between states, although to different degrees and in different ways. The existence of regionally unstable interstate relations does not require concrete manifestations of nationalist aggression by governments. The very *threat* of potential aggression by revisionist states seeking the recovery of, or interfering with, diaspora[1]-inhabited territory is sometimes sufficient to breed mistrust and violence.

The first type of nationalism, associated with minority-majority demographic clusters, is *irredentist-type nationalism*, which represents the preferences of nationalists within a *homeland state* for higher levels of self-determination for conationals within a *kin state*.[2] At its strongest, irredentist nationalism seeks to eliminate control of a foreign government (kin state) over a diaspora group and the incorporation of that group and the territory it inhabits within the homeland state. I tend to employ the term irredentist-"type" nationalism, however, to connote the fact that policies may be designed to promote higher levels of conational self-determination[3] rather than seeking overt annexation of a territory.

A precondition for the existence of irredentism, as it is commonly used, is that a segment of a national group exists in significant numbers in two or more states. For the sake of clarity, *the usage of the terms irredentism and irredentist-type nationalism in this work will only be associated with demographic situations in which the shared nation constitutes the majority of the population in at least one state and a minority of the population of another* (i.e., "minority-majority" transborder demographics). On the other hand I label examples such as the Kurdish situation, whereby the nationality in question never forms the majority of a single state's population, as a distinct category of "minority-minority" nationalism.

I refer to the second type of transborder nationalism, associated with majority-majority demographic populations, as *contending government* nationalism. Contending government nationalism exists when two or more governments claim legitimate ethnonational representation of the peoples and territories of the same nation. Concerned primarily with the division of state control within a larger national community, contending government nationalism can be broken down into stronger and weaker forms. Hechter (2000) refers to the strongest form as "unification nationalism." Unification nationalism, brought to fruition, implies the transfer of power from two or more state authorities to a single state authority—either peacefully or through violent "regime change" and absorption. Governments may also be willing to accept more limited territorial gains that fall short of the wholesale destruction of another state. As with irredentist-type situations, the presence of a common nation residing on both sides of an international border promotes limited annexations within contending government demographic situations.

Contending government nationalism occurs between states that might be considered administrative divisions of a larger nation, meaning borders themselves lack the same strength of legitimacy accorded to states with borders dividing more divergent populations. Although this work focuses primarily on irredentist-type nationalism, the importance of contending government nationalism in terms of the larger scope of transborder national issues will be frequently noted and periodically analyzed, where appropriate, alongside the primary focus on irredentism. As such, the cursory treatment of contending government dyads will provide an important starting point for further research investigating the highly destabilizing effect that such nationalism introduces into interstate relations.

A third form of transborder nationalism involves ties between minority groups within different states. Although such ties are interesting in their own right, the international implications of transborder minority-minority groups are less profound than those involving irredentist-type (as defined earlier) and contending government demographics, because, in most cases, one would not expect such shared minorities to have high levels of control over the foreign policy decisions *within either* of the states in which they reside. Thus, while irredentist-type and contending government transborder situations represent a systematic source of foreign policy grievance for the states involved, these same states cannot be expected to behave as aggressively when only minority groups are involved. Because much of this work involves issues of state structure and foreign policy preferences, I only accord cursory treatment to shared minority demographics due to the presumed

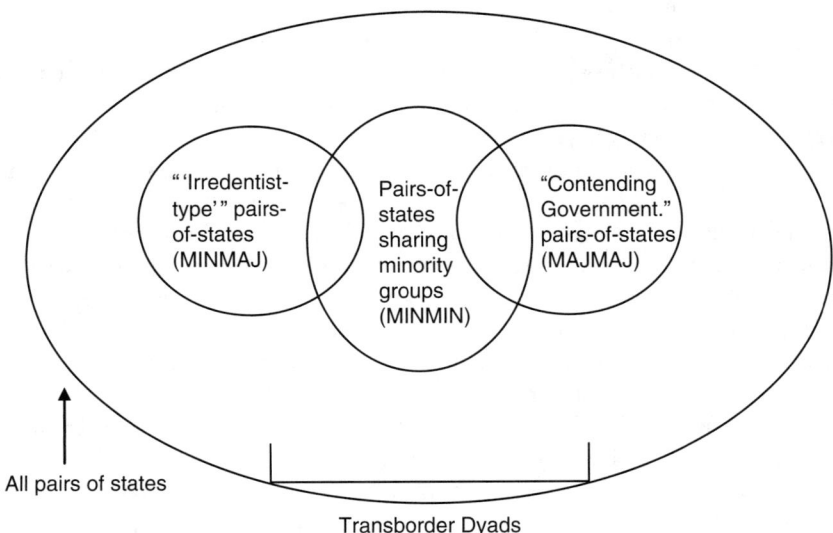

Figure 1.1   Transborder Dyads in the International System

lack of access to policy formulation and execution of minority groups. Henceforth, when I refer to *transborder nationalism* (unless otherwise stated) I am referring to irredentist-type and contending government nationalism.

Employing criteria I describe in chapter 5, only a minority of the pairs of countries (henceforth referred to as dyads) in the world share a politically relevant transborder nationality.[4] Even when restricting the sample to contiguous dyads, only about 40 percent of dyads fall into one of the three categories of transborder groups described earlier. Figure 1.1 provides a visual representation of transborder demographics, as labeled throughout this work, within the larger context of all contiguous pairs of states.[5]

Transborder Nationality and International Conflict: A General Model

Two sets of causal mechanisms are related to heightened conflict rates specifically among irredentist-type and contending government dyads. The first set of conditions involves the *influence of norms* in causing higher rates of conflict among these relevant transborder dyads during different periods and relative to nontransborder (and minority-minority) dyads overall. To elucidate what is described as the "baseline" level of dispute among dyads, I model three basic combinations of international and societal (or "local") norms and their expected influence on state behavior. While norms are certainly not the *only* influence over the foreign policies of states, this work argues that they may represent a systematic factor influencing state behavior.

When the influence of *international norms of sovereignty*, which promote peaceful interstate relations, impact executive foreign policy decision making to a greater extent than *localized norms of self-determination*, which are associated with preferences for nationalist foreign policy goals, relations between states will tend to be peaceful. This is generally the case with dyads (pairs of states) that are *not* characterized by transborder demography.

When the opposite is true and domestic norms of national self-determination are clearly stronger than international norms of sovereignty, relations will tend to be strongly conflictual. This is most evident in irredentist-type dyads when a diaspora group is involved in rebellion against a kin state—a situation which invokes very high levels of nationalist sentiment among domestic audiences in a homeland state.

The last combination concerns situations when international norms of sovereignty and domestic norms of nationalism/self-determination are either both strong or both weak—roughly "canceling one another out." In this situation it is difficult to determine what policies a state will pursue (a situation referred to later as foreign policy "indeterminacy"), creating high levels of intradyadic distrust. This situation characterizes the most frequent state of affairs within transborder dyads.

Under conditions involving roughly equivalent international and societal-level normative pressures, it is important to understand how decision makers decide whether to pursue more aggressive or more passive policies. According to Saideman (2001: 219), when "the norm of territorial integrity competes with the norm of self-determination," the situation is such that it "allows states to consider

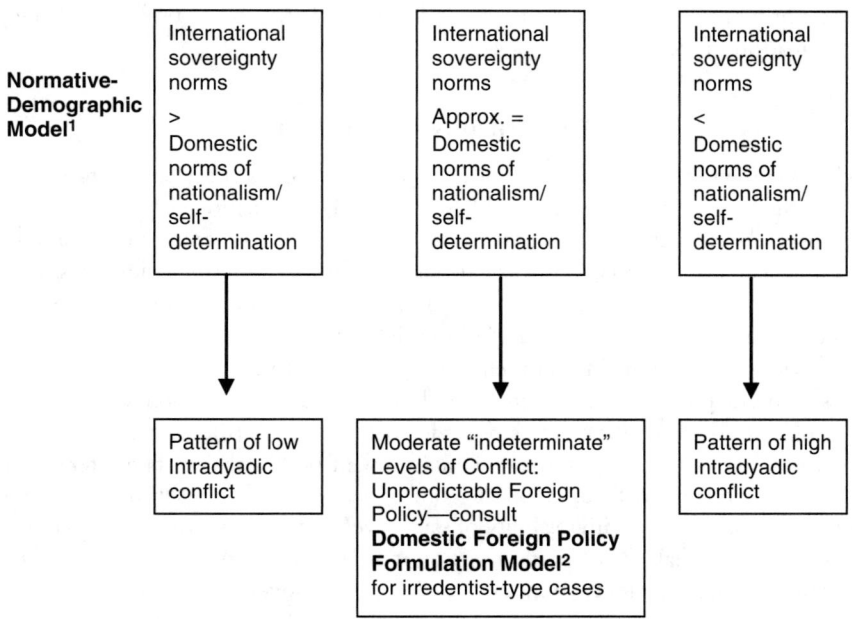

Figure 1.2 Theoretical Framework and Interrelation of Models

Notes:
1. The Normative-Demographic Model is described in chapter 3.
2. The Domestic Foreign Policy Formulation Model is described in chapter 4.

other factors, so domestic political concerns may become more important." Along this line of analysis suggested by Saideman, this work examines not only normative issues in international relations, but also seeks to understand some of the domestic considerations that may "tip" policies toward either peace or aggression in situations when normative prescriptions for action are muddled.

The second part of the model attempts to unravel the processes associated with uncertain foreign policy outcomes in transborder states by focusing on the particular circumstances and domestic structures within irredentist-type homeland states that affect decision making. Although such dyads are expected to be more conflictual in general than nontransborder dyads, specific factors, such as the presence of military influence over homeland state policy or the relative political and economic conditions of diaspora groups, may provide a greater impetus for dispute initiation within the greater framework of already tense bilateral relations.

Thus, the joint causal model (summarized in figure 1.2) suggested in this work has both (1) a normative-demographic component, which explains how overall patterns of bilateral relations exist that are conditioned by norms deriving their impact from the nature of transborder demographics, and (2) a domestic component, which deals specifically with situations wherein it is unclear how foreign policy will be manifested due to conflic-ting international and domestic normative pressures on executives. This general model is analyzed and explained in greater depth in chapter 2 (the normative-demographic model) and chapter 3 (the domestic foreign policy formulation model).

The Structure of This Work

This volume begins by establishing the conceptual framework necessary to understand the theoretical mechanisms that cause transborder nationalist preferences to manifest themselves in international relations. Chapter 2 describes how domestic nationalism arises and creates societal demands on executive decision makers to adopt aggressive policies that translate into bilateral hostility among transborder states. The chapter introduces a working definition of nationalism and describes how individual nationalist sentiment ultimately helps foster collective action, creates domestic pressures on executives, and translates into foreign policy preferences for aggression in situations of transborder nationality. Furthermore, the chapter explores the international normative environment within which state interactions take place, particularly focusing on the conflict between norms of self-determination and norms stressing the inviolability of state sovereignty. As a term largely synonymous with nationalism, self-determination represents the antithesis of international norms of state sovereignty, because the idea of state sovereignty validates the rule of a state controlled by foreigners over members of other nationalities.

Chapter 3 introduces the normative-demographic model that explains why irredentist-type and contending government demographics are associated with higher dispute rates among states sharing similar nationalist groups. When nations are divided by state borders, state leaders will be pressured from below by societal norms of nationalism and self-determination and from above by international norms of sovereignty. This tension often results in unpredictable foreign policies enacted by "majority" national states, and distrust and defensive forms of aggression by states sharing a national group with them. This chapter suggests a series of testable hypotheses examining the link between demographics and interstate relations, with the understanding that intangible normative factors link these tangible factors to interstate behavior.

While norms condition state behavior, specific foreign policies vary depending upon mediating domestic considerations, particularly in terms of how political structures channel the interests of various domestic audiences. Chapter 4 examines factors influencing the decision-making processes of homeland state leaders within irredentist-type contexts, including: the role of military influence on decision making; the degree to which executives are insulated from foreign policy failures; how diaspora rebellion affects public pressures on an executive; how relative balances of power constrain potential policy options. The domestic foreign policy formulation model presented in this chapter suggests factors that are particularly useful in understanding foreign policy behavior by homeland irredentist states in particular circumstances for which the normative-demographic model does not account.

Chapter 5 presents a series of empirical tests of the theories presented in the earlier chapters. It begins by defining how key concepts are operationalized into a series of key and control variables that are used to test the hypotheses of the earlier chapters. Next, the chapter describes the econometric methods through which these variables are tested. Last, the empirical results of the models are presented and the implications of the findings are discussed with an eye toward utilizing the findings as the theoretical basis for the case studies found in the following chapters.

Chapters 6–8 introduce several case studies to illustrate the domestic and international mechanisms characterizing cases in which transborder nationalism is a factor influencing international interactions. Each case study involves a focused comparison of the relations among two or three states, and the underlying national dynamics involved in these relations over several decades.

Chapter 6 examines the role of irredentist-type nationalism in the trilateral relations of Somalia, Kenya, and Ethiopia. I contrast the bilateral relations of Somalia and Ethiopia with those of Somalia and Kenya. In both cases a significant Somali diaspora groups resided over the borders in Ethiopia and Kenya. However, due to factors such as the relative economic conditions of these diaspora and the timing of diaspora militancy, relations between Somalia and these two states took different paths. Relations between Ethiopia and Kenya, which lack a transborder nationality, are also contrasted with the irredentist-type dyads. Finally, the chapter also examines differences in Somali policies during different periods that arise due to changes in societal normative pressures, government structures, and international constraints.

Chapter 7 examines relations among India, Pakistan, and China over the past decades. While China and India went to war in the early 1960s, the depth of hostility between these two states has paled in comparison to that existing between India and Pakistan. Clearly, a major part of the reason for continued Pakistani hostility lies in the outstanding irredentist grievances held by the Pakistani state concerning Kashmir. Though India and Pakistan have witnessed periods of relative peace during the past decades, however, this chapter will explain why Pakistani leadership has adopted different foreign policies during different periods.

Chapter 8 traces the bilateral relationship of Turkey and Greece, in particular focusing on the period since the First World War. The relations between these two states are particularly interesting because the subject of interest—the presence of transborder national groups and their effect on interstate affairs—actually varies during the century. Prior to the 1920s, both states had a large diaspora from the other present within their borders. Due to forced expulsion and later a more orderly population exchange under the auspices of the League of Nations, the size of the diaspora population within each state shrank greatly. The elimination of outstanding issues surrounding treatment of each state's diaspora brought about an era of peace between the two states that lasted 30 years. Friendly relations, however, have been absent for much of the last half century due to introduction of the Cyprus issue, which it will be argued introduced diaspora-oriented conflicts similar to those that had existed before the 1920s.

Finally, chapter 9 summarizes the findings and suggests some possible implications for the future, including suggesting some potential emerging international trouble spots. The chapter also suggests potential steps that might be taken by states involved in irredentist disputes or outside actors that would mitigate the explosive nature of these situations. The recommendations represent a direct extension of the theoretical and empirical findings of earlier chapters, as well as more nuanced lessons derived from the case studies. With creative and forceful international diplomacy, the destabilizing impact of transborder nationalism on international affairs can be mitigated—at least to some degree.

Transborder Nationalism as a Major Correlate of Interstate Conflict—Final Introductory Thoughts

The vitriol accompanying disputes in the Middle East, Kashmir, the Korean peninsula, and many other regional hotspots simply cannot be readily explained by any of the major contemporary international relations paradigms—because they are qualitatively different from most interactions within the state system. While

Table 1.2 Major Wars and Transborder Nationality (1946–1990)

War	Start Date	End Date	Description
First Kashmir	July 17, 1948	January 1, 1949	MINMAJ
Palestine	May 15, 1948	July 18, 1948	MINMAJ
Korean	June 24, 1950	July 27, 1953	MAJMAJ
Russo-Hungarian	October 23, 1956	November 14, 1956	–
Sinai	October 29, 1956	November 6, 1956	MINMAJ
Assam	October 20, 1962	November 22, 1962	–
Vietnamese	February 7, 1965	April 30, 1975	MAJMAJ
Second Kashmir	August 5, 1965	September 23, 1965	MINMAJ
Six Day	June 5, 1967	June 10, 1967	MINMAJ
Israeli-Egyptian	March 6, 1969	August 7, 1970	MINMAJ
Football	July 14, 1969	July 18, 1969	MAJMAJ
Bangladesh	December 3, 1971	December 17, 1971	MINMAJ
Yom Kippur	October 6, 1973	October 24, 1973	MINMAJ
Turko-Cypriot	July 20, 1974	July 29, 1974	MINMAJ
Vietnamese-Cambodian	May 1, 1975	January 7, 1979	MINMAJ
Ethiopian-Somalian	August 1, 1977	March 14, 1978	MINMAJ
Ugandan-Tanzanian	October 30, 1978	April 12, 1979	–
Sino-Vietnamese	February 17, 1979	March 10, 1979	MINMAJ
Iran-Iraq	September 22, 1980	August 20, 1988	MINMAJ
Falklands	March 25, 1982	June 20, 1982	–
Israel-Syria (Lebanon)	April 21, 1982	September 5, 1982	MINMAJ
Sino-Vietnamese	January 5, 1987	February 6, 1987	MINMAJ
Gulf War	August 2, 1990	April 11, 1991	MAJMAJ

transborder dyads represent only a minority of all possible pairings of states, a disproportionate number of international military crises—large and small—witnessed over the past two centuries have been manifestations of irredentist-type and contending government nationalism. The drive toward the unification of national groups under singular representative governments have had a profound effect on the course of international events—from the unification of Italy and Germany through the fall of the Ottoman and Habsburg empires to the decolonization movement of the postwar period and up until the present.

During the Cold War, demographic patterns interacting with nationalist motives played a role in many of the major wars that took place between 1945 and 1990. In other words, the Cold War did not "bottle up" nationalism, as is commonly assumed, in many regions of the world. Table 1.2, taken from the Correlates of War database project, displays the major international wars that occurred between the end of the Second World War and the end of the Cold War and codes these conflicts according to the type of transborder relationship existing between the major antagonists.[6] Irredentist-type demographics are indicated by the letters MINMAJ, indicating the presence of a national minority in one state and a related national majority in another. Similarly, contending government situations are indicated by the letters MAJMAJ. Although one could certainly argue that transborder demographics were not always the primary causal mechanism leading to every war listed in table 1.2, the correlation between transborder demographics and international wars is striking.

Considering that the MINMAJ and MAJMAJ characterizations in table 1.2 can only be applied to approximately one-third of the contiguous state pairings in the international system, one cannot ignore the fact that over three-quarters of the major wars in the five decades following the Second World War were sparked between states that may be described as such. As will be argued in this work, major wars only represent extreme examples of what turns out to be consistently hostile and militant interactions among states sharing national groups. Correlation does not necessarily indicate causation, however, and the following chapters seek not only to establish transborder nationality as a major influence in determining the behavior of states, but also to tease out a more complete story of how and why nationalist preferences develop and how such preferences are manifested in aggressive foreign policies around the globe.

PART I

CHAPTER 2

NATIONALITY, NATION, AND ETHNICITY

Due to the role nationalism plays in international relations, patterns of increased hostility between states often arise when those states share a common national group. In reviewing alternate understandings of nationalism, this chapter establishes the central common elements that make the concept an important causal factor in modern international relations. In particular, it seeks to provide an understanding of nationalism that is both parsimonious enough to be analytically useful, yet broad enough to provide explanatory leverage over a wide variety of situations.

The chapter first establishes how nationalism, which represents the injection of politics into a cultural context, differs from the apolitical concept of ethnicity. Next, the chapter looks at the conditions leading from the development of communal nationalist preferences to the translation of such preferences into potentially revisionist state behavior within the international arena. Finally, the chapter examines why members of the international communal are selectively tolerant of such challenges to the status quo due to the normative ambiguity surrounding the concept of national self-determination.

The politics of nationalism is the politics of identity. *Webster's New Dictionary and Thesaurus* lists one definition of identity as "who or what a person is." Such a broad conception, however, does not do justice to the constructivist aspects of social identity. As a social construct, identity is necessarily a relative term—one cannot form self-identity without gauging ones traits vis-à-vis others whom one observes. Views of identity concerning one's self and others form through a process of social comparison that results in perceptions of distinctiveness as well as similarity and connection.

Some group identities, such as those based on political affiliation or class, are apt to change from generation to generation—or within a given generation. *Ethnic identity*, however, is unusual in that it is more stable than most other types of identity. Born into an ethnic group, one almost certainly dies a member of the same ethnic group. *National identity*, on the other hand, is somewhat more fluid than ethnic identity, because such identification melds relatively fixed cultural identities with political ones. Before seeking to define contentious terms such as nation and nationalism, however, it is useful to briefly discuss the term "ethnicity" as a starting point for the more political concept of nationality.

Ethnicity—An Inclusive Label

Charles Tilly is well known for his quotation describing the nation as "one of the most puzzling and tendentious terms in the political lexicon" (1975: 6). Scholars tend to be somewhat more united, however, in their conceptions of ethnicity than their conceptions of nationality. What ties most modern descriptions of "ethnicity" together is a focus by scholars on the inclusiveness of the term. Connor (1994: 105) notes the danger of describing "linguistic, racial, or religious" in such a way that "there is a risk of concluding that each term is describing a separate phenomenon." Similarly, Smith (1991: 8) notes that "the similarities between religion and ethnic identity need to be stressed" because they both "stem from similar cultural criteria of classification."

Horowitz (1985: 69), however, downplays the role of culture, claiming that it is not an "ineluctable prerequisite for identity to come into being." This view is due to the fact that he views ethnicity as a fundamentally ascriptive label bestowed more or less at birth based upon factors that may have little to do with culture (such as physiognomy). Horowitz's critique is important because it warns against relying too much on culture as the sole defining feature of ethnicity. Someone traveling to another land might adopt another culture, for instance, but still be branded a member of the ethnic group from which he or she originated. Nevertheless, Horowitz ultimately adopts a multifaceted understanding of ethnicity that may include a variety of ascriptive criteria.

The degree of subjectivity involved in ethnic identity sometimes arises as a topic of dispute among scholars, but most accept that ethnicity lies, at least to some degree, in the eye of the beholder. Few, if any, scholars adhere to the "primordialist" doctrine in its purest sense, which views ethnic national ties as fundamentally innate. Even Clifford Geertz, the anthropologist most associated with the doctrine, describes national ties as primordial *sentiments* rather than intrinsic biological attachment (Connor 1994: 103). The majority of scholars, if not all, subscribe to the original tenet of Max Weber that an ethnic group is a "subjective belief" in "common descent . . . whether or not an objective blood relationship exists" (1968: 389). The emphasis on subjectivity and inclusivity underlies both constructivist and rationalist approaches to identity.

The subfield most associated with questions of identity is constructivism. Constructivists emphasize subjectivity and the endogenous nature of identity formation in the context of "intersubjective understandings" that create insider-outsider divisions. However, the range of potential constructivist arguments is vast due to differences in opinions concerning the sources from which intersubjective understandings arise. Ethnic consciousness may arise from instrumentalist elite manipulation, as emphasized by Anderson (1983), or through a series of historical social interactions which are perhaps best understood through anthropological study (Tilly 1997: 512). Due to the generality of constructivism, it often tends also to be cited as the approach utilized, if not necessarily by name, by those who shy away from philosophical and semantic debate in order to concentrate more on the behavior of ethnic groups.[1]

Despite their presumed focus on "objective" analysis, rational-choice approaches also assume that ethnicity is a malleable and inclusive concept. Rationalists stress the ways in which ethnicity and nation are utilized as organizing concepts that bestow individual benefits while overcoming collective action dilemmas. Rational-choice approaches often involve some form of formal modeling and arguments such as "nationalism will ebb and flow with permanent changes in long-term real interest rates . . . because the ability of governments to raise the needed revenues to finance [projects in national communities] will be . . . affected" (Breton and Breton 1995: 113) and "maintaining a continuous supply of [joint goods] requires the establishment of social *controls*—monitoring and sanctioning institutions—that discourage free riding" (Hechter 2000: 22, emphasis in the original).[2] For the rational choice theorist, ethnicity and nationality (which is actually their primary focus[3]) are not so much identities than organizing mechanisms. Therefore, rational choice analysis lends itself readily to arguments suggesting instrumental uses of nationalist rhetoric by agents who engage in "the manipulation of collective identity . . . to achieve power or to enforce social discipline" (Tilly 1997: 507). For rationalists, the term ethnicity encompasses a wide variety of groups that may be motivated by different factors of identity. While not always providing a great deal of leverage of the term ethnicity itself, rational choice approaches are particularly useful in that they frequently examine how ethnicity serves as a factor that assists in overcoming collective action dilemmas—a topic that will be addressed shortly.

Distinctions between Nationality and Ethnicity

In order to untangle the differences between ethnicity and nationality, it is important to come to an understanding of what a nation is. However, in order to define a nation, we must first define its distinguishing feature—namely, the pursuance of national self-determination, or, simply put, nationalism. While the previous statement might seem tautological, I am stressing an important point. Factors classifying ethnicity primarily consider *who a person is*, while factors classifying nationality consider not only who a person is but *what they want* as well. Nations are associated with nationalists and nationalism; ethnic groups are not associated with ethnocists or ethno-ism. Most scholars would concur with the assertion of Breuilly (1982: 35–36) that nationalism "clearly builds upon some sense of cultural identity," as is usually the case with ethnic identity, but that it also represents a "political ideology."

Understanding nationality as a political identity helps clarify scholarly debates of the past. Kohn (1944) is particularly credited with emphasizing the difference between "Western" nationalism, historically the dominant paradigm in Great Britain, France, the United States, and Canada, and "Eastern" nationalism, which most heavily influences thought in Eastern Europe and, implicitly, the rest of the world. Despite the seemingly dated terminology and simplified schema, Smith (2001: 40) argues against dismissing Kohn on the grounds that the basic "kernel of truth," that nations might either be conceived of as "voluntarist" or "organic," continues today in the concepts of "civic" and "ethnic" nationalism. Similar to the thoughts presented in the introduction of this work, Smith states that

> [w]hereas the Western concept laid down that an individual had to belong to some nation but choose to which he or she belonged, the non-Western or national concept allowed no such latitude. Whether you stayed in your community or emigrated to another, you remained ineluctably, organically, a member of the community of your birth and were for ever stamped by it. (p. 11)

The desire to classify different types of nationalism, however, obscures the real question of how one should differentiate national from ethnic identity. Connor (1993: 42) eventually provides the key criteria for differentiating ethnicity from nationality by stressing the aforementioned difference between ascription and self-awareness:

> We can describe the nation as a self-differentiating ethnic group. A prerequisite of nationhood is a popularly held awareness or belief that one's own group is unique in the most vital sense. In the absence of such a popularly held conviction, there is only an ethnic group.

Connor's statements also suggest an important point. While national groups naturally differ from one another, it is the process of differentiation itself that makes nationality so salient. Establishing the boundaries of ethnicity lies largely in the realm of anthropology, while establishing the boundaries of nations lies largely in the realm of politics.

For the purposes of this work, a nation differs from an ethnic group in three fundamental ways. First, because the concept of nation is political in nature, a nation is more voluntarist in nature than an ethnic group. Thus, whereas membership in an ethnic group tends to be ascribed, membership in a nation is much more a question of self-identification. Second, members of a nation desire high levels of self-determination for the group, whereas members of an ethnic group may seek little or none. Without nationalism, there can be no nation. Third, members of a nation must share certain cultural referents and group cultural norms, whereas this is not necessarily true for an ethnic group (although it usually is). Ethnicity may be ascribed according to criteria other than culture, such as physiognomy or language, to a group whose members may not view themselves as a collective. No one, however, ascribes national status to groups—groups become nations through the development of the collective preference to pursue higher levels of group self-determination.

The Defining Features of Nationalism and Nations

Defining nationalism has traditionally been a tricky business because the focus placed on obtaining a nation-state has obscured other manifestations of nationalism that lie short of the maximalist desire to alter state borders. *Nationalism represents, in the broadest sense, a desire to mitigate the degree of foreign influence and control exercised over the members and perceived territory of a nation.* Obtaining control over the institutions of a state is certainly a goal of many nationalists—but once a state is "captured," are we to say that members of a nation can no longer be nationalist? Absolutely not. The erection of trade barriers and the nationalization of industries, for instance, are acts that mitigate foreign influence over the nation, and thus, represent measures that are nationalist in nature. Nationalism can range from the harmless efforts of the French to prevent the incorporation of foreign syntax into the French language to the genocide against Jews (and other groups) committed by Nazi Germany The common thread that ties nationalism together throughout the ages is not simply the drive for statehood, but rather the mitigation of that which is alien.

Governments formed as the result of nationalist processes can be either democratic or nondemocratic—a source of confusion for many attempting to define the precise nature of the ideology represented by nationalism. Like freedom of speech or many other liberal values, nationalism may be viewed as the promotion of a negative right. Just as knowledge of the content of a specific political message is not a necessary condition for understanding the right to free speech, neither is knowledge of the specific forms of government acceptable to a given group of nationalists necessary to understand nationalism. To a greater or lesser degree, nationalism entails the rejection of that which is foreign, just as freedom of speech rejects that which is censorious. However, like free speech, nationalism entails a continual process of debate—particularly concerning the form and nature of the nation and what is foreign to it.

Despite rough agreement on the key aspects of concepts of nationality, nation, and nationalism, there remains great latitude for disagreement among scholars. If, as I have suggested, nationalism entails defense of the nation against that which is foreign, how might one define a nation?

For the purposes of this work, a nation is a self-defined multigenerational cultural group seeking to acquire or preserve a high degree of self-determination vis-à-vis powers and influences not considered part of the nation. Self-definition is important because it is an essential ingredient for collective action. A nation is multigenerational because the development of the symbolic referents that underpin cultures and facilitate collective action (as described later) takes at least decades to become second nature to social interactions among a community.

While it can be said that nationalism is the drive to mitigate that which is foreign, the definition of the term 'foreign' is contextual. Mann (1995: 59) points to the Spanish Civil War and describes how Nationalists and Republicans both asserted that they were the true standard-bearers of the Spanish nation. Political movements may sometimes adopt views whereby "opposed class and political movements, religious deviants and troublesome regionalists" are seen as "'foreign,' outside the nation." Thus, group boundaries establishing who is foreign to the nation may be stretched from ethnic groups such as Jews to political groups that are seen as standard-bearers of foreign ideas. There are many historical examples in which "definitions of the nation were fundamentally political rather than national" (p. 62). Mann's emphasis on melding nationality with ideology is crucial to understanding why nationalism should not be thought exclusively as a desire to eliminate the rule of one national group over another—it represents a generalized desire to eliminate not only direct foreign control, but also cleanse the nation of "alien" governance.

Making Sense of Nationalism as a Political Phenomenon

Nationalism arises as a potent political phenomenon when communal norms are accompanied by the development of the ability of nations to act collectively. Although the specific nature of nationalist motivation may vary, the role of the nation in promoting *a desire for* collective behavior is indisputable. Nationalism promotes collective action in a manner unparalleled by most "belief systems" due to the intensity of *norms of reciprocal obligation*.[4] These norms are so intense because they are instilled from birth as part of the communal setting that characterizes a nation. This sense of obligation entails defending one's conationals against that which is foreign, and the expectation that one will be protected in turn. The obligation to defend the nation means defending conationals against physical, political, or cultural repression—against government by foreigners and foreign forms of government. It means an obligation to protect not only life and liberty, so to speak, but also property—property conceived of as the national property—a defined territory considered historically connected to the people. In essence, the scope of this shared obligation also defines the scope of the nation.

Despite instilling a preference for collective action on behalf of conationals, nationalism itself does not create collective action. Collective action also requires leadership, organization, coordination as well as the material means for executing desired policies. States become valuable tools for promoting and pursuing nationalist goals because they provide the enforcement tools that help overcome potential collective action within a national community. At the same time, well-organized groups within the state, such as the armed forces, can pressure state leaders to mobilize the population as a whole in the pursuance of nationalist objectives abroad. Thus, while nationalist preferences within a populace can be tapped by state leaders to pursue aggression abroad, it is equally likely that well organized groups in society with strong nationalist preferences and an ability to influence executive decision making can pressure executives into more risk-acceptance foreign policies than would otherwise exist.

Finally, the existence of specific nationalist goals (I use the term "nationalist referents") facilitates collect preferences and action on behalf of conationals by offering greater clarity and focus to national grievances and goals. As has been noted, nationalism can take many different forms and exist to different degrees, depending upon the nature of the alien "threat" that nationalists seek to redress. Leaders and politicians often seek to activate and organize previously latent nationalist sentiments when a specific source of foreign influence or control over the nation can be identified and challenged. As will be explained in greater detail in the next chapter, the existence of conationals under alien rule adds an element of specificity to nationalist sentiment—representing a concrete cause around which nationalists may rally.

Nationalism, Self-Determination, and International Norms

Thus far, this chapter has focused upon how nationalism emerges as a political phenomenon. Nationalist movements, however, do not operate in a vacuum.

When interstate relations are involved, the international community often has a stake in defending the status quo against the revisionism represented by nationalist goals. Ambrosio (2001) has argued that the primary factor interceding between the formulation of irredentist nationalist goals and their actualization is the level of tolerance for those goals displayed by the international community. His parsimonious model provides a convincing explanation that accounts for many of the differing outcomes within international nationalist-type disputes. However, it does not address why third-party states sometimes adopt higher or lower levels of tolerance toward the behavior of revisionist states. The remainder of this chapter explores how the ambiguity of international norms of self-determination leads to their *selective* invocation in pursuance of nationalist goals and the *selective* willingness of the international community to overlook transgressions of state sovereignty and territorial integrity in some international disputes.

The terms nationalism and national self-determination are often used interchangeably; this creates a certain semantic confusion. The major difference between the two terms lies in the fact that nationalism is generally regarded as an ideology driving specific political situations whereas national self-determination is regarded as a norm with more universal applicability. Similar to the definitions I have offered, scholars who frame their arguments in terms of self-determination focus more on the negative right implied in the term (freedom from foreign control and influence) rather than attempting to define things in the affirmative manner of nationalist scholars (attempts to obtain a state, unified economy, etc.). Writing on self-determination, Buchheit (1978:2) asserts that "the moral appeal of the principle seems to arise from a recognition of the harsh treatment and exploitation that have historically been the fate of groups ruled by 'alien' people" and that those seeking self-determination do so in the belief that "'alien' government will always be harsher, less receptive . . . and supportive of alien values."

Nationalism is both a localized phenomenon and a phenomenon that threatens the international system by challenging traditional state-centered constituent norms of sovereignty and territorial integrity. Self-determination, on the other hand, is a constituent norm advocated by the international community, even though it largely suggests the same basic goals as local nationalism—namely, that culturally similar peoples be accorded freedom to pursue their own political destiny. Nationalism represents an affective preference of members of individuals and national groups, whereas self-determination suggests an international normative prescription for appropriate governance that is validated to a greater or lesser extent by the international community.

Self-determination as an international norm gained prominence from the "bottom-up" as a legitimization of localized nationalism by liberal and Marxist scholars and leaders during the period surrounding the First World War. The bottom-up derivation of nationalism as an international norm is important to grasp because, as the following discussion will argue, self-determination remains only an incompletely realized international norm and offers only vague prescriptions of appropriate international behavior. The concepts of sovereignty[5] and territorial integrity, on the other hand, are largely "top-down" norms conceived by international society in order to maintain order in the international system. As such, these norms have filtered into society only to the degree that publics tend to demand respect for the borders of their own states, while not necessarily acknowledging the universality of the abstract concept of sovereignty when more tangible issues are involved. *While self-determination, a norm emanating from below, remains only partially realized as a norm at the international level, respect for territorial integrity and sovereignty, somewhat abstract norms emanating from above, are only partially realized within domestic political cultures as relevant prescriptions for state behavior.*

Although the international community provides certain sanction to the idea of self-determination, a long-running tension between norms of self-determination and state sovereignty has existed through much of the past century. This tension has been most apparent during the periods after the World Wars, including the era of decolonization, when the greatest changes to the state system were evident and state leaders engaged in spirited debate over accepted behavioral norms between states and the degree to which the international community may interfere with affairs within states.

Internationalist leftist groups made many of the first noteworthy efforts of the twentieth century to promote self-determination as an international norm. Lenin viewed the right of national self-determination as an intermediate step to the achievement of international socialism. As an extension of his anti-imperialist views, Lenin saw the right to secede, specifically, as the method through which nations could achieve the equitable status upon which international socialism could be built (Cassese 1995:17). Although Lenin clearly subordinated the drive for national self-determination to the needs of the global socialist movement, his widespread appeals on the national question greatly affected the arguments put forth by the USSR and other Marxist-Leninist states throughout the century and, therefore, played a major role in the international process of developing international norms of self-determination.

At the same time that Lenin was openly propounding his views on the matter of national self-determination, Woodrow Wilson was developing his own philosophy on the subject. For Wilson, national self-determination was an extension of democracy, which primarily entailed the right of peoples to choose their own government freely (Cassese 1995: 19). The difference between Wilsonian and Leninist views largely reflect the differences between ethnic and civic conceptions of self-determination that are still debated by contemporary scholars.

After the Second World War, the concept of self-determination was increasingly included in international treatises. With the establishment of the UN, the lack of specificity reflected in the emerging norm of self-determination was evident in Article 1(2) of the UN charter itself, which simply stated the UN goal of developing "friendly relations among nations based on respect for the principle of equal rights and self-determination of peoples." Other provisions, however, watered down this principle—particularly Article 73, which provided for colonial rule of "non self-governing territories" in the "interests of the inhabitants." Clearly, inclusion of the principle of self-determination in the UN charter meant little in concrete terms, and served mainly to perpetuate the norm of self-determination as a vague, easily manipulated rhetorical device. With the acceleration of the decolonization process in the late 1950s and 1960s, however, the idea of self-determination was never far from the center of international debate.

In international legal terms, much of the discussion concerning self-determination took place following the announcement of the UN Covenant on Human Rights of 1948 and during the drafting processes, until 1966, of the associated UN Covenant on Economic, Social and Cultural Rights and the UN Covenant of Civil and Political Rights. Following a tradition established by its early leaders, the USSR was the first major advocate of including national self-determination in these treatises. Although the Commission on Human Rights, where much of this debate took place, rejected early Soviet-sponsored resolutions suggesting the inclusion of self-determination in further treatises, the scope of the norm of self-determination came under increased scrutiny throughout the early 1950s.

In a telling pattern concerning the flexibility of the term self-determination, various states in the debate defined their position on the scope of the norm through the lens of their own specific interests. Debates on the council were split roughly between the states that argued for a narrow definition of self-determination that would only apply to colonial territories, and those who supported a broader definition that would include any large national group governed by another. A handful of colonial states, including Great Britain, France, and Belgium opposed any provision. Still other states, such as Chile, argued the norm should extend far enough to include the idea of economic self-determination, including rights to expropriation and nationalization of state resources (Cassese 1995: 51). States with national minorities but no colonial holdings, such as the Soviet Union, supported a narrow definition focusing on the imperial question. Other states, such as Afghanistan which was engaged at the time in an irredentist dispute with Pakistan over Pashtun territories, supported broader interpretation of the norm.

Supporters of the incorporation of the broader, yet vaguer, definitions of self-determination eventually won out, at least on paper. Many Western states, in the end, supported the broader definitions of self-determination in order to dilute what otherwise would have been a more pointed attack on colonialism as well as to head off any serious consideration of provisions that would extend the norm so far as to include the economic principles of self-determination advocated by some states. What emerged from the decade and a half process of debate was a series of international agreements that included provisions for the self-determination of peoples. Perhaps most noteworthy has been the United Nations Covenant on Civil and Political Rights, which reads:

1. All peoples have the right of self-determination. By virtue of that right they freely determine their political status and freely pursue their economic, social and cultural development.
2. All peoples may, for their own ends, freely dispose of their natural wealth and resources without prejudice to any obligations arising out of international economic co-operation, based upon the principle of mutual benefit, and international law. In no case may a people be deprived of its own means of subsistence.
3. The States Parties to the present Covenant, including those having responsibility for the administration of Non-Self-Governing and Trust Territories, shall promote the realization of the right of self-determination, and shall respect that right, in conformity with the provisions of the Charter of the United Nations.

Other international agreements ratified since 1960 mention the concept of self-determination,[6] but none has been as influential as the Covenant in establishing the concept of self-determination as a *right*. At the same time, none has been particularly illuminating in defining precisely how far self-determination ought to be extended. No treaty directly denies the extension of self-determination to national minorities—thus leaving the door open for nationalist groups challenging the status quo in the name of self-determination as well as the selective tolerance of such calls by third parties.

The Implications of Normative Ambiguity

State sovereignty and the associated ideals of noninterference and territorial integrity remain the dominant norms of the international system—of this there is little doubt. However, the lack of common agreement on the precise meaning of self-determination and the extent of its applicability has important implications for both the international community as well as within domestic politics. While the international community has refused to grant recognition to national movements seeking their own states, one cannot assume that calls for self-determination by governments have no affect on transborder situations. Although territorial conquest or interference in the affairs of the territory of one state by another is likely to provoke an international backlash when that territory is home to a foreign population, greater international tolerance exists when a conational population is present.

Essentially, there exists a hierarchy of international acceptability concerning the permissibility of aggression by one state against another. Near-universal condemnation generally accompanies the conquest and occupation of territory inhabited by a population that views the conquering state as alien. Conquest of sparsely populated territories or territories inhabited by willing conationals is also widely seen as a violation of international norms, but is less likely to provoke an international outcry.

A good example involves differing international sentiments toward the Israeli occupation of the Golan Heights versus the occupations of the West Bank and Gaza strip. While the international community is relatively indifferent to the annexation of the sparsely populated Golan Heights, Israeli occupation of territories with large populations of Palestinians draws frequent international protest. In other words, international opinion is more concerned with the occupation of foreign peoples than foreign territory. In the same vein, one would expect the occupation of territories predominately populated by conationals to draw less international ire than other types of conquest. As I describe in the case study examining India-Pakistan-China, for example, international sympathy for Pakistani calls for Kashmiri self-determination led to more muted international reaction to Pakistani aggression than one would normally expect.

Outright invasion of one state by another is only the strongest expression of state revisionism and aggression. States seeking possession of a foreign state's territory would rather compel the acquiescence of that state to the territorial transfer. The ceding of territory and populations willingly from one state to another is the most internationally acceptable path to irredentist or transborder nationalism goals. This fact lends itself to strategies of subversion pursued by revisionist states against neighbors that are home to conational populations. The most common and regular method of pursuing irredentist-type and contending government nationalist goals entails the incitement of secessionist or revolutionary movements within a state targeted for aggression rather than overt military force. For instance, Pakistan has frequently infiltrated militants into Kashmir in the hope of aiding secessionist forces. This strategy, referred to as *secessionist-merger*, promotes the independence of a coveted territory, whose inhabitants will presumably choose to merge with a homeland state in the future. The contending government version, which I label *overthrow-merger*, was the longstanding strategy of the North Vietnamese government, which sought to install a communist government in the South which would eventually choose unification with the North (which, in fact happened, although with more overt intervention than Hanoi's leadership would have originally preferred).

In the end, the potential for nationalist-type aggression by revisionist states toward their neighbors remains a source of insecurity and distrust in many areas of the world. When states pursue nationalist objectives in spite of prevailing international opinion concerning the sanctity of territorial boundaries, it is often possible to find at least a handful of supportive, and perhaps influential, allies. The possibility of achieving a modicum support within the international community for state revisionism undertaken in the name of national self-determination enhances the probability that a state will adopt a more aggressive stance toward its neighbors.

Conclusion

The preceding discussion differentiated nationality from ethnicity in order to emphasize the political role played by nationalism. Nevertheless, as a self-defined political identity, nationality is very difficult to describe empirically. Ethnicity, on the other hand, is more amenable to description by outsiders, as it is primarily an "ascribed" label bestowed from without. The empirical section in chapter 5 of this work utilizes ethnicity to proxy nationality, with the understanding that while not entirely congruent, the politicized manifestations of ethnicity generally result in a group that views itself as a national entity—especially in the non-Western world. Although the later empirical analysis uses politicized ethnicities as "units of analyses," the political mechanisms underlying group interactions, in lieu of a better term, can best be described as nationalist.

A major purpose of this chapter has been to establish why actualizing nationalist goals becomes a common preference among a national group. Nationalism represents the drive of culturally similar and politically active groups to mitigate the influence of foreign influence upon them. The desire for national self-determination, which begins under varied historical circumstances when national awareness comes about for different groups, is perpetuated culturally from generation to generation through norms of reciprocal obligation, which allow collective action to take place.

The chapter also discussed how the international community interprets local nationalist movements through the lens of "self-determination." Although recognized variously as a right and a principle, the norm of self-determination remains vague, allowing for different interpretations both internationally and domestically. The rhetorical power of norms of self-determination coupled with the ambiguity of such norms means that states invoking self-determination within the context of interstate disputes often achieve a measure of international and domestic support for aggressive policies that infringe upon the boundaries of other states.

The juxtaposition of nationalist preferences arising within society and the generally, but not absolutely, constraining influence of international norms stressing sovereignty and territorial integrity sets the stage for the next chapter, which posits a model linking demographics to normative causality. The model argues that transborder nationality leads to the growth of domestic nationalism, which places political pressure on foreign policy decision makers, who must weigh the preferences of domestic constituents against the prescriptions of international normative considerations. Similarly, in some situations, particularly those characterized by contending government demographics, international constraints on aggressive behavior may be weaker, once again leading to greater instability among states with conational populations.

CHAPTER 3

SOVEREIGNTY AND SELF-DETERMINATION: CONFLICTING NORMS AS THE BASIS FOR INTERNATIONAL CONFLICT

This chapter explains why norms of self-determination associated with nationalist preferences are likely to break down respect for norms of state sovereignty by potentially revisionist states within transborder dyads. It argues that conflictual bilateral relations will develop between states sharing a common national group due to the fact that norms of sovereignty are perceived as selectively and circumstantially vulnerable to transgression by nationalistically-oriented states. As Carment and James (1998: 79) suggest, issues involving self-determination may lead to "the breakdown of certain clearly defined norms in the international system." Unlike chapter 4, which examines specific domestic conditions that help explain variation in foreign policy aggression by homeland states in irredentist situations, this chapter addresses the underlying conditions that foster bilateral instability and mistrust within transborder dyads. This chapter and the next present a series of arguments leading to the formulation of testable hypotheses that I assess empirically in chapter 5.

The presence of conflicting norms in transborder states at the international and societal levels increases the chances for interstate conflict. Within nontransborder situations, international norms of sovereignty are not severely challenged by societal/local nationalism, and, therefore, systematically tend to dampen aggressive behavior among states striving to behave legitimately in the eyes of the international community. But in transborder situations, local nationalism (or self-determination) places public pressure on an executive[1] to make decisions that are at odds with international norms of sovereignty. The collision of these norms translates into unpredictable state behavior and bilateral instability that contrasts sharply with the generally peaceful state of affairs existing between most states.

Kacowicz (1994) undertakes perhaps the most specific scholarly attempt to reconcile the relationship between conflicting norms and bilateral international conflict and finds that a lack of congruence on basic normative understandings between states hinders the prospect of peaceful territorial exchanges. He admits, however, that operationalizing a variable indicating normative incompatibility through "content analysis" techniques is an imprecise process heavily dependent on researcher judgment (p. 228). Furthermore, Kacowicz includes a variety of conflicting norm types, including some overly broad categorizations such as "reciprocity versus peaceful settlement." Although Kacowicz draws attention to the key role played by normative incompatibility in fostering difficulties in bilateral state relations, the following pages address this question in greater depth.

To begin, it is important to understand how I utilize the term "norm" in this work. Goertz and Diehl (1992: 638) suggest that the term describes either behavioral regularity within state interactions or the *normative* role played by "issues of justice and rights." The term norm, as used here, refers primarily to the second, deontological, meaning.

Goertz and Diehl also assert that international norms affect international behavior in a wholly separate manner than perceptions of state interest—or, in their words "self-interest is the null hypothesis of the study of norms" (1992: 644). Thus, for Goertz and Diehl, only given the absence of self-interest can one draw a causal link between international norms and state behavior.

Unfortunately, self-interest is far from an objective term, and a sharp distinction between self-interest and norms is hard to draw under many circumstances. Norms do not only influence state preference—selective invocation of norms may also correlate with preexisting state interests. Norms serve not simply to discourage aggressive behavior that a state might otherwise prefer. Norms may also encourage and justify aggression under circumstances when calculations of self-interest are unclear.[2]

The measurement of norms is frustratingly elusive because norms are intangible, requiring them to be theoretically anchored to other, more objective, factors in order to be assessed. In this work, the impact of norms of territorial integrity on international relations are argued to arise from demographic realities that foster differing perceptions of international morality among different nations and state populaces. Thus, while the presence of a transborder nationality itself does not directly translate into conflict, such a presence promotes the normative (mis)understandings that enhance the propensity for such conflict. In short, where a state sits demographically directly influences where it stands normatively.

Figure 3.1 describes the causal reasoning underlying the normative-demographic model I use to describe and analyze bilateral relations within transborder dyads.

Since one cannot readily measure the direct connection between norms and conflict except in the contextual sense that is undertaken in the chapters addressing specific cases, the first task is to establish the intermediary links between:

1. Demographics and conflicting norms;
2. Conflicting norms and interstate distrust; and
3. Distrust and heightened levels of conflict. In doing so, the theory makes a case for the viability of an empirical approach that treats demographic variables as proxies for underlying normative considerations that breed varying levels of conflict.

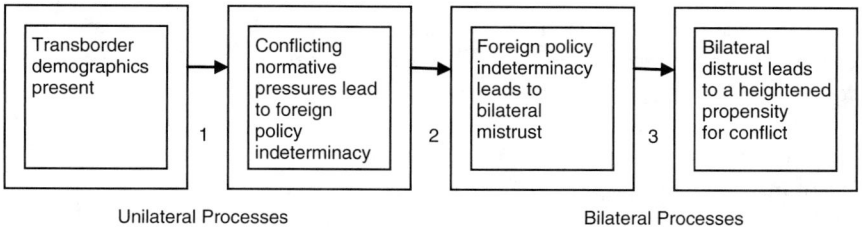

Figure 3.1 Causal Chain Linking Transborder Demographics to Bilateral Instability

From Demographics to Foreign Policy Indeterminacy

In their efforts to clarify the causal mechanisms linking the presence of international and societal norms to state behavior, constructivist minded scholars have, in recent years, sought to characterize the relative strength of norms based on at least two factors: *specificity* and *commonality* (Legro 1997).[3] Specificity refers to the degree of clarity with which a norm can be said to prescribe (or proscribe) state behavior. *Commonality* describes the size of the worldwide audience that accepts a norm as a prescription of appropriate state behavior. Norms of low specificity or commonality are useless as theoretical constructs, as they are too narrowly observed or too vague to systematically affect state behavior. Defining the level of commonality and specificity that characterizes a norm is clearly a somewhat ad hoc process. Still, when considering the *relative* strength of norms vis-à-vis one another, the terms specificity and commonality can be quite useful.

Boekle et al. (1999) present a useful model that describes how norms may act as causal variables affecting foreign policy decisions. According to the model, leaders stand at the nexus of international and societal normative expectations. For the authors, international norms are defined as those "expectations of appropriate behavior which are shared within international society or within a particularly subsystem of international society by states, its constituent entities" (p. 13). Societal norms, or at least those with a high degree of commonality, are similar to the concepts of "political culture" and "national identity" and defined as "expectations of behavior, which can be said to be shared not only by individual societal groups but by 'society' as a whole" (p. 17).

The predictive capability of constructivist theory is high when international norms and societal norms are congruent and both have at least "medium" levels of specificity and commonality. In this case, the behavioral prescriptions of norms on foreign policy reinforce one another and have a strong causal effect. According to their model, norms predict foreign policy behavior when a norm is weak or absent on either the societal or international level, but present (with at least medium levels of specificity and commonality) on the opposite level. In these cases, however, the predictive capability of norms is lower than the case of normative congruence on both levels.

Two instances, however, yield little predictive capability regarding the affect of norms on foreign policy behavior. The first instance occurs when no clear norms exist at either the international or the societal level. The second instance occurs when international norms and societal norms are in conflict. In the second case, leaders are torn between two polar opposite sets of expectations, rendering prediction "just as impossible as when these expectations of behavior are completely absent" (Boekle et al., 1999: 10). Table 3.1 summarizes their basic model.

This model has important ramifications for the role of sovereignty and self-determination norms in assessing international relations behavior. As has been discussed earlier, self-determination represents a norm that "contradicts" norms emphasizing territorial integrity and state sovereignty. As norms propounded for centuries by international organizations and agreements, territorial integrity and sovereignty represent strong international norms due to their high degree of both specificity and commonality. Self-determination, however, tends to represent a weak international norm, with a high degree of commonality—indicated in multiple international agreements as a desirable right and goal—but characterized by a low degree of specificity, as reflected within the continual international debates concerning the extent and nature of the right.

The existence of a transborder national group, however, promotes the specificity of self-determination as a norm *on the societal level*, because it provides a concrete referent upon which national grievances may be focused. The previous chapter emphasized the broad-based nature of nationalism and self-determination—how it can mean many things to many people with only the rejection of foreign influence as a common element. The existence of conationals under alien rule, however, provides a rallying point in society around which the specific application of the norm of self-determination may be applied. For instance, while the average Spaniard might have a difficult time defining self-determination in precise terms, the average Pakistani is quite likely to cite Kashmir when addressing the same question. Thus, while self-determination remains an underspecified norm on the international level, it represents a very specific principle to groups with conationals abroad.

As the specificity of self-determination goals increase on the societal level, the specificity of norms of territorial integrity/sovereignty correspondingly decrease as they are no longer considered absolute in their prescriptions of appropriate action. Thus, nationalism norms tend to override respect for international norms at the societal level *when* there is actually a *specific* nationalist cause around which to rally.

Table 3.1 International and Societal Norms, Predictive Relationships

International Level	*Societal/National Level*	Relationship	*Predictive Capability*
norm present	norm present	Congruent	High
norm present	norm absent		Medium
norm absent	norm present		Medium
norm present	norm present	Contradictory	None
norm absent	norm absent	Neither[1]	None

Note:
1. This is my addition to the model—clearly if a norm is absent on both levels, it can not be considered contradictory or congruent.

Consequently, state leaders initiating nationalist oriented conflicts are rarely at a loss for public support, at least at the outset.

Table 3.2 illustrates the predicted contours of a state's foreign policy in transborder versus nontransborder contexts. The first example in table 3.2 reflects the muted role of self-determination norms when transborder groups are absent. In such a case, self-determination (or similarly speaking, nationalism) is a largely unspecific term, which equates to the "absence" of the norm as a causal mechanism. The second example illustrates the role of norms in an irredentist-type transborder state, where the circumstance of a divided nation adds a high degree of specificity to the idea of nationalist self-determination within society, making it a relevant causal variable. The third example illustrates normative considerations in a contending government state, within which societal nationalism and international normative constraints are both lower than in an irredentist-type state (I describe the reasons for this later).

The model indicates that the context of bilateral relations will assume different dimensions depending upon whether or not a transborder group is present. The absence of specific referents around which to express self-determination among nontransborder nations yields a situation within which state leaders will systematically tend to yield to the dictates of the international norms and respect the territorial integrity and sovereignty of other nations. In the presence of an irredentist-type transborder group, the self-determination norm has a much higher degree of specificity on the societal level, both mutually constraining an executive while, at the same time, allowing that decision maker the freedom "to choose the norm which best justifies his or her behavior" (Boekle et al, 1999: 10). Likewise, when contending government nationalism is involved, the weakening of perceived international constraints on aggression coupled with weaker societal-level nationalism creates a similarly indeterminate outcome. *The indeterminacy of foreign policy expectations sets transborder situations apart from nontransborder situations.* The factors that might influence a decision maker's ultimate course of action under such a circumstance are numerous—and I explore several of these "tipping" factors in the next chapter. The important point, however, is that as local self-determination pressures increase,

Table 3.2 Predicted Effect of Norms on State Behavior

	International Level	*Societal Level*	*Prediction*
Nontransborder State	Territorial integrity norm is overriding (high specificity)	Self-determination norm is absent (low specificity)	Territorial integrity is dominant (pattern of less conflict)
Irredentist-type State	Territorial integrity norm is overriding (high specificity)	Self-determination norm is overriding (high specificity)	Indeterminate role for norms
Contending Government State	Territorial Integrity Norm weakened vis-à-vis self-determination (medium specificity)	Nationalist norm weaker than within irredentist-type situations (medium specificity)	Indeterminate role for norms

international norms of territorial integrity and respect for sovereignty become less influential as factors that constrain state behavior. This increases the propensity of a state to engage in aggressive behavior.

To illustrate the point further, one might apply an analogy frequently cited when analyzing the effect of norms on behavior. Were a motorist to pull up to a traffic light on an empty road with no police in sight, it is likely that, despite a certain urge to run the light, the motorist would respect the legitimacy of the law and wait for the light to change. What if the motorist were in a hurry, however, because he or she was late for an event? In this case, respect for the law would conflict with the specific value the motorist placed on punctuality. Some motorists would wait for the light to turn, others would not—but overall more motorists would run the light in such a situation than they would in the absence of a pressing engagement.

The foreign policies of states wherein the dominant nationality (if one exists) lacks significant transborder ties will be systematically more peaceful due to international proscriptions against the violation of the territorial sanctity of a foreign state. The indeterminacy of foreign policy within transborder situations, on the other hand, translates into a breakdown of the territorial integrity norm as a systematically stabilizing influence. Whether or not a particular norm plays a role in formulating the decision maker's preferences or is simply cited to justify preexisting interests is not the relevant question in this situation, because either may be the case. The clash of international and societal norms within homeland states increases the degree of uncertainty concerning a state's future behavior and ultimately renders bilateral relations within transborder dyads unstable over the long term.

Although reasonably stable over the long term, international and societal normative pressures are subject to change under certain circumstances. For instance, during periods of diaspora rebellion within irredentist dyads, as will be noted later in association with hypothesis 1N, nationalist pressures within society are expected to strongly increase, and will tend to strongly outweigh international normative considerations. In other cases, it is possible for nationalist pressures from below to dramatically decrease. As described in the case study of chapter 6, the fracturing of Somali society during the 1980s led to a drastic reduction of societal pressures on Somali decision makers, leading to a dominant role for norms of sovereignty and the opportunity for Somali leaders to pursue more peaceful policies toward their neighbors than in the past.

International normative pressures may wax and wane as well. For instance, Ambrosio (2001) suggests that the inattention of the international community (i.e., weakness in the application of international norms) to situations such as the Azerbaijan-Armenia dispute represented the primary condition facilitating irredentist conflict. Later, in chapter 8—which comprises the case study examining Greece and Turkey—I suggest that international norms not only failed to suppress Greek irredentist aggression during the First World War, but instead encouraged such behavior.

From Foreign Policy Indeterminacy to Bilateral Mistrust

While it is in some sense mentally awkward to think of "indeterminate" foreign policies as resulting in relatively more conflictual outcomes than those that are systematically peaceful, the essence of international "instability" lies in the that idea that certain potentially revisionist states are, in fact, unpredictable in their behavior. Bilateral mistrust exists between states sharing national groups because the government of a kin state (that is home to part of the national population that comprises another state's dominant nationality) fears that a neighboring homeland state will not respect interstate borders or state sovereignty. Kin states, being potential targets of nationalist-oriented state aggression, will often vocally stress international norms of territorial integrity as both a means of currying international support and as a way of reminding putatively revisionist states of their obligations to the international community.

Domestic nationalist sentiments present leaders of homeland states with increased incentives to threaten or take military action against kin states, while kin states consider the perceived threat posed by the homeland state when formulating foreign policy. In other words, the mere presence of a transborder group may lead not only to higher levels of aggression by homeland states but may also lead to increased levels of "defensive" aggression by kin states whose leaders are wary about the threat that nationalist pursuits may pose to their borders and sovereignty.

Strict Walzian neorealist interpretations suggest that the primary factor states consider when assessing the intentions of their neighbors is the difference in material (particularly military) capabilities (Brooks 1997: 135). Attempting to refine realist theory, however, Walt (1987) focuses attention on the role of relative threat, rather than relative capability, as the central focus of a state's security-seeking behavior. Walt claims that one cannot determine systemically "which sources of threat will be most important in any given case" (p. 22). If the state leadership in a country that is home to a portion of a national group perceives a strategic threat emanating from a state dominated by the same group, however, it is likely that they will adopt a more aggressive foreign policy in order to deter potential revisionist behavior. National demographic patterns, like patterns of geography or military capabilities, have an effect on bilateral interactions across the globe because they lend themselves to the breakdown of territorial integrity as a systematically restraining norm.

Just as outright military aggression poses a threat to the security of the targeted state, so too does the potential threat posed by milder forms of subversion. Often states aid and abet dissident or insurgent groups in an effort to actualize higher levels of self-determination for conationals abroad. In its most extreme, these strategies seek to achieve "secessionist-merger" outcomes in the irredentist context and "overthrow-merger" outcomes in the contending government context. While a revisionist state attempts to realize its foreign policy preferences by aiding national kin in an inflammatory manner, a state that is the target of such policies may defend against such threats with equally conflictual responses in order to deter support for insurgent groups. Thus, a continuum of policies exist that may lend themselves to bilateral distrust and instability in transborder national dyads, from milder subversive forms to full scale wars.

From Bilateral Mistrust to Bilateral Conflict

Wendt (1999: 257) suggests that the prevailing "culture" of international relations within specific "sub-systems" may be crucial to understanding the nature of interactions between states within particular regions. Within his writings, mutual respect (or lack thereof) for state sovereignty—described exclusively in terms of the right of other states to exist—is the defining characteristic of international cultures. When international norms are absent, a Hobbesian, kill or be killed, state of mutual enmity exists between states. However, Wendt would characterize most conflicts arising from transborder national situations as disputes between "rivals" rather than "enemies" because contention centers on geographically limited territories rather than the existence of a foreign state (p. 284).

If the perception exists that international norms will not restrain regional conflict, one would expect states to pursue higher levels of aggression. Given a regional subculture within which international norms are expected to be weak, states that may not otherwise hold revisionist interests (such as kin states in irredentist dyads) "*behave* 'as if' [they] were deep revisionists[s]" in order to protect their own security (p. 262, emphasis in the original). Due to the challenge posed to international norms of sovereignty and territorial integrity by popular nationalism, regions in which transborder demographics are more common will more closely reflect the "dog-eat-dog" world envisioned by neorealist scholars.

The presence of outstanding nationalist disputes limits cooperation between states and hinders them from transcending enemy/rivalry type relationships because leaders in revisionist and target states alike understand the cultural "rules of the game" and the potentially conflictual implications when national self-determination exists as a source of state grievance. Those rules involve the potential disregarding of norms of territorial integrity by revisionist states at opportune moments, or the pursuance of pure power politics when the demarcation of territories is unclear to all sides.

Hypotheses Associated with the Link Between Norms, Demographics, And Conflict

Having established how dyadic demographics and international conflict are linked by normative considerations, the next section poses a series of hypotheses that may be tested in order to find out whether transborder dyads tend to represent a particularly conflictual subset of relationships within the international system. The first set of hypotheses suggests relationships between transborder nationality and disputes in general. The second set refines this relationship by suggesting relationships between specific types of international disputes (territorial, political, or regime-change) and transborder nationality.

Thus far I have argued that nationalism, and the related idea of national self-determination, are norms shared throughout entire nations and within the international community as a whole. The desire to minimize alien influence over the nation is shared at the societal level and reinforced through culturally ingrained norms of reciprocal obligation that are passed on through different generations. Absent a concrete referent around which to rally nationalism (such as the presence of a national diaspora), these norms tend to be latent and nonspecific. When transborder groups are absent, nationalism at the societal level will tend to be unspecific in nature. Norms of territorial integrity and sovereignty at the international level will then tend to promote systematically more peaceful relations.

In irredentist-type transborder situations (I deal with contending government situations later), there exists a concrete transborder grievance around which nationalists may rally, increasing the specificity of the norm in such a manner that it becomes relevant to decision makers representing the nation. In such situations, decision makers are "trapped" between international norms calling for the respect of territorial integrity and sovereignty of other states and societal norms pressing for the maximization of self-determination for all parts of the nation. Within such situations, decision making is more unpredictable and indeterminate in comparison to situations where transborder groups are absent.

Under certain circumstances, societal pressures for self-determination will clearly outweigh international normative considerations beyond a level which we might think of as resulting in an "indeterminate" effect on behavior. Nationalism in irredentist homeland states increases in intensity when diaspora groups seem most endangered or most desirous of self-determination. Diaspora groups engaged in rebellion against the kin state within which they reside are both signaling their extreme discontent with the territorial status quo as well as positioning themselves as an "at risk" minority.[4]

In the context of irredentist-type dyads witnessing diaspora rebellion, the calculus of normative causality differs from those situations in which no rebellion exists. Instead of a situation in which international norms tend to outweigh societal norms in their causal influence, such as nontransborder situations (international norms > societal norms), or a situation in which the outcome is more or less indeterminate (international norms = societal norms), as is the general state of affairs within transborder situations, one might suggest that within cases involving irredentist diaspora rebellion nationalist pressures from society would often tend to outweigh international considerations (international norms < societal norms). Reconsidering figure 3.1 in this instance, one might replace the term "indeterminacy" with "hostility" and "mistrust" with "enmity." Thinking back to the analogy of the traffic light on an empty road, one might consider what a motorist would do in a crisis—for instance were the motorist taking a passenger to a hospital for emergency care. Under such conditions, the pressing desire to help one's passenger would almost inevitably outweigh the more abstract normative prescription calling for the motorist to wait for the light to change. Unlike the indecision that would characterize a lesser emergency, the appropriate behavior in such a crisis would seem fairly clear.

Similarly, the first hypothesis—1N—suggests that if a crisis existed in a foreign state that involved a conational group, more abstract international principles would take a backseat to societal pressures on a government to engage in national "rescue" behavior.

Hypothesis 1N: Contiguous states containing a state with a majority national group in one state and a same-national minority in the other (irredentist-type, MINMAJ) will tend to experience more international militarized disputes than similar dyads if the same-national minority population is or has recently engaged in armed rebellion.

Hypothesis 1N suggests a pattern of systematic conflict within irredentist-type dyads witnessing diaspora rebellion. The next hypothesis brings us back to the idea of systematic "indeterminacy," which lends itself to bilateral instability even in the absence of diaspora rebellion. Homeland states seek "protection" of conationals through the pursuance of policies designed to elevate diaspora self-determination, while kin states seek to defend themselves against threats to state sovereignty. Both states will suspect the intentions of the other because normative disagreements hinder mutual understanding and promote distrust of one another's intentions.

Hypothesis 2N: Contiguous dyads containing a state with a majority national group in one state and a same-national minority in the other (irredentist-type) will tend to have more militarized international disputes than other dyads even in the absence of rebellion.

While most of the preceding section concerns irredentism-type demography and nationalism, the logic concerning the creation of distrust under normatively ambiguous circumstances can extend to transborder "contending government" situations. Nationalist/self-determination norms *within society* are weaker within contending government situations than irredentist ones, because aggressive policies are likely to harm conationals. However, *international* norms stressing sovereignty and territorial integrity are often weaker as well.

The goal of a revisionist contending government leader is to portray aggressive policies to the world community in the context of an intranational rather than interstate dispute. In contrast to irredentist situations, contending government aggression resulting in the destruction of a neighboring state does not leave behind an aggrieved rump state that might plead its case before the international community—only governments in exile that gradually loose legitimacy and visibility as the annexation gains international acceptance. Furthermore, even in situations of limited annexations, occupation is facilitated by conationality—and thus would, in time, no longer be viewed internationally in the same manner that it would if the occupation involved a foreign nation.

Contending government dyads are often the most Hobbesian in the world due to the perceived lessening of international constraints in such disputes and the consequent challenge to norms of territorial integrity and sovereignty they present. Varying levels of international constraint tend to play a central role in promoting or dissuading aggression in contending government cases than in irredentist-type disputes.[5] North Korea's invasion of South Korea, North Vietnam's invasion of South Vietnam, and Iraq's invasion of Kuwait were all undertaken by leadership that calculated that the international community would view such action in context of an intranational rather than an interstate dispute.

Within contending government situations, states not only behave "indeterminately" themselves, but also expect their conational majority neighbors to do so as well. Contending government foreign policy interactions theoretically mirror one another in terms of the preferences of state leaders for territorial conquest or regime change.[6] A different dynamic takes place within irredentist-type dyads as kin states are unlikely to hold counter claims on the homeland state's territory, as is the case within contending dyads.

While both types of dyads are affected by the threat that norms of self-determination pose to norms of territorial integrity, irredentist-type dyads contain a unilaterally revisionist (homeland state) and, by a unilaterally defensively oriented (kin state), while the states within contending government dyads are better characterized as both bilaterally revisionist and defensively oriented. Even though the systemically unstable bilateral outcomes that result may seem similar due to the fact that kin states in irredentist-type dyads will initiate many disputes for defensive reasons, one would expect the causality to be somewhat different. While irredentist-type situations promote relatively high levels of foreign policy revisionism on a more purely "nationalist" basis due to societal pressures on leadership, contending governments are faced with severe *bilateral* strategic dilemmas deriving from the weakness of international norms concerned with sovereignty and territorial integrity and the consequent threat that this poses to the territory and existence of both states.

Figure 3.2 provides a graphic representation of the fundamental systemic difference in interactions in irredentist versus contending government situations.

Based on the preceding discussion describing the inherently unstable bilateral relations that one would expect to exist systematically among contending government (majority-majority) dyads, the next hypothesis suggests:

Hypothesis 3N: Contiguous dyads that share an ethnic group, and in which members of that group form a majority of the population in both states (contending government), will tend to have more militarized international disputes than other dyads.

For the sake of comparison with hypothesis 1N, which suggests that diaspora rebellion within irredentist dyads will lead to greater interstate conflict, it is useful to assess whether the presence of ethnonational rebellion in all dyads leads to

Irredentist-type Systemic Interactions

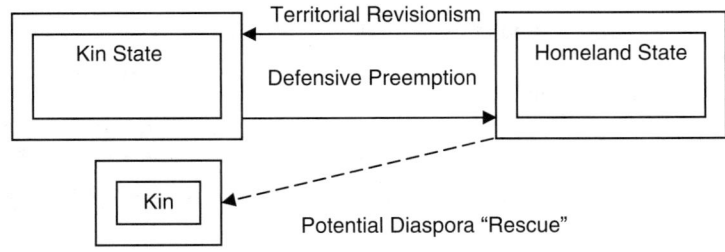

Contending Government Systemic Interactions

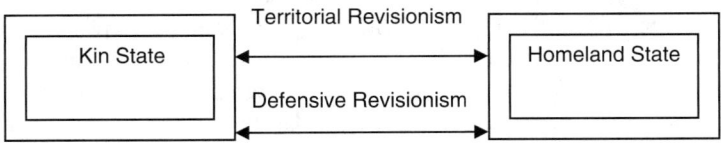

Figure 3.2 Irredentist-type and Contending Government Systemic Interactions

higher rates of international disputes. This assures that one is not simply witnessing results based solely on the presence of rebellion, but also the hypothesized unique nature of rebellion within irredentist-type dyads. More than simply a control variable, however, the effect of ethnonational rebellion on international conflict is central enough to the topic at hand to merit a hypothesis suggesting its role in provoking interstate disputes. Whether rebellion encourages leaders to engage in foreign policy adventurism in order to foster national unity and divert attention from other domestic issues, or whether an embattled domestic situation encourages outside states to take advantage of a "soft target," liberal and realist theory both seem to suggest that ethnic rebellion[7] would increase dyadic conflict propensity. Therefore, the next hypothesis states:

Hypothesis 4N: Ethnic rebellion will increase dispute rates among contiguous dyads regardless of the presence of a transborder group.

The following hypothetical linkages refine the relationship between nationalist international politics and conflict by suggesting that the issues involved in transborder national dyads systematically differ than those fostering conflict among nontransborder states. The first major issue that separates nationalist conflict from other types of interstate conflict is the territorial aspect of such conflicts. Irredentist-type conflicts concern not only the desire of homeland states to extend state control over conationals in another state, but also to retrieve the territories that their conationals inhabit. Contending governments desire either to annex other national territorial states in their entirety or to absorb limited territories that are more easily assimilated due to national similarity. While Huth (1996: 22) finds that irredentist-type situations only make up about 15 percent of the cases in his ongoing territorial dispute dataset, his coding does not indicate the intensity of such disputes or the frequency of military conflicts within such ongoing feuds. Indeed, he (p. 109) and Huth and Allee (2002) find that ethnic ties are a specific determinant of military disputes within their broader categorization of interstate territorial disputes. Thus, the following hypothesis:

Hypothesis 5N: The presence of militarized *territorial* disputes between pairs of states will be positively associated with the presence of a transborder nation group that is a either a majority of the population in both states (contending government, MAJMAJ) or a majority in one and a minority in the other (irredentist-type, MINMAJ).

The most acrimonious Hobbesian type disputes described by Wendt (1999) are those that seek to destroy the state apparatus of a neighboring country. Aggressors in these instances do not even recognize the legitimacy of another state's government, and, in adopting such a view, often claim their own right to rule the population and territory of the foreign state. One would not generally associate such conflict with irredentist-type disputes, whereby one state may claim the territory and associated population of part of a foreign state, but recognizes the right of the kin state to govern other territories and populations not claimed by the homeland.

The situation is different with contending government scenarios. When two different states govern different sections of a larger national population and each offers a different perspective on the appropriate governance of that nation, conflict may arise as a result of mutual competition and mutual fear. Furthermore, the ability to feasibly absorb the population of another state, coupled with a certain hesitation on the part of the international community under some circumstances to intervene in intranational affairs, provides one of the few practical opportunities in the international system for leaders desirous of pursuing large-scale annexations.

At the same time, questions of ideology often become central within contending government situations due to issues of legitimate governance. Incentives for bilateral aggression derive from the view of a "competing government" as a rival for both national legitimacy and strategic dominance. Rivalry for national legitimacy is based on the idea that one government must better represent national preferences than the other—meaning that the existence of one government represents a threat to the other's claim to legitimate national authority. Strategically driven aggression takes place because of each state's desire to enhance its sphere of authority over the nation and national territory while mitigating or eliminating the power of the other state. Ideological differences that promote rivalry among such governments drive both the struggle for legitimacy and strategic supremacy. As the ideologies of contending governments converge, one would expect distrust and instability to decline to the point at which the two states may decide to merge voluntarily if the leaders of one the states can be convinced to give up power willingly. Thus, the very fact that a contending governments dyad exists suggests that ideological differences between conational governments are still present within that dyad. Thus:

Hypothesis 6N: The presence of militarized disputes relating to the *forced overthrow of one state government by another* will be positively associated with contending government dyads, but not irredentist-type dyads. Furthermore, joint-democracy should greatly reduce the tension inherent in these dyads.

A last broad categorization of militarized disputes involves clashes over policy, rather than over territories or the legitimate governance of those territories. Such disputes are more amenable to negotiated settlements than those involving territory or the populations that inhabit them. While territorial disputes render it difficult for democratic leaders to make concessions and seek negotiated settlements (Huth and Allee 2002: 285–286; Walter 2002: 82), disputes centering around "policy" matters can be expected to be more responsive to the presence of joint democracy and the structural and normative processes that underlie democratic peace theory. At the same time, leaders of states in transborder dyads are unlikely to react to disputes involving nonterritorial and nongovernmental issues any differently than leaders within nontransborder dyads as such issues do not relate to nationalist preferences. Thus:

Hypothesis 7N: Unlike the impact of shared democracy (democratic peace), which is expected to have a significant pacifying effect on international conflict involving *policy disputes*, the presence of a transborder nationality will not be associated with militarized conflict stemming from (non territorial/non governance) policy disagreements.

Conclusion

This chapter has argued that a direct pathway exists between transborder national demographics and international conflict. Heightened levels of conflict exist because the presence of transborder demographics lends itself to the development of conflicting norms concerning the legitimacy of state borders versus those of national unity. In the absence of transborder demographics, nationalism and self-determination norms among societies are muted due to the lack of a concrete referent upon which to focus nationalist sentiments. When interstate borders divide nations, however, self-determination norms within society are much more specific in their applicability. The rise of nationalism places pressure on decision makers from below, while international norms of territorial integrity and sovereignty place restrictive pressures on leaders from above. As a result, the influence of norms can be described as indeterminate in comparison to the systematically peaceful role of international norms given the absence of transborder nationality. Consequently, mutual bilateral distrust develops as a consequence of shared understandings associated with the expectation of future threatening behavior conducted by neighboring states that interpret legitimate governance in an alternate manner.

I will empirically assess the hypotheses discussed in this chapter in chapter 5. The first hypotheses presented earlier (1–4) suggest that transborder dyads are systematically associated with higher levels of conflict than other, nontransborder dyads. The final hypotheses (5–7) suggest a series of propositions concerning the types of disputes with which one would most expect transborder dyads to be associated. The hypotheses suggest that territorial disputes are associated with both irredentist and contending government dyads, whereas regime-change type disputes are only associated with contending government situations. Furthermore, the hypotheses suggest that democratic peace theory is comparably poorly suited for understanding territorial disputes. On the other hand, democratic peace theory is most useful in understanding the most prevalent forms of militarized disputes, which involve differences in policies rather than territory or governance.

Having examined the normative issues that create the background conditions for higher levels of international disputes in transborder dyads, I move in the next chapter to establish a better understanding of specific conditions under which one would expect homeland states to act more or less aggressively. As we have noted in this chapter, normative incongruence on the societal and international level breeds indeterminacy in a manner such that homeland states may essentially act, over the long term, as if norms of territorial integrity and sovereignty did not exist at all. However, even in such a hypothetical situation, states would still engage in greater or lesser amounts of aggression during different periods.

The next chapter focuses primarily upon factors conditioning aggressive behavior by homeland states within irredentist-type dyads, largely to the exclusion of states within contending government situations. The reasons for focusing on irredentist-type situations are primarily methodological, including: (1) the fact that majority-majority dyadic relations are primarily undirected and interactive (i.e., there is no distinct revisionist and targeted states), with specific domestic structures and issues likely playing less of a role promoting conflict than mutual perceptions of insecurity attributable to the potential breakdown of international norms; (2) the difficulty in categorizing contending government dyads as a unified whole in terms of domestic casual preferences and mechanisms; and (3) the scope of this work is simply too small to consider the causal similarity between irredentist and contending government dyads while utilizing case studies to illustrate both instances. In future research, however, the domestic processes in contending government states merit consideration.

CHAPTER 4

THE DETERMINANTS OF AGGRESSIVE BEHAVIOR IN IRREDENTIST-TYPE SITUATIONS

The preceding chapter argued that when transborder national groups are shared between two states and the population of at least one state consists of a majority of that national population, one might expect overall higher levels of bilateral hostility. Ultimately, this hostility rests upon the instability caused by the indeterminate behavioral expectations of potentially revisionist state leadership, who are pressured by international norms calling for the respect of territorial integrity and sovereignty, while, at the same time being subject to public pressures to act to maximize national self-determination for all segments of the national population. This indeterminacy suggests a higher baseline level of hostility among transborder dyads in comparison to those without transborder groups, which will tend to be systematically peaceful as international norms remain relatively unchallenged by societal pressures.

However, the fact that norms create a situation of indeterminacy for decision-making leaders leads to the question: How do state leaders formulate foreign policy under conditions dominated by conflicting norms? Even among transborder dyads, which one would expect to be more conflictual than nontransborder dyads, there exist periods within which potentially revisionist states pursue more peaceful or more aggressive patterns of behavior. This chapter examines structures, processes, and factors that influence decision-making outcomes in irredentist states in an effort to analyze how, even under conditions of normative incongruence and indeterminacy, foreign policy preferences may manifest themselves aggressively or passively under different circumstances.

The basic model of domestic processes includes three major factors: affective motivations, domestic structure, and international military constraints. By the term "affect" I mean the conditions of a diaspora group and whether domestic audiences are likely to regard the diaspora as threatened, repressed, or otherwise discontent relative to conditions in the homeland state. A diaspora that enjoys favorable political and economic conditions relative to those of homeland conationals is less likely to attract appeals for self-determination by homeland groups because members of the diaspora may find secession or incorporation into a homeland state unappealing.

Domestic structures influence decision making by either imposing constraints upon or facilitating certain executive decisions. Some domestic structures may encourage aggressive behavior from leaders by exposing them to the influence of domestic nationalist pressure groups while other structures may hinder aggressive behavior by presenting a series of checks and balances or veto points that obstruct executive preferences for aggression.

International military constraints are the last consideration and the most straightforward. A homeland state with irredentist designs on territory controlled by a much stronger kin state will think twice before adopting policies that could potentially provoke reprisals by the stronger state. Efforts to "protect" or liberate the nation may not only lack feasibility under such circumstances, but might also pose a threat to the continued security of the homeland itself.

Up to this point I have considered the various factors believed associated with dispute initiation interactively. In other words, the presence of all three conditions—diaspora discontent, domestic structures amenable to aggression, and military feasibility are expected to encourage aggression when all three factors are "favorable." One factor, however, that is not expected to be interactive is that of diaspora uprising, or rebellion. As argued in the previous chapter, diaspora rebellion changes the general calculus of behavior expected from a state by changing the relative pressures emanating from the international community and society from a state of indeterminacy to one that generally favors aggression. Therefore, the effect of diaspora rebellion is expected to operate independently of the other factors in the model. The foreign policy formulation model appears in figure 4.1.

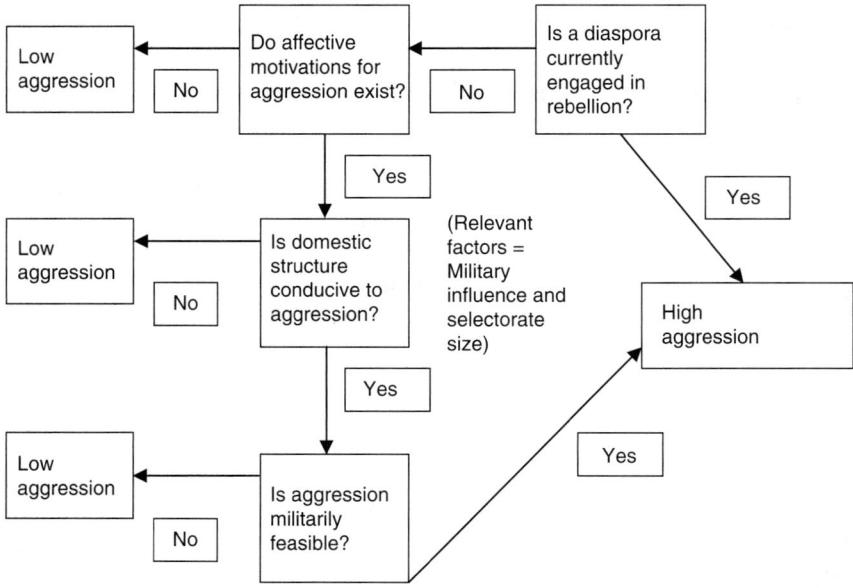

Figure 4.1 Foreign Policy Formulation in Homeland States

The following sections first examine how the factors in the model may act independently. A hypothesis summarizing the potential causal impact of each factor on state conflict accompanies each description. Later I examine how one might expect these factors to work in tandem with one another.

Affective Motivations and Homeland State Conflict Initiation—Diaspora Rebellion

I discussed diaspora rebellion earlier in terms of its impact on bilateral state relations. Here I discuss diaspora rebellion in the context of dispute *initiation*. Because I expect the presence of rebellion to supersede other considerations in foreign policy decision-making processes, it is important to include such rebellion in analyses of state foreign policies.

Chapter 2 described the concept of "reciprocal obligation" that underpins the affective desire to aid conationals that are perceived as oppressed. This cultural component of nationalism is fundamental in the development of affective preferences that lead publics and leadership alike to support ethnonational "rescue" strategies when diaspora groups become engaged in military operations with foreign governments. Just as many rationalist theorists begin with the understanding that individuals are motivated by power or wealth, I make the assumption that individuals are motivated by the desire to successfully protect conationals from harm by outside groups.

Given the presence of diaspora rebellion, homeland audiences will demand leadership take action on behalf of those abroad. If a nationalist rebellion takes place next door to a homeland state controlled by co-nationals, it can be expected that broad support for aid to rebel groups will develop in that homeland state. This chapter's first hypothesis deals with extreme forms of kin discontent manifested in armed uprising and its anticipated propensity to elicit "rescue" behavior by homeland states:

Hypothesis 1D: A homeland state is more likely to initiate a dispute against a kin state when a national kin are engaged in rebellion against the kin state.

It should be further emphasized that hypothesis 1D differs from the earlier normative hypothesis 1N—discussed in chapter 3—in that it is unidirectional, dealing with conflict initiation by irredentist homeland states, rather than bilateral. While it is likely that both conflict initiation and bilateral relations are influenced by diaspora uprisings in irredentist-type dyads, it is important for the model to test the effect on conflict initiation because the effect of such rebellion is expected to be dramatic enough to strongly influence other factors involved with conflict initiation. For instance, diaspora discontent (described later) and diaspora rebellion are likely correlated. Failing to statistically control for diaspora uprisings would provide a false impression as to whether the economic and political conditions that are expected to lead to diaspora discontent are sufficient to breed dispute initiation regardless of the presence of armed rebellion. In fact, the model in figure 4.1 suggests that diaspora rebellion represents a qualitatively different, and much more direct, factor encouraging dispute initiation than other factors—something which becomes clearer in the interactive model described later in this chapter.

Affective Motivations and Homeland State
Conflict Initiation—Diaspora Discontent

Diaspora groups are less likely to be satisfied with their political situations when they are relatively disadvantaged compared to conationals living within the homeland. In terms of economic well-being, it means that national kin residing in a wealthier kin state[1] are less inclined to support the irredentist designs of a homeland state. Homeland audiences and leaders, realizing this, are less likely to seek revisionism abroad—at least in irredentist situations. In many, and probably most, kin states, national diaspora—being ethnic "outsiders"—are economically marginalized when compared to the dominant group in their state. Unfortunately, specific subnational data actually describing the conditions of diasporas, other than the overall conditions of the state in which they live, does not exist in many cases. Still, the relative economic conditions of a homeland state compared to a given diaspora-inhabited kin state may provide a rough idea as to whether that diaspora group would benefit or suffer economically were it to be incorporated into the homeland state.

The exclusion of conationals from political processes in kin states is also a strong motivation for nationalist grievance among homeland audiences. Mousseau (2001) and Hegre et al. (2001) find an inverted U-shape association between ethnonational insurgency and democracy, suggesting that both higher levels of democracy and repression mitigate the potential for ethnic uprising. Political repression, however, only suppresses the means of expressing discontent through rebellion—not discontent itself. Sambanis (2001) finds that domestic ethnic conflict is strongly influenced by democratization in a standard linear-type manner. Although these studies focus on ethnonational rebellion, it is sensible to assume that even in the absence of rebellion that higher levels of political oppression would be linked to nationalist discontent among minority groups.

It thus seems a reasonable assumption that diaspora who live in states that are politically more repressive or economically less developed than their homeland state will desire incorporation into the homeland state more than groups living in states that are both politically freer and economically better-off than their homeland. On the other hand, those diaspora groups who perceive themselves as having a higher standard of well-being in their kin state than would be the case were they incorporated into a homeland state will agitate less for nationalist goals. As will be described in chapter 6, for instance, the relative success of the Kenyan state compared to the deteriorating conditions in Somalia muted the voices of Somali separatists in Kenya.

Finally, from an instrumental point of view, subversive activities embarked upon by homeland states in regions inhabited by conational diaspora groups may rely on the support of such groups. Although the theory herein suggests that affective factors concerning the status of diaspora groups are the primary motivation for conflict initiation, a lack of support for homeland intervention can nevertheless present an important constraint. This lesson was learned the hard way by Pakistani leadership during the 1965 invasion of Kashmir (described in chapter 7) when Kashmiri Muslims, who had been perceived as discontent, actually cooperated in large numbers with local authorities to thwart their would-be liberators.

Thus, the next hypothesis suggests that homelands will act more nationalistically when the political and economic conditions in the homeland state are favorable to those in the kin state targeted by homeland nationalists.

Hypothesis 2D: A homeland state is more likely to act aggressively toward a kin state when either the relative economic wealth or level of political freedom in the kin state is less than that of the homeland.

Domestic Audiences and Domestic Structures

The preferences of domestic groups and the nature of the political structures that channel these preferences are both important in determining expected foreign policy outcomes. My two main points of investigation concerning irredentist-type dyads involve the role of potentially influential domestic audiences in influencing leadership decisions to pursue greater or lesser degrees of military aggression, and the general institutional environment within these interactions take place.

The model hypothesizes that the final foreign policy decision maker will be an executive leader.[2] Leaders may be more or less nationalistically inclined, making it difficult to assume that they will pursue any systematic choice of action in irredentist-type situations on their own. What leaders have in common, however, is a preference to stay in power. This common assumption in political science, which relegates the leader to somewhat of a political "weather vane" role by assuming he or she is beholden to the preferences of domestic audiences, will be held as an underlying assumption in this work as well.

Leaders face potential audience costs (Fearon 1994) based upon their foreign policy performance.[3] This straightforward concept of audience costs suggests that the failure to stand firm or escalate matters militarily during a crisis will lead to a diminished political position at home. Although Fearon's examination of audience costs takes place in the context of temporally limited international crisis situations, he does not address the fact that bottom-up domestic pressures exist in the absence of such crises as well. Leaders may provoke crises themselves when they fear that the domestic benefits of initiating a potentially risky crisis outweigh the costs of doing nothing. In this sense, crises develop not necessarily through a process of rational self-selection based on potential success, as suggested by Fearon, but rather because international or domestic events raise the potential costs of inaction by increasing the amount of political pressure placed on an executive.

The potential influence of different bottom-up linkages is associated with the nature and strength of the institutions governing a country. Bueno de Mesquita et al. (2003) suggests that the "political survival" of executive leaders is contingent upon the adoption of appropriate policies that best suit the size of the "selectorate."[4] By selectorate, the authors refer to those upon whom an executive potentially relies to retain power. In highly autocratic situations, the selectorate will be a relatively small group of politically connected individuals while in full democracies the selectorate will include most citizens of voting age. While the selectorate model is useful, it suffers from the common rationalist assumption that only material gains will satiate domestic audiences.

Nevertheless, narrow selectorates are associated with weak institutions with few veto points designed to check executive power. Therefore, if a leader decides that his or her domestic situation is best furthered through aggression (i.e., I have assumed such action would be normally taken on behalf of the leader's narrow group of supporters) there will not likely be significant roadblocks posed by institutional constraints or other segments of society. Audience costs resulting from the potential failure of aggressive policies are also more limited in autocracies due to the restriction of the political process (although the threat of assassination or revolution naturally exists), and this may make an executive more risk acceptant.

In comparison to more open systems, political systems consisting of a narrow selectorate tend to face lower audience costs in the event of foreign policy failure fostering more risk acceptant policies on the part of leaders. Thus, our first "domestic" hypothesis states:

Hypothesis 3D: Irredentist (homeland) states within which a leader is more able to insulate himself from public opinion and institutionalized "veto points" will tend to be more conflictual than systems within which a leader faces greater public accountability.

A country's military establishment may exert major influence over the continued tenure of the executive within some states. The placation of this domestic audience may or may not involve material gain for military elites, but it almost always involves satisfying nationalist preferences that can be expected to be more intense than the rest of society. The audience cost paid by an executive that does not satisfy the preferences of an influential military can be severe, including forcible removal from office.

While one would normally associate a strong military role in government policy with autocratic government, it is possible in certain democratic states for a weak civilian-military divide to exist. Such situations often involve military meddling in democratic processes at opportune times, followed by a subsequent retreat to the background of politics. Pakistan and Turkey are two examples of states in which democracy has coincided to a certain extent in recent historical periods with strong military influence. Altogether, however, cases of weak civil-military divides in democratic states are rarer than in nondemocratic states.

Due to their clear hierarchal organization and their possession of the means of violence, militaries are potentially the most able actors in almost any society to influence leadership decisions. The central questions involving irredentist-type national situations are whether militaries will choose to involve themselves in foreign policy decision making and, if so, whether those pressures tend to be more aggressive or passive. While one may argue that militaries frequently regard their role as apolitical in the strictest sense (Huntington 1957: 68), protecting the nation is generally seen as "above politics" and the main calling of a state's armed forces.

By controlling the means of violence in society, all militaries at least present the threat of forcing civilian adherence to military preferences on political issues. The policy preferences of military officers will affect, to some degree, the preferences of leadership in almost any state. However, the degree of military influence in policymaking varies widely across the globe—from almost nonexistent in secure states with strong distinctions in civil-militaries spheres of authority to almost exclusive in states run by military officers that exclude civilian authorities.

Many writers on civil-military relations stress the important role that nationalism plays in training state militaries and regard state armed forces as strong bastion of continuing nationalist sentiment (Perlmutter 1969: 403; Janowitz 1977: 139). Finer (1962: 9) presents one of the starkest pictures of the role of nationalism in the military, suggesting that "the inculcation of extreme nationalism . . . is universal in the training of all but the very few ideological or religious armies . . . This accompanied by systematic disparagement of the foreigner."[5] Posen (1993: 81,121) suggests that political elites consciously seek to inculcate a nationalist ideology in the armed forces that stresses "the uniqueness and inclusiveness of one's own collective relative to next door" in order to "increase the intensity of warfare and specifically the ability of states to mobilize . . . the spirit of self-sacrifice of millions of soldiers."

While military sentiment often "opposes reckless, aggressive, belligerent action" by civilian leaders (Huntington 1957: 79), soldiers are particularly motivated and receptive to using force in defense of the nation, even when such force represents aggression against another state. Posen (1993: 124) focuses on the "defensive impulses of nationalism" and suggests that as military influence on public policy increases, so to does the tendency to "inflate" enemy images and foreign threats to the nation. Schofield (2000: 135) similarly notes the propensity of military leaders to overstate the existence of foreign threats and to recommend "a rapid escalation of hostilities" if conflict should break out.

Praetorian states are those in which the military tends to intervene heavily in politics and potentially dominate political decision making (Perlmutter 1969: 383). Due to the strong nationalist preferences of modern militaries[6] their hierarchal structure, which lends itself to collective action; the societally "ordained" role of soldiers in defending the nation; the propensity of military perspectives to inflate threats; exaggerated perceptions of "windows of opportunity" for the successful application of force (Schofield 2000: 135); and a preference for rapid escalation of disputes, one would expect that "praetorian" states react more aggressively toward kin states in irredentist-type dyads. Thus:

Hypothesis 4D: Periods within which military influence over policymaking is strong within irredentist-type homeland states will tend to be more conflictual than periods when military influence is weaker.

The Feasibility of Military Aggression

The last condition conditioning decision-making behavior in irredentist-type homeland states, military feasibility, is rather straightforward. Realist/neorealist theory suggests that power imbalances are most likely to lead to international conflict (Morgenthau 1948; Waltz 1979; Mearsheimer 2001). Under classic realist theory, homeland states would thus be more likely to act aggressively if they possessed greater military capabilities than neighboring kin states.

While considerations of relative military power are likely relevant to interstate aggression, it may not be military *imbalances* that foster aggression. Organski and Kugler (1980) suggest a theory of "power transition," whereby opportunities for attempted militaristic revisionism are generally absent in terms of the general status quo balance of state capabilities. However, when an aggrieved state finds its capabilities increased relative to its neighbors for one reason or another, the potential for conflict increases as the aggrieved state finds itself more able to project power at its neighbor's expense. At the same time, the stronger status quo state encounters increasing incentives for a preemptive strike in order to prevent another state from eclipsing its military capabilities.

Balance of power, whether of the static realist-neorealist or power-transitional variety, may not be strictly determined by the military capabilities that each state controls. Geographic considerations, such as the presence of the Taiwan straights separating Taiwan from mainland China, may hinder the potential for aggression and serve to equalize power imbalances. What is most important when considering whether military threats or actions initiated by a homeland state toward a kin state are feasible is whether such actions are perceived as feasible. In other words, the objective realities of military power are often impossible to determine, except in the broadest sense.

According to Vasquez (1993), the prime underlying condition that determines whether states go to war concerns the inability to accurately assess relative capabilities. In respect to a situation wherein there is a clear discrepancy in military power; one would expect war to be rare—especially when the potential initiator is the weaker state. This work, however, focuses primarily on conflicts involving much lower levels of violence than war. In order to justify lesser degrees of aggression, a weaker state need not be able to defeat a strong state militarily. Rather, the weaker state must merely be able to deter overt military retaliation taken in response to more limited aggression. Limited forms of aggression become more "feasible" if the homeland state leadership feels that retaliation would be costly for a stronger neighbor. If the balance of power heavily tilts in favor of a kin state, however, retaliation can be expected to become less costly, meaning that even low levels of violence initiated by weaker states become a markedly unwise gamble—and unfeasible from a common sense standpoint. Thus, the next hypothesis suggests:

Hypothesis 5D: A homeland state is more likely to act aggressively toward a kin state when it possesses a feasible deterrent to military retaliation by the kin state.

The Interaction of Domestic Factors

Figure 4.1 suggests that aggression is likely when three basic conditions: (1) affective motivations; (2) domestically conducive structures; and (3) military feasibility fall into line. In terms of preferences, it has been suggested that diaspora uprisings will independently affect conflict initiation while the relative economic/political conditions of diaspora will be important in conjunction with other variables. In terms of domestic structure, the focus was upon whether a narrow or wide "selectorate" exists and whether the military is influential in policymaking. Military feasibility addresses whether states are capable of defending themselves against retaliation by neighboring states. Earlier, I suggested that these different factors may act independently of one another. In this section, I offer a series of propositions suggesting how these factors may work in conjunction.

Considered dichotomous variables, the five major factors that are analyzed are: (1) diaspora uprising (yes or no); (2) diaspora conditions (better or worse); (3) selectorate size (narrow or not narrow); (4) military influence (high or not high); and (5) military feasibility (yes or no). These variables can be combined in 32 different ways, each with a potentially different outcome. The task at hand involves simplifying those 32 different outcomes in a manner that takes into account the relative importance of each of the factors in relation to one another.

The first and most basic variable conditioning the level of conflict initiation that one would expect from an aggrieved homeland state concerns military feasibility. It certainly stands to reason that the 16 combinations of variables within which military threats or action are not feasible will tend to be associated with low levels of dispute initiation—no matter the value of the other variables. Therefore, my next hypothesis suggests:

Hypothesis 6D: When considering combinations of variables associated with irredentist-type behavior, dispute initiation by putative irredentist homeland states will be less common when military feasibility is absent.

Along with military feasibility, the most important factor to consider concerns whether or not a diaspora is engaged in rebellion. Domestic politics that influence foreign policy decision making may be divided into two circumstances: crisis and noncrisis situations. Brecher (1977: 42) defines a foreign policy crisis as "a situational change in the external or internal environment which creates in the minds of the incumbent decision makers of an international actor a perceived threat from the external environment to [the] basic values to which a responsive decision is deemed necessary." In the context of this discussion, a responsive decision is required due to the perception that the fate of a conational group hangs in the balance due to the presence of violent confrontation between that group and a foreign government. Diaspora rebellion creates a foreign policy "crisis" situation that fosters widespread bottom-up domestic audience pressures on leaders in homeland states.

A leader during such a crisis situation must weigh the relative cost of inaction versus the potential for foreign policy failure. Whether or not a large or small selectorate exists, it is almost certain that the potential cost of inaction will be large as different segments of society "rally around the nation." To the self-interested executive, it is largely irrelevant whether domestic audience pressure is exerted from other elites, from potential revolutionaries or assassins, from parliaments, or from civilian interests groups. Because audience pressures will be widespread across most segments of society in crisis situations, one would expect that domestic structures and the specific nature of domestic audiences matter less during situations of diaspora rebellion. At the same time, because a diaspora (or segment, at least, thereof) has clearly signaled a desire for greater self-determination, one would also not expect the relative political/economic conditions of diaspora to be a particularly important consideration under such circumstances. Finally, risk-acceptant behavior associated with diaspora rebellion "crisis" may even override considerations of military feasibility—although it is not clear under what conditions the domestic costs of inaction would outweigh the potential costs of reckless endeavors abroad. In general, however, one would largely expect that crisis situations associated with diaspora uprisings and the concurrent rise of widespread, intense nationalism across a variety of domestic homeland audiences would largely represent a category unto itself that renders other variables largely mute. Thus:

Hypothesis 7D: The presence of diaspora rebellion will be associated with higher dispute initiation rates regardless of the values of other factors.

Having addressed "crisis" situations brought about by diaspora rebellion, I now turn to factors associated with noncrisis situations. The next two hypotheses address the interactive, left side of figure 4.1 that associates the joint presence of diaspora discontent, domestic structural conditions favorable to nationalist aggression, and military feasibility with higher levels of conflict initiation.

The first factor in determining whether aggressive policies of conflict initiation are likely to be pursued once again concerns the relative status of states that are home to diaspora groups in comparison to the conditions within homeland states. In the absence of an uprising, the relative socioeconomic and political conditions faced by diaspora become a determining factor in whether or not leaders face domestic pressures to adopt a confrontational posture with neighboring kin states. Since conflictual behavior by a homeland state is undertaken in support of conational self-determination, the presence of widespread desire for self-determination on the part of a diaspora is a key motivation for aggression.

Another factor addressed in the model concerns military feasibility. Once again, this factor rests on the idea that, in the absence of a crisis situation, the homeland state leadership will consider the relative strength of their military versus that of a state that is home to a conational population. When the balance of power heavily favors the potential target of aggression, it is likely that decision makers will largely forsake any aggressive designs on behalf of diaspora groups.

If militarized aggression is feasible and a diaspora group is desirous of self-determination, the question then becomes whether certain domestic structures will promote higher levels of aggression than others. The theory has suggested two factors that might provide a nationalist impetus to foreign policymaking. The first factor concerns the weakness of the civil-military divide in decision-making processes in irredentist homeland states. The preceding section noted how most theory and research suggests that nationalist preferences in the armed forces of most states exceed those of the general population. High-ranking members of the armed forces are also aware of the general opportunities for military aggression, and prefer to adopt offensive postures when times of military feasibility present themselves—with the understanding that in the future balances of power may sway against the homeland state. For military leaders, diaspora discontent enhances the prospect of future conflict that may or may not take place on favorable terms—and, as such, military leaders will prefer to act sooner rather than later. When diaspora discontent and military influence over policy dovetail, states will more frequently initiate aggressive foreign policies as long as such policies are militarily feasible. In other words:

Hypothesis 8D: When relatively poor economic/political conditions exist in a kin state, but diaspora rebellion is absent, a homeland state is more likely to act aggressively toward the kin state when military influence over policy within the homeland state is high and aggression is militarily feasible.

A second domestic structural factor that may influence the rate of conflict initiation by homeland states in irredentist-type situations concerns the size of the "selectorate" to which an executive is accountable. Rather than (or in addition to) the influence of the military over policy, states with insulated decision-making processes may tend to act more aggressively (when a diaspora is perceived as desirous of a higher degree of self-determination and when military feasibility is present). Assessing the role of higher levels of government insularity allows us to determine whether the degree of accountability to state citizens affects conflict initiation rates, and whether one can primarily attribute potentially higher dispute initiation rates to this insularity. Thus, in contrast to hypothesis (8D), which suggests a weak civil-military divide as the main impetus for aggression in irredentist-type situations, the next hypothesis (9D) suggests that the restriction of executive accountability to a small group of citizens is mainly responsible for increased nationalist aggression within irredentist-type situations:

Hypothesis 9D: Low levels of democratic accountability will enhance the propensity for conflict initiation by a homeland state when relatively poor economic/political conditions exist in a kin state; diaspora rebellion is absent; and military action is feasible.

Conclusion

This chapter has established a theory of conflict initiation by homeland states in irredentist dyads. The chapter began with a model that suggested that three conditions affect the propensity of homeland states to adopt militarily aggressive foreign policies. These three conditions include: (1) the perceived status of diaspora groups within foreign states and the level of desire for greater self-determination; (2) the presence or absence of domestic structures and audiences leading to the enhancement or mitigation of conflict likelihood; (3) the military feasibility of conducting aggressive policies without fear of successful overwhelming retaliation by the target of such policies.

Diaspora preferences for greater levels of self-determination are most clearly signaled when militant diaspora rebellion exists, an event that is expected to influence conflict initiation largely independently of other considerations. The economic and political conditions of diaspora relative to the kin state are also expected to act as important indicators of the desirability of self-determination by diaspora groups.

Certain domestic structures are expected to lead to potentially more aggressive policies by homeland states in irredentist-type dyads. The first structure leading to higher conflict initiation propensities concerns the degree of military influence over policy. The second concerns the public accountability of executive decision making and whether or not a narrow "selectorate" exists.

I also discussed the importance of military "feasibility," defined as the ability of a potentially aggressive state to impose substantial costs upon another state seeking military retribution in response to aggressive policies. One would expect states that are substantially less powerful than their neighbors to temper aggressive behavior aimed at achieving nationalist goals.

Although the model implies a set of interactive conditions, I assess the five factors both independently and interactively. Hypotheses 1D—5D suggest that homeland states within irredentist dyads will initiate disputes more commonly when (1) an uprising occurs among a kin group in a neighboring state; (2) the state in which a kin group resides is more politically repressive or economically underdeveloped; (3) military influence over policy making within a homeland state is high; (4) a homeland state has a "narrow selectorate," or (5) military action is feasible. Hypotheses 6D–9D suggest a series of logical interactions among these variables, which include:

1. The preeminence of military feasibility. In the absence of military feasibility, other factors are expected to be largely irrelevant.
2. The presence of diaspora rebellion is expected to largely eclipse the influence of other considerations. In these "crisis" cases, domestic audience costs are extremely large across most segments of society, forcing an executive to formulate aggressive policies no matter what the form of domestic political structure or constellations of political audiences within the state.
3. In the absence of diaspora rebellion, the relative political and economic condition of diaspora groups will assume an essential ingredient to the formulation of homeland foreign policy. Kin groups must be perceived as desirous of self-determination or merger with homeland states in order to attract aggressive policies on their behalf. This condition is often not met when the conditions in a kin state are relatively better than those in the homeland.
4. When the relative conditions of a kin group are poor, but no diaspora rebellion is present, high military influence over policy will increase the propensity of a homeland to initiate disputes (when militarily feasible).
5. The ability of executives within narrow selectorates to "buy off" their bases of support in the event of foreign policy failure makes such leaders more

risk-acceptant and increases the propensity for conflict initiation (when militarily feasible).
6. The next chapter tests the hypothetical propositions of the two previous chapters through a series of regression analyses. The results obtained from the regression analyses will determine the analytical foundation for the case studies that comprise the second part of this work.

CHAPTER 5

EMPIRICAL ASSESSMENT

This chapter tests the hypotheses of the previous chapters in order to determine whether patterns emerge concerning the nature of transborder national politics. I divide the chapter into three sections. The first section explains the basic research design utilized in constructing the econometric models and introduces the dependent and independent variables utilized in these models. The second section reveals the results obtained from the empirical testing. The third section provides a detailed discussion of the implications of the statistical findings. Appendices 5.1, 5.2, 5.3 and 5.4 provided at the end of this chapter describe, in greater depth, the statistical methodologies and variables employed for this study.

Time Frame and Units of Analysis

Most of the models employed in this chapter examine the period from 1951 to 1991. The time frame represents an historical era that is often characterized in terms of suppressed or "bottled up" ethnic tensions among states. The era covered includes the entire Cold War period with the exception of the earliest years.

Each case within the dataset represents a dyad-year (i.e., a pair of states during a given year). Data is organized using two different types of dyadic frameworks. The earlier hypotheses in chapter 3 concerning bilateral relationships among states sharing national groups are analyzed using undirected dyads. Undirected dyads are insensitive to issues concerning which state initiated given conflicts. Thus, the analysis focuses on the overall relations of states with the assumption that both revisionist and (status quo-oriented) defensive types of aggression will take place in roughly equal proportions—rising and falling in tandem with the causal variables in question. This undirected dyadic framework examines all sets of contiguous dyads in the world with the intention of establishing whether transborder dyads represent a uniquely conflictual subset of all international dyads in accordance with the theory presented in chapter 3.

Theories concerning factors associated with irredentist-type homeland state initiation (chapter 4) are assessed with a restricted dataset that only includes dyads associated with irredentist-type (minority-majority) demographics. In order to examine levels of dispute initiation within irredentist-type dyads, I utilize a directed dyad format. Directed dyads are useful because monadic mechanisms can be examined within potentially revisionist states in order to determine why one state initiates a dispute against another state.

Dependent Variables

I utilize information derived from the well-known Correlates of War dataset to code the following dependent variables that describe the presence or absence of aggressive behavior by and between states:

1. *Militarized International Disputes* (MID): The dependent variable MID indicates the public issuance of a military threat by high officials of one state against another during an international disagreement, a public show of force, or an actual military engagement. The variable is simply a dichotomous variable with 1 indicating that a dispute occurred between states of a dyad during a particular year and 0 when one did not.
2. *Fatal Disputes* (FATAL): The dependent variable FATAL indicates that at least one fatality has occurred in the course of a Militarized Interstate Dispute. Utilizing this variable eliminates many of the less serious MIDs—sometimes referred to collectively as "tuna-boat chases." As the results will show, eliminating the "white noise" of lesser disputes has little effect on the results derived.
3. *Territorial Disputes, Governmental Disputes, Policy Disputes* (TERRMID, GOVMID, POLMID): The Correlates of War data project provides information subdividing MIDs into three distinct types—territorial, governmental (regime change), and policy based. This allows for the analysis of different independent variables within different dispute scenarios. As the results will show, different types of disputes are sometimes associated with different underlying factors.

Demographic Independent Variables—Concepts and Operationalization

Up until this point, theoretical discussion has centered upon nationality and nationalism as the factors influencing political action. Unfortunately, because nationality is largely self-attributed (see chapter 2), it is not possible to code transborder nationality per se for use in empirical testing. One can, however, utilize the proximate concept of politicized ethnicity, a term that is much more ascriptive in character, to help us understand how nationalism functions in transborder situations.

Although not a prerequisite of nationhood, most nations have a particular ethnic identification.. The larger and more geographically concentrated an ethnic group, the more likely its members are to regard themselves as a nation. Ethnic groups that form a majority of the population in a state will almost certainly view themselves as a nation or at least as part of a larger nation divided into separate states. Since this analysis primarily concerns itself with groups that form the majority of the population of states—and the relationship of those groups with kin groups in other states—those who identify themselves as a nation will generally be identifiable by the fact that they are also the majority ethnic groups in a state.

Appropriately operationalizing data involving ethnicity also poses a challenge, however, because alternate conceptions of ethnicity exist.[1] Shared language, physical attributes, religion, culture, symbols, and historical understandings all have greater or lesser relevance for group identity depending upon the unique circumstances of each community. Our primarily interest in ethnicity, however, is to use its features to proxy nationality as closely as possible. Thus, relevant politicized ethnic groups are those that are, at least potentially, able to "make demands in the political arena . . . in a form of interest group politics" (Brass, 1991: 19).

When establishing the role of ethnicity in domestic and international affairs it is essential to remain rooted in politics. Thus, when considering how to define "ethnicity" as a useful term for this study, it is important to focus on the politically relevant aspects of identity. Groups such as Hindus and Muslims in India and Pakistan, while not literally "ethnic" groups, share a common communal identity in many areas and are united by common political bonds. The idea of a political ethnic identity represents the linkage between the neutral anthropological traits of a group and the potential for that group to exercise political pressure and influence.[2]

I choose relevant ethnic groupings for this study based on their inclusion in major research efforts that are aimed, in large part, toward understanding the political dynamics within states. Therefore, the datasets include ethnic groups that merit attention due to their potential political influence. By strictly adhering to the data presented in these well-established research efforts, the potential for haphazard operationalizations of "relevant" political ethnic groupings is mitigated.

I code the existence of a transborder group from four sources. If a minority is included in the Minorities at Risk dataset (1999), I consider it a relevant ethnic group.[3] The criteria for including an ethnic group are that the group consists of at least 1 percent of a population of 500,000 or greater and meets one of four "at risk" criteria.[4] The major advantage of utilizing the Minorities at Risk coding lies in the fact that many smaller, geographically concentrated groups are represented in the database that might otherwise fall "under the radar" when examining the relative population size of groups within states. The disadvantage lies in the fact that only groups that meet specific political factors are included, which may result in the omission of groups that lack a history of political activism but have the potential of coalescing into important political actors.

In establishing the presence of relevant transborder groups, I have also drawn upon several alternate sources. A group is also considered a relevant ethnic group if it is listed by either the *CIA World Factbook* (2000) or Vanhanen's ethnic/linguistic/religious/racial division data (1999). Finally, if a transborder linguistic group, that has not already been coded, is listed in the *Ethnologue* (2000), it is included in the list of transborder groups.[5] A group is considered politically relevant only if it consists of at least 3 percent of a country's population[6] as listed in Vanhanen (1999), the *CIA World Factbook* (2001), or the *Ethnologue* (2000). Inclusion in the Minorities at Risk dataset is considered sufficient evidence of political relevancy itself, so there is no minimum percentage requirement for such groups.

Key Demographic Variables

Once rules have been established for the appropriate coding of ethnonational groups, the following demographic variables can be derived as ethnonational demographics are examined in the context of state dyads:

1. Majority-Majority (MAJMAJ)
2. Minority-Majority (MINMAJ)
3. Minority-Minority (MINMIN)

The MAJMAJ variable reflects contending government demographic situations, while the MINMAJ variable represents irredentist-type situations. A MINMIN variable is also included in the model. Although I theorize that dyads consisting solely of transborder minorities (without a majority in either state) will be no more conflictual than other dyads, it is worth assessing as a basis of comparison with the MAJMAJ and MINMAJ variables.

The three types of transborder dyads are coded using three criteria: (1) whether a transborder ethnic group is present (i.e., does one group exist in two contiguous states)[7]; (2) whether the group is politically relevant in both states; and (3) whether that group represents a majority or minority of the population in each state of a dyad. Each transborder group represents the majority of the population of both states of a dyad (MAJMAJ); a majority in one state and a minority in the other (MINMAJ); and/or a minority in both states (MINMIN).[8] The MAJMAJ variable is simply coded 0 or 1, depending on whether a majority of an ethnic group exists in both states. The MINMAJ variable is coded 0, 1, or 2, depending on whether a minority-majority cluster exists—and whether it exists once or twice in a dyad.[9]

I code the minority-minority variable as a dummy variable (0 or 1) in the model rather than coding such groups using ordinal variables that indicate the actual number of shared minorities. The reason for this coding decision is twofold. First, minority group labels can be aggregated and disaggregated in various ways, making operationalizing minority an imprecise procedure. For example, one might describe Thailand and Burma as sharing a minority of Hill Tribes. As suggested in the Minority at Risk project, these tribes can be described as a coherent, but loose ethnopolitical units. However, one could also disaggregate those Hill Tribes into Karen, Hmong, and other specific ethnolingual groups. Or one could continue to disaggregate these groups into their subunits, and consider Pwo Karen, Pao' Karen, S'Gaw Karen, Hmong Daw, Hmong Njua, and so on, to be included in the total. Depending on how one aggregates such groups, one could say that one, six, or twenty transborder minorities exist. Without the information to finely distinguish how tightly knit such ethnic associations are, one is forced to accept the minimal level of relevant information—namely, whether a transborder presence exists or not. These variables are used to assess the hypotheses listed in chapter 3. Following the theory of chapter 4, the directed dyads utilized to assess conflict initiation patterns are restricted to dyads characterized as MINMAJ.

Other Key Independent Variables[10]

The preceding chapters have argued the importance played not only by transborder demographics, but by potential rebellion by diaspora groups within irredentist-type dyads. Diaspora rebellion solidifies the domestic consensus regarding the importance of nationalist action within the bilateral context as well as increasing preferences for national "rescue" strategies when focusing upon foreign policy formulation in irredentist homeland states. Thus within both the bilateral normative-demographic models and the dispute initiation models, a dummy variable indicating a national *kin uprising* (RELEVANT) is coded 1 when a diaspora group within the minority state of a MINMAJ dyad is engaged in armed resistance against its government, and 0 otherwise.[11]

The presence of an ethnic rebellion may lead to increased intradyadic hostility even without the presence of a transborder dyad, making the inclusion of a dichotomous *ethnic uprising* (UPETHNIC) variable both necessary and theoretically interesting in its own right. Ethnic uprisings may affect bilateral stability as states may adopt more aggressive foreign policies in order to divert attention from domestic ethnic struggles. "Hot pursuits" of rebels into adjacent states can lead to increased friction between neighbors. Neighboring states might also seek to exploit rebel movements for politically opportunistic reasons (to pressure another government, divert its resources, seek to exploit resources within rebel territory, etc.) This variable is used within the normative-demographic model to assess hypothesis 4N.

Several important variables are expected to impact the incidence of dispute initiation. Each of these dichotomous variables is tested within two econometric models—first within a model examining the individual effects of each variable and then another assessing the interactive effects of different combinations of the variables.

The first of the variables describes the role of *military influence* (MILITARY) over foreign policy of homeland states in irredentist contexts. Military influence is assumed present when (1) a military government exists; (2) a civilian head of state represents a figurehead for a military government; or (3) a civilian government is in control, but a military coup has occurred during the previous half decade (representing the potential for renewed military intervention in politics). The potential effect of military influence over foreign policy is examined in the discussion preceding hypothesis 3D in chapter 4.

Another variable concerning domestic structures that potentially impact foreign policy outcomes is that of selectorate size, or more specifically, as coded, the presence of a *narrow selectorate* (SELECTORATE). In general, political systems consisting of a narrow selectorate (generally speaking, more autocratic states) are expected to face lower audience costs in the event of foreign policy failure fostering more risk acceptant policies on the part of leaders. The presence of a narrow selectorate is coded as a 1 if a state is coded as less than a -5 within the Polity IV dataset project. Such a coding distinguished states with publicly insulated leaders from leaders of democracies or of systems with mixed characteristics, such as those characterizing weakly autocratic states.

Another variable hypothesized to influence dispute initiation by homeland irredentist states is that of expected *diaspora discontent* (DISCONTENT). The coding of this variable assumes that diasporas will be more desirous of retrieval by a homeland state if the kin state in which they reside is either (1) relatively more politically repressive; or (2) relatively worse off economically. The presence of either one of these conditions is expected to increase the nationalist preferences of decision makers, as described by the theory preceding hypothesis 2D.

Finally, the dispute initiation concerns the matter of *military feasibility* (FEASIBLE). The lack thereof is assumed to present an important constraint on aggressive dispute initiation, whether an irredentist issue is at stake or not. Although irredentist-type disputes are heavily influenced by affective factors, basic rationality dictates that a leader will hesitate to engage in aggressive behavior without the ability to credibly deter conventional retaliation. Aggressive policies are considered feasible by the military only so long as the state initiating such policies possesses at least one-fifth of the material military capabilities possessed by the target of such policies.

Control Variables[12]

A number of control variables are included into the model in order to assess potentially alternate explanations for conflict that are not described in the primary models and theories. Some of these control variables are important in order to mitigate problems of spatial and temporal serial correlation associated with pooled time-series data sets. The inclusion of the *peace-years* variable mitigates serial correlation in the data by controlling for unobserved variation in dyadic behavior that may be associated with past values of the dependent variable. *Regional variables* are also included in each regression to control for unobserved causal factors associated with the geographical region of the dyad. Regional variables are included in each regression, but the results are not displayed.

Several variables assess the role of liberal and realist paradigms in determining the nature of international conflict, with a particular eye toward comparing these variables with the normative-demographic variables used in the undirected dyad regressions. Two key realist concepts reflected in the bilateral model concern whether the existence of a *dyadic alliance* (ALLIES) or the ratio of *relative military capabilities* (CAP) influence bilateral conflict. Variables utilized by liberal scholars of international relations are utilized as controls as well, including a variable testing the concept of *democratic peace* (DEMAUTLO) that indicates the lower Polity score within a dyad as well a variable assessing the role of *economic interdependence* (DEPENDLO) that indicates the degree of trade engaged in by the more economically isolated member of each dyad.

Other variables are included in the bilateral model because they relate to theories of ethnonational conflict, although are not considered central to the theories presented herein. *Interaction terms* assessing the presence of ethnonational rebellion within contending government (MAJMAJ) and transborder minority (MINMIN) dyads are assessed alongside the primary focus on diaspora rebellion in irredentist dyads. The effect of high levels of *ethnic heterogeneity* within at least one state (of a dyad) are assessed for a variety of interesting theoretical reasons (see appendix 5.1 for further explanation) as well as the fact that such dyads may be expected to be more likely to contain transborder groups, making the variable a useful control on the variables of primary theoretical importance.

Other control variables are mainly associated with the directed dyad model dealing with dispute initiation. A main reason several of these variables are included involves the desire to test for instrumental motivations for conflict initiation—factors that have thus far not been described in terms of their potential relation to conflictual preferences among homeland states within irredentist-type dyads. Homeland state leaders may engage in aggressive behavior, for instance, when engaged in a rivalry over territories containing *economically importance resources* (ECONHUTH) or if such territories are regions of *strategic importance* (STRATHUTH). Furthermore, leaders may engage in diversionary aggression in order to strengthen their position among their constituents, especially during periods of economic decline. The concept of diversionary aggression, suggesting that leaders will play the nationalist card in foreign policy in order to deflect attention from domestic problems is assessed by examining recent economic performance, or, more specifically, the recent *three year change in GDP* (GDP3).

Last, I assess the relative constraints and opportunities created by the presence or absence of economic ties and large-scale rebellion. Similar to the idea of economic interdependence and the potential restraints posed by higher levels thereof, the effects of overall *intra-dyadic trade* (BITRADE) as well as the general *economic openness* (and thus susceptibility to international sanctions) of homeland irredentist states are also assessed (TRADEGLOBE). In order to control the idea that aggressive policies fostered by diaspora rebellion may be initiated due to the vulnerability of the state engaged in civil conflict, a variable indicating (not necessarily ethnonational based) *large-scale rebellion* (UPBIGK) within a kin state is included.

Normative-Demographic Variable Results

The results of the empirical tests assessing the normative-demographic hypotheses of chapter 4 are listed in table 5.1. Examining the first columns, the MID and FATAL models reveal strong associations between shared ethnicity and conflict. The choice of dependent variable appears to matter little, as the results of both models are roughly similar. Two variables show relatively weak levels of significance in one model and fall below $p = .10$ in the other. The existence of ethnic rebellion in the presence of a shared minority group results in a $p = .08$ significance level in the MID model and $p = .14$ in the FATAL model. The control variable indicating levels of bilateral trade achieves significance at $p < .10$ in one model (FATAL) but not the other (MID), which suggests that in more serious disputes the potential for disrupted trade relations becomes more of a factor than in less serious ones.

The MAJMAJ (contending government) and MINMAJ (irredentist-type) variables are significant at $p < .05$ in both models, with the MAJMAJ variable is significant at $p < .01$. The MINMAJ variable is significant in the absence of specific ethnic uprisings among diasporas within kin states, but the presence of such uprisings is both significantly associated with conflict at $p < .01$ and yields a much higher coefficient.[13]

Table 5.1 Normative-Demographic Model Results

	MID	FATAL	TERRMID	POLMID	GOVMID
KEY VARIABLES					
Minority-Majority Dyad (irredentist scenario)	.439 (.192)**	.491 (.239)**	1.022 (.313)***	.162 (.265)	−.065 (.653)
Minority-Majority Dyad with Diaspora Rebellion	1.203 (.350)***	1.400 (.284)***	1.341 (.408)***	−.322 (.392)	1.863 (1.22)
Majority-Majority Dyads (contending government)	.889 (.221)***	1.401 (.284)***	1.089 (.386)***	−.226 (.297)	2.176 (.608)***
Minority-Minority Dyads	−.009 (.213)	−.191 (.293)	.244 (.400)	−.256 (.370)	−.561 (.994)
Ethnic-based Uprising$_{(t-1)}$	.149 (.120)	.154 (.168)	−.074 (.295)	.375 (.175)**	−.008 (.006)
CONTROL VARIABLES					
Majority-Majority Dyad X Ethnic-based Uprising$_{(t-1)}$	−.219 (.326)	−.135 (.802)	.180 (.701)	.492 (.563)	−.869 (1.06)
Minority-Minority Dyad X Ethnic-based Uprising$_{(t-1)}$	.354 (.204)*	.466 (.315)	−.079 (.452)	.457 (.364)	—(!)
Ethnic Heterogeneity (higher level)	−.004 (.002)**	−.007 (.003)**	−.004 (.004)	−.005 (.003)	−.008 (.006)
Allied States$_{(t-1)}$	−.579 (.177)***	−.699 (.205)***	−.566 (.337)*	−.650 (.227)***	−.271 (.592)
Capability Ratio$_{(t-1)}$	−.005 (.002)***	−.010 (.004)**	−.037 (.017)**	−.002 (.001)	−.001 (.003)
Democracy-Autocracy$_{(t-1)}$ (lower score)	−.056 (.013)***	−.051 (.018)***	−.020 (.028)	−.062 (.090)***	−.151 (.058)***
Trade Dependency$_{(t-1)}$ (lower score)	−17.7 (11.2)	−28.4 (15.6)*	3.531 (13.6)	−34.44 (20.3)*	−11.98 (35.1)
Peace Years	−.137 (.012)***	−.091 (.013)***	−.197 (.033)***	−.077 (.012)***	−.261 (.074)***
CONSTANT	−1.360 (.247)***	−2.734 (.333)***	−2.384 (.478)***	−2.430 (.342)***	−5.124 (.763)***
N	11604	11604	11604	11604	1160
Wald Chi-Sq	430.57	354.57	219.39	145.27	75.49

Notes:

★ p < .10, ★★p < .05, ★★★p < .01 All tests are one-tailed regional controls utilized in all models.
(!) No ethnic uprisings occurred in cases of shared minority dyads engaged in GOVMIDs.

As mentioned earlier, and in contrast to earlier findings (see Woodwell 2004), ethnic uprisings accompanying shared minority groups are (rather weakly) related to increased intradyadic hostility in the MID model, indicating that spillover-type effects may result in increased instability within such situations. Uprisings in general are not associated with higher dispute rates in either model, suggesting that interstate instability arising from civil conflict is most associated with the presence of a shared ethnic group rather than the simple presence of conflict itself.

Among other control variables, increasing levels of ethnic heterogeneity in at least one state of a dyad, is, as suggested by Marshall (1997), significantly ($p < .05$) associated with lower levels of hostility within dyads. The same holds true for the presence of higher levels of joint democracy, which is associated with lower levels of disputes as well ($p < .01$). The variable indicating balance of capabilities is similarly significant ($p < .01$), although not in the way that strict realist theory would suggest. Rather than enhancing the propensity for conflict, increasing differences in military capabilities are actually associated with lower levels of hostilities. This suggests greater support for theories of power transition, which argue for increased conflict when state capabilities are similar, rather than the increase in conflict suggested by classical realism when state capabilities are more unbalanced. Last, the role played by the presence of a military alliance between states in a dyad is strongly significant at $p < .001$ and yields a sharply negative coefficient.

Overall, the results suggest that international relations may be understood in terms of normative-demographic considerations as well as in terms of both liberal and realist factors. The demographic variables that were hypothesized to be associated with interstate conflict are found to be consistently significant in the models. At the same time, liberal variables involving joint democracy and, to a lesser degree, joint trade display a tendency to mute conflict as their value increases. The two realist control variables are both shown to be significant, although the variable indicating balance of capabilities suggests a higher chance of conflict arising as capabilities converge rather than diverge.

While the first two columns examine all types of disputes in the international system, the third, fourth, and fifth columns disaggregates disputes into territorial, policy, and regime change conflicts. A clearer picture of the relationship between normative-demographic and liberal variables within the international system emerges when viewing the results of these models.

The TERRMID, POLMID, and GOVMID models yield intriguing results. Irredentist-type and contending government situations are both significantly associated with territorial disputes ($p < .01$ and $p < .10$, respectively). Once again, MINMAJ situations are particularly associated with higher levels of intradyadic hostility when a diaspora uprising is present ($p < .01$). GOVMID disputes, wherein the very legitimacy and right to rule of a particular government is in question, are significantly associated with contending government situations (MAJMAJ, $p < .01$), but not irredentist-type ones. The tendency of jointly democratic "contending governments" to either merge or coexist peacefully is manifested in the significance of joint democracy in the GOVMID model as well ($p < .01$).

POLMID disputes, that may involve a variety of policy disputes not related to territory or governance, are not related to either irredentist-type or contending government dyads. To what, then, are policy disputes related? Most importantly, these disputes are related to shared democracy (p < .01), although ethnic heterogeneity and ethnic uprisings in the absence of transborder groups also yield significant, negative results (p < .05 for both). However, whereas shared ethnicity is not associated systematically with policy disputes,[14] neither is shared democracy related to territorial disputes in any significant manner.

The results suggest that international politics is essentially guided by three sets of relationships: (1) issues involving policy differences (POLMID), which are unaffected by nationalist/normative mechanisms, but strongly related to the presence or absence of joint democracy; (2) questions of territorial control (TERRMID), which may be strongly affected by nationalism and normative issues, but seem not to be affected by the presence or absence of joint democracy; and (3) governance issues (GOVMID), which are associated with both shared (majority) national groups and the level of joint democracy. *In other words, liberal variables concerning the effects of joint democracy are only systematically associated with conflicts in the world related to policy and governance, not territorial disputes.*

In order to clarify the specific effects of significant variables found in the models in tables 5.2 and 5.3 reveal how such coefficients can be expected to translate into higher or lower propensities of disputes in terms of percentages. Starting from a baseline level of conflict, I alter each significant variable in turn in order to assess the effect on dispute propensity. All continuous variables are set at their mean, and all dummy and ordinal variables are set at zero (thus, I assume no ethnic rebellion, transborder ethnic groups, or alliance are present). The dyad is also assumed to be divided between regions—the benchmark variable for the regional controls used in these models.

Table 5.2 The Effect of Significant Systemic Variables on Bilateral MID and FATAL Probability

	MID Proportional Baseline Change	FATAL Proportional Baseline Change
Majority-Majority Dyad (MAJMAJ = 1)	−129%	−294%
Minority-Majority Dyad—No Rebellion (MINMAJ = 1 and RELEVANT = 0)	−52%	−62%
Minority-Majority Dyad—w/Rebellion (MINMAJ = 1 and RELEVANT = 1)	−338%	−527%
MINMIN = 1 and Ethnic Uprising = 1	−40%	Not significant
Ethnic Heterogeneity + 1 Standard Dev.	−12%	−21%
ALLIES = 1	−43%	−50%
Capability-Ratio × 2	−1%	−17%
Democracy raised + 1 Standard Dev.	−31%	−29%
Bilateral Trade + 1 Standard Dev.	Not significant	−22%
Peace Years + 1 Standard Dev.	−76%	−64%

Such a "typical" dyad is predicted, for instance, to have a baseline dispute probability of 4.3 percent for any type of MID and 1.0 percent for fatal MIDs. The tables display the predicted changes in absolute and relative probability from the baseline as each variable is altered either from 0 to 1 (for dummy variables) or one standard deviation (for continuous and ordinal variables, with the exception of capability ratio, which is simply doubled due to the extremely high value of its standard deviation).

More than anything else, these tables drive home the degree to which contending government and irredentist demographic situations increase intradyadic hostility. Dispute rates multiply when transborder national groups are present. Overall disputes rise by over 300 percent, and fatal disputes by 500 percent, when a diaspora uprising occurs within an irredentist situation.[15] Within territorial disputes, the percentage increases to almost 900 percent. Even in the absence of uprising, the tables reveal that, across all dyads one might anticipate about 50–60 percent more disputes in irredentist-type dyads than one would encounter in other contiguous dyads. In contrast to the effects of joint democracy, which has a modest but widespread impact on interstate relations, transborder demographics tend to have a more explosive influence, albeit only in situations were such situations exist.

Table 5.3 The Effect of Significant Systemic Variables on TERRMID, POLMID, and GOVMID Probability

	TERRMID Proportional Baseline Change	GOVMID Proportional Baseline Change	POLMID Proportional Baseline Change
Majority-Majority Dyad (MAJMAJ = 1)	+193%	+779%	Not significant
Minority-Majority Dyad—No Rebellion (MINMAJ = 1 and RELEVANT = 0)	+174%	Not significant	Not significant
Minority-Majority Dyad—w/ Rebellion (MINMAJ = 1 and RELEVANT = 1)	+895%	Not significant	Not significant
Ethnic Heterogeneity + 1 Standard Dev.	Not significant	Not significant	−14%
Ethnic Uprising = 1	Not significant	Not significant	+43%
ALLIES = 1	−43%	Not significant	−47%
Capability-Ratio × 2	−6%	Not Significant	Not Significant
Democracy raised + 1 Standard Dev.	Not significant	−64%	−34%
Peace Years + 1 Standard Dev.	−87%	−94%	−55%

Finally, it is interesting to note the role of the peace-years control variables in the results listed in table 5.3. The effect of adding one standard deviation of peace-years (about 11 years for MIDS and FATAL) is particularly strong in the TERRMID (−87 percent) and GOVMID (+94 percent) models. This indicates how particularly amenable such issues are to enduring rivalries. However, once conditions change such that peace is maintained for a significant period of time between two states with transborder issues, one can expect a major reduction in future intradyadic hostility.

The More Things Change . . .

The recent availability of new data now allows for the theory tested between the years 1951 and 1991 to also be assessed for the first 10 years of the post–Cold War period from 1992 to 2001. Reflecting the variables found in table 5.2 that were

Table 5.4 Factors Affecting Bilateral MIDS during the Period 1992–2001 in Comparison with the Period 1951–1991

	Coefficient (Standard error) p-value (1992–2001)	Coefficient (Standard error) p-value (1951–1991; from table 5.1)	MID Proportional baseline change (1992–2001)	MID Proportional baseline change (1951–1991; from table 5.2)
Majority-Majority Dyad	1.15 (.48) p < .02	.89 (.22) p < .01	+192%	+129%
Minority-Majority Dyad—No Rebellion	.59 (.30) p < .06	.44 (.19) p < .03	+76%	+52%
Minority-Majority Dyad—w/Rebellion	.91 (.39) p < .02	1.20 (.35) p < .01	+300%	+338%
Ethnic Heterogeneity	.001 (.004) p < .82	−.004 (.002) p < .03	Not significant	−12%
Allies	−.13 (.25) p < .61	−.58 (.18) p < .01	Not Significant	−43%
Capability-Ratio	.000 (.000) p < .27	−.005 (.002) p < .01	Not Significant	−1%
(Lower) Democracy	−.037 (.25) p < .13	−.056 (.13) p <.01	Not Significant	−31%
Peace Years	−.072 (.012) p < .01	−.138 (.012) p < .01	−64%	−76%
Number of Cases (dyad years)	3553	11604	3553	11604

found to be significant in both the MID and FATAL models over the period 1951–1991, the following analysis shows how these variables were related to MIDs over the period 1992–2001.

As the results show in table 5.4, demographic variables remain a systematic determinant of interstate behavior during the post–Cold War era. While one might have expected an "explosion" of interstate nationalist aggression during the post–Cold War period, the results indicate a marked degree of continuity in the nature of bilateral state relations during more recent years. Due in part to the smaller sample size, it is no surprise that the significance levels of the key demographic variables are somewhat weaker during the period 1992–2001. However, the coefficients of these variables, and the associated percentage increases in dispute behavior associated with the presence of transborder groups, are quite similar when the Cold War and immediate post–Cold War eras are compared.

Perhaps even more striking is the fact that the demographic variables (and the number of years since a previous dispute) are the only strong predictors of state behavior during the period 1992–2001. Variables involving ethnic heterogeneity, alliance bonds, and relative capabilities appear to have little bearing on dispute rates over the decade. Joint democracy, while more significant than most of the variables, also appears to be a weak predictor of conflict in the post–Cold War period in comparison to the demographic variables. Overall, the results display a strong and continuing role of ethnonational demographics and nationalism in the conduct of interstate affairs.

Domestic Foreign Policy Formulation Results

Table 5.5 displays the results obtained when testing variables associated with the homeland dispute initiation hypotheses discussed in chapter 4. Once again, the MID and FATAL models display similar results, with the major difference being that military feasibility is significantly associated with MIDs ($p < .05$), but not fatal MIDs—a result that defies ready explanation. Perhaps disputes that are serious enough to merit the initiation of large-scale violence on the part of homeland states create larger audience costs that make such states more risk acceptant. This is, however, largely conjecture, because one would not expect such states to march to full-scale war under circumstances of certain defeat.

The two key variables significantly associated with disputes in both the MID and FATAL models are military influence over policy ($p < .01$ and $p < .05$, respectively) and diaspora uprising (both $p < .05$). When either or both of these factors exist, one would expect an increase in the propensity of a homeland state to initiate disputes with neighboring kin states. Surprisingly, variables associated with narrow selectorates and diaspora discontent are not found to be significant at $p < .10$. However, it must be noted that in the FATAL model, narrow selectorate is significant at $p = .101$, indicating a rather systematic association between dispute initiation and narrow selectorates in fatal disputes.

Several of the control variables are significantly associated with dispute initiation as well. Instrumental-type factors including the strategic ($p < .01$ and $p < .05$) and economic value (both $p < .01$) of a territory are strongly associated with dispute

Table 5.5 Domestic Foreign Policy Formulation Model Results (For Putatively Irredentist Homeland States)

	MID	FATAL
KEY VARIABLES		
Military Influence$_{(t-1)}$	1.472 (.279)***	.891 (.388)**
Narrow Selectorate$_{(t-1)}$	−.011 (.455)	.704 (.429)
Diaspora Discontent$_{(t-1)}$	−.023 (.316)	.273 (.310)
Diaspora Uprising$_{(t-1)}$	.615 (.285)**	1.026 (.477)**
Military Feasibility$_{(t-1)}$	.935 (.458)**	.311 (.566)
CONTROL VARIABLES		
Global Trade$_{(t-1)}$	1.204 (1.16)	1.496 (1.03)
Intradyadic Trade$_{(t-1)}$	1.345 (1.89)	−3.016 (3.42)
Strategically Valuable Territorial Dispute$_{(t-1)}$	1.400 (.358)***	.788 (.650)**
Economically Valuable Territorial Dispute$_{(t-1)}$	1.118 (.433)***	1.341 (.365)***
Economic Growth 3 years$_{(t-1)}$	2.263 (1.12)**	2.054 (1.57)*
Large Uprising in kin state$_{(t-1)}$	−.365 (.353)	−.214 (.333)
Ethnic Heterogeneity	.002 (.006)	.004 (.006)
Peace Years	−.194 (.070)***	−.103 (.040)***
CONSTANT	−2.689 (1.04)***	−5.750 (1.06)***
N	1681	1678
Wald Chi-Sq	286.63	609.15

Notes:
1. All tests are one-tailed and regional controls are utilized in all models.
2. *p < .10, **p < .05, ***p < .01.

initiation rates among homeland states, clearly indicating that even in irredentist-type disputes, homeland preferences cannot be entirely explained in terms of nationalist attachments.

Diversionary theories, at least in the context of irredentist-type dyads, are not supported by the results. Quite the opposite seems true, with economic growth actually associated with higher conflict propensity (p < .05, and p < .10). Although the effect is somewhat modest, the results that "encapsulation" effects, whereby a state encountering economic stagnation or decline is less likely to initiate conflict, seems more likely to occur in irredentist-type situations. In addition, the modest positive association between global trade and dispute initiation in the MID and FATAL models (p = .30, p = .15) suggest that dispute initiators tend not to be "hermit kingdoms" in any sense but, rather, relatively open, modernizing states.

While several of the key and control variables are significant, this fact alone tells one little about what makes the domestic politics of irredentist-type situations different than those of other dyads. The table 5.6 pares down the domestic politics model into a core model encompassing only significant and jointly significant variables and compares these variables to conflict initiation by all other (nontransborder) states.

By comparing the first and second columns with the third and fourth columns, one notices that three of the variables are significant across the board. This is true of variables concerning the strategic and economic value of disputed territory as well as the question of the military feasibility of aggression. Thus, the case studies will consider these variables, but it should be kept in mind that while they hold explanatory power for the actions of potentially irredentist homeland states, the same factors affect the actions of revisionist (transborder or nontransborder) states in general as well.

Two of the key variables differ significantly in the irredentist-type context when compared to other dyads. The first is military influence. While the effect of

Table 5.6   Core Models—(Domestic Foreign Policy Model)

	Irredentist-MINMAJ		ALL DYADS except Transborder Dyads	
	MID	FATAL	MID	FATAL
KEY VARIABLES				
Military Influence$_{(t-1)}$	1.341 (.264)***	.932 (.379)**	−.193 (.227)	−.197 (.339)
Narrow Selectorate$_{(t-1)}$	NS	.619 (.417)	.740 (.237)***	.988 (.460)**
Diaspora Uprising$_{(t-1)}$	.613 (.258)***	1.122 (.444)**	NS	NS
Military Feasibility$_{(t-1)}$	.883 (.409)**	NS	1.110 (.361)***	1.418 (.484)***
CONTROL VARIABLES				
Strategically Valuable Territorial Dispute$_{(t-1)}$	1.311 (.302)***	.852 (.320)***	1.614 (.387)***	1.721 (.310)***
Economically Valuable Territorial Dispute $_{(t-1)}$	1.101 (1.13)***	1.229 (.327)***	.846 (.344)**	1.216 (.408)***
Global Trade$_{(t-1)}$	1.204 (1.16)	1.760 (.98)*	−.837 (1.12)	−1.364 (2.49)
Econ. Growth 3yrs. $_{(t-1)}$	2.400 (1.18)***	1.967 (1.10)***	−.840 (.589)	−.543 (1.28)
Peace Years	−.195 (.065)***	−.111 (.042)***	−.161 (.019)***	−.106 (.022)***
CONSTANT	−2.547 (1.18)***	−5.434 (.489)***	−3.341 (.459)***	−6.081 (.66)***
N	1729	1728	14485	14485
Wald Chi-Sq	110.44	355.14	199.22	319.03

Notes:
1. All tests are one-tailed.
2. All models use regional controls.
3. *p < .10, **p < .05, ***p < .01.
4. NS = The values were not found to be significant in the full model, displayed in table 5.5.

military influence over policy is strongly associated with increases in homeland state dispute initiation in irredentist dyads, no such association exists in dyads in general (the sign even indicates a negative influence). Narrow selectorates, while only weakly associated with fatal conflict initiation by homeland states (p = .13), are strongly associated with dispute initiation in other cases (p <.01 for MIDs, p <.05 for fatal MIDS).

In terms of the control variables examining economic growth and global trade, there is also a marked discrepancy between irredentist homeland dispute initiation and other dyads. While global trade and economic growth, in particular, increase conflict initiation propensity in irredentist-type situations, in other cases, these factors are found to be insignificant (and display negative signs).

Once again, the coefficients in table 5.6 are difficult to interpret as displayed. Transformed in the same manner as the results shown in tables 5.2 and 5.3, table 5.7 indicates the baseline probability changes for the variables found in the above models.

Table 5.7 Domestic Foreign Policy Core Model—Baseline Probability Changes

	IRREDENTIST DYADS		ALL Nontransborder DYADS	
	MID Proportional Baseline Change	FATAL Proportional Baseline Change	MID Proportional Baseline Change	FATAL Proportional Baseline Change
Military Influence = 1	+273%	+154%	Not significant	Not significant
Narrow Selectorate = 1	Not significant	+86%	+109%	+168%
Diaspora Uprising = 1	+83%	+206%	N/A	N/A
Military Feasibility = 1	+139%	Not significant	+315%	+312%
Strategic Territorial Rivalry = 1	+262%	+134%	+394%	+458%
Econ. Territorial Rivalry = 1	+195%	+241%	+132%	+237%
Global Trade + 1 SD	Not significant	−19%	Not significant	Not significant
3 yrs GDP change + 1 SD	+26%	+21%	Not significant	Not significant
Peace Years + 1 Standard Dev.	−94%	−71%	−82%	−69%

Interactive Domestic Results

The variables described earlier (Military Influence; Narrow Selectorate; Diaspora Discontent; Diaspora Uprising; and Military Feasibility) are hypothesized to affect dispute initiation separately. However, it is useful to see the effect of these variables in tandem with one another. In other words, we would like to know how these variables interact when they occur (or do not occur) concurrently. Utilizing tree modeling software (described in further detail in appendix 5.4), a tree with 20 terminal nodes is created representing potentially significant *combinations* of key variables[16] (Military Influence; Narrow Selectorate; Diaspora Discontent; Diaspora Uprising; and Military Feasibility).

Of the 20 terminal nodes, three nodes are not associated with any MID initiation, leaving 17 combinations of variables for the analysis. When analyzed through similar statistical methods as the earlier analysis (including the use of a peace-years variable) I find that of these 17 combinations, seven are found to be statistically significant—six in a positive direction and one in a negative direction. In total, there are six variable combinations associated with higher rates of dispute initiation than one would normally expect from homeland states in typical irredentist dyads and four combinations (including the three with no MIDs) can be said to be associated with fewer disputes. The three interactive variables that witness no MIDs[17] represent the following combination of factors:

1. No Uprising; Discontent; Low Military Influence; Not Narrow Selectorate; Not Feasible
2. No Uprising; Military Influence; Not Narrow Selectorate; Not Feasible
3. Uprising; Low Military Influence; Not Feasible

The clearest pattern among these cases is the lack of "feasibility" in dispute initiation. Even in the presence of a diaspora uprising, military feasibility plays a strong role in dissuading leaders from pursuing aggressive policies. The remaining variable combinations are tested and the results are shown in table 5.8.

The one significantly negative variable ($p < .10$) is not particularly surprising, because it reflects a combination values of variables that were each found separately to lead to a decreased chance of dispute initiation (No Uprising; No Discontent; No Military Influence; not Narrow Selectorate; and Not Feasible).

Six nodes represent statistically significant combinations of variables that are associated with an increased propensity for homeland state conflict initiation. The first four are associated with the presence of a diaspora uprising:

1. Uprising; No Discontent; Military Influence (coefficient = 2.17 $p < .00$; example: Syria → Israel 1970–1990)
2. Uprising; Discontent; Military Influence (coefficient = 2.62 $p < .00$; example: Somalia → Ethiopia 1976–1980)
3. Uprising; No Discontent; Low Military Influence; Narrow Selectorate; Feasible (coefficient = 2.39 $p < .00$; example: Egypt → Israel 1966–1975)
4. Uprising; No Discontent; Low Military Influence; Not Narrow Selectorate; Feasible (coefficient = 0.92 $p < .05$; example: Pakistan → India 1990–1991)

Table 5.8 Classification Tree Interactive Regression Results

Interactive Variable Combination	MID
UP; D; MI	2.174 (.626)***
UP; D; nMI; NS; F	.872 (.766)
UP; D; nMI; nNS; F	.194 (.488)
UP; nD; MI	2.636 (.349)***
UP; nD; nMI; NS; F	2.400 (.844)***
UP; nD; nMI; nNS; F	.919 (.467)**
UP; nMI; nF	**NO MIDS**
nUP; MI; nNS; nF	**NO MIDS**
nUP; D; MI; NS; F	2.700 (1.24)**
nUP; D; MI; NS; nF	2.064 (1.77)
nUP; D; MI; nNS; F	1.600 (.514)***
nUP; D; nMI; NS	.306 (.638)
nUP; D; nMI; nNS; F	−.083 (.680)
nUP; D; nMI; nNS; nF	**NO MIDS**
nUP; nD; MI; NS; nF	−.378 (.949)
nUP; nD; MI; NS; F	−.579 (.952)
nUP; nD; MI; nNS; F	.393 (.865)
nUP; nD; nMI; NS	−1.518 (1.15)
nUP; nD; nMI; nNS; F	−.477 (.757)
nUP; nD; nMI; nNS; nF	−1.456 (.778)*
Peace Years	−.262 (.060)***
CONSTANT	−1.518 (.415)***
N	1945
Wald Chi-Sq	220.02

Notes:
1. UP = Diaspora Uprising, nUP = no Diaspora Uprising; D = Diaspora Discontent, nD = No Diaspora Discontent; MI = High Military Influence, nMI = no High Military Influence; NS = Narrow Selectorate, nNS = Not Narrow Selectorate; F = Militarily Feasible, nF = Not Military Feasible.
2. * $p < .10$, ** $p < .05$, *** $p < .01$.
3. All tests are one-tailed.
4. The "No MIDs" outcomes were found in the use of the classification tree—they are provided in the regression results above for illustrative purposes (i.e., because of the perfect prediction of these categories, they were not included in the regression).

The results of these variable interactions reveal one very clear fact—in the presence of a diaspora uprising, other factors, including domestic institutions, matter less. This is evident in the variety of factors represented within the significant variable combinations. Combinations 1 and 2 in table 5.8 reveal the interesting pattern that in the presence of diaspora uprising and military influence, questions of military feasibility or selectorate size are so irrelevant that they are "pruned" from the tree. Considering that these are the only significant outcomes not requiring the presence of a positive military feasibility value, they seem to indicate a particular risk acceptance on the part of military influenced governments during crisis situations. The only other conclusion that one may draw is that while selectorate size seems irrelevant in terms of statistical significance, the presence of a much smaller coefficient in combination four compared to combination three might indicate that wider selectorates at least dampen the level of elevated conflict, even if such heightened aggression can be expected to exist.

Of even greater interest are the two nodes significantly associated with higher conflict levels when rebellion is absent:

1. No Uprising; Discontent; Military Influence; Not Narrow Selectorate; Feasible (coefficient = 1.60; p <.00; example: Turkey → Greece, 1980–1985)
2. No Uprising; Discontent; Military Influence; Narrow Selectorate; Feasible (coefficient = 2.70; p <.05; example: Iraq → Iran, 1970s)

Here one notes that in the absence of rebellion, the presence or absence of a narrow selectorate once again does not particularly matter. However, when compared to other cases within which a diaspora uprising has *not* occurred, the pattern of *Military Influence + Discontent (+ Military Feasibility)* stands out as an important combination of variables associated with higher dispute initiation rates for homeland states. Thus, as opposed to the earlier finding suggesting that relative kin state political or economic conditions (discontent) were a largely insignificant factor, the results of the interactive analysis indicate that these factors are important under particular circumstances when military influence over policy is strong. Similarly, while military influence was found to have a strong influence across all cases in earlier noninteractive regressions, the classification method reveals that military influence is particularly important in situations when diasporas are not engaged in rebellion, but suffer under relatively poor economic or political conditions compared to those of the homeland.

Summary of Results and Implications for Theory

Table 5.9 lists the hypotheses from chapters 3 and 4 that are confirmed by the preceding analysis. This discussion will be divided into two sections as per table 5.9. The first section will discuss the implications of results obtained from testing the normative-demographic hypotheses. The second section will discuss the results obtained from testing hypotheses associated with irredentist homeland state behavior.

Normative-Demographic Implications of Transborder Nationality and Nationalism

The results of the normative-demographic models highlight the important role that transborder national demographics play in bilateral state relations. National[18] demographic spillover into bordering states yields much higher rates of dyadic conflict if at least part of a national group constitutes a majority of the population in one of the states. According to the results of this analysis, in cases where two contiguous states share a majority group (MAJMAJ), or one state is home to a majority and the other a minority of the same population (MINMAJ), marginal dispute rates increase

Table 5.9 Hypothesis Outcomes and Associated Variables

Hypothesis	Variable	Relation to Disputes found as variable increases
Normative-Demographic Hypotheses (undirected dyads)		
1N Irredentist dyads with Diaspora Rebellion	RELEVANT	Increase in MID, FATAL, and TERRMID models
2N Irredentist-type Dyads (controlling for Diaspora Rebellion)	MINMAJ	Increase in MID, FATAL, and TERRMID models
3N Contending Government	MAJMAJ	Increase in MID, FATAL, TERRMID, and GOVMID models
4N Ethnic Rebellion (in general)	UPETHNIC	Increase in POLMID model
5N Territorial Disputes—association with MINMAJ and MAJMAJ	MAJMAJ MINMAJ (DEMAUTLO)	Increase Increase (Not Significant)
6N Regime Change Disputes – association with MINMAJ and MAJMAJ	MAJMAJ MINMAJ (DEMAUTLO)	Increase Not Significant (Decrease)
7N Policy Disputes—association with DEMAUTLO	(MAJMAJ) (MINMAJ) DEMAUTLO	(Not Significant) (Not Significant) Decrease
Domestic Irredentist Hypotheses (directed dyads)		
1D Diaspora Rebellion	RELEVANT	Increase
2D Diaspora Discontent	DISCONT	Not Significant
3D Narrow Selectorate	SELECTORATE	Increase (but results are weak in FATAL, not significant in MID)
4D Military Influence	MILITARY	Increase
5D Military Feasibility	FEASIBLE	Increase

Continued

Table 5.9 Continued

Hypothesis	Variable	Relation to Disputes found as variable increases
6D Military Feasibility in interactive model outcomes	Combinations including FEASIBLE (= 1)	Absent military feasibility, none of the interactive combinations is positive and significant
7D Diaspora rebellion will increase dispute initiation while other factors will be largely irrelevant within interactive model	Combinations including RELEVANT (= 1)	Diaspora rebellion increases dispute initiation in 4 of 6 interactive outcomes with no systematic pattern among other variables
8D No Uprising + Poor Diaspora Conditions + Military Influence + Military Feasibility	Combination including RELEVANT (= 0); DISCONT (= 1); MILITARY (= 1); and FEASIBLE (= 1)	Increase
9D No Uprising + Poor Diaspora Conditions + Narrow Selectorate + Military Feasibility	Combination including RELEVANT (= 0); DISCONT (= 1); SELECTORATE (= 1); and FEASIBLE (= 1)	Not significant

greatly over their benchmark values, particularly when fatalities are involved. This is borne out throughout this study in both the case of contending government (majority-majority) and irredentist-type (minority-majority) dyads.

An important factor differentiating irredentist-type and contending government dyads is the manner in which kin state populations are viewed. Whereas irredentist-type nationalism increases in intensity when diaspora groups are viewed as oppressed, nationalism in contending government situations is muted by the fact that aggressive policies may harm conationals. This mitigates the instinct to engage in militant "rescue" strategies in the presence of kin state rebellion, as it requires conflict to be directed at conational populations rather than foreign nationalities. The analysis reflects this distinction. It is clear that diaspora rebellion in minority-majority dyads significantly increases the chance of international disputes, while a similar effect is not found within contending government dyads.

Surprisingly, uprisings in shared minority situations were found to significantly, albeit somewhat modestly, increase MID and FATAL dispute propensities within dyads sharing rebellious minority groups. Contrary to the findings of Woodwell (2004), the results suggest that spillover effects from ethnonational domestic rebellion may play a role in disrupting normal state relations.

The types of disputes involving irredentist-type and contending dyads differ as well. Irredentist-type dyads are only systematically related to territorial disputes, whereas contending government dyads are associated with both territorial and regime change disputes. Both types of dyads are involved in disputes, however, that tend to be less common, but more inflammatory, than the "policy"-type disputes most associated with democratic peace theory and the associated lack of joint democracy.

Overall, the results suggest that ethnonational demographics play a strong role in international relations. Although norms of sovereignty and territorial integrity tend to outweigh those of self-determination as a guiding international principal, the weakness of traditional status quo international norms vis-à-vis self-determination allows for the selective invocation of nationalist rhetoric as a situational pretext for interstate aggression. More than simple rhetoric, norms of self-determination appeal in fundamental ways across broad audiences in homeland states, and the desire to unite with kin populations in neighboring states often becomes a cultural mantra that guides many foreign policy choices.

The next section discusses the results concerning the domestic political structures and issues underlying the cultivation of territorial revisionist aims in irredentist-type dyads. While the theoretical background and empirical results that I have discussed suggest that irredentist homeland populations will usually hold preferences for unification with kin populations, the intensity of those preferences and the manner in which they are manifested in foreign policy outcomes can be expected to vary depending upon a number of institutional and situational factors.

Homeland Revisionist Behavior within Irredentist-Type Dyads

The analysis of factors related to dispute initiation by homeland states in irredentist-type dyads confirms the broad contours of the theoretical arguments of chapter 4, while sharpening understanding of the model presented in figure 4.1. In terms of the *interactions* presented in the model, the empirical analysis indicates that the presence of diaspora rebellion represents a category of its own, which, when it exists, largely overrides the consideration of other factors. I have suggested this is likely due to intense and widespread domestic audience costs that necessitate action by executives in almost any homeland state, no matter what domestic structures are present.

At the same time, the coupling of diaspora discontent, state structures favoring aggression, and the presence of military feasibility is shown to be an important combination leading to systematically higher levels of aggression when the "state structure favoring aggression" involves a weak civil-military divide. On the other hand, the presence of an insulated executive decision maker, as described in the concept of a narrow selectorate, represents a very weak link in the causal schema when compared to the role of military influence.

When examined individually (and controlling for other factors), several variables stand out as systematically influencing the initiation of international disputes within irredentist-type dyads. Some of these variables are influential in the initiation of disputes no matter the demographic context; others are influential only within irredentist-type situations. Table 5.10 compares the factors associated with dispute initiation in all contiguous dyads with those factors associated uniquely with homeland state dispute initiation.

The effect of military influence on dispute initiation within irredentist-type dyads is one of the most important findings of this study. The greater the influence

Table 5.10 Factors Associated with Increased Dispute Initiation Solely within Irredentist-type Dyads and within Both Irredentist-type and "General" (Non-Transborder) Dyads

Irredentist-type Dyads	Both Irredentist-type and General Dyads
Uprising of National Diaspora in kin state	
Military Influence over Foreign Policy	
Economic Growth— Previous Three Years	
Higher Global Trade (weakly supported)	
Strategic Territorial Rivalry	Strategic Territorial Rivalry
Economic Territorial Rivalry	Economic Territorial Rivalry
Military Feasibility	Military Feasibility
Narrow Selectorate (weakly supported)	Narrow Selectorate (much more strongly supported in general dyad than irredentist dyads)

of the military over policy within a homeland state, the greater the potential for violence within irredentist dyads.

As mentioned in chapter 4, military influence differs from the influence of other domestic audience due to several major factors: (1) the fact that militaries represent bastions of strong nationalist sentiment, sentiment that is constantly reinforced by the state in order to increase combat effectiveness by inculcating a spirit of self-sacrifice (Posen 1993: 81); (2) the enhanced ability of military decision makers to organize collective action to pressure for aggressive policies abroad; and (3) the preferences of military leaders for taking decisive aggressive action within the context of military crises in order to gain quick military advantage on the battlefield. Because the degree of military influence within a homeland state can be expected to wax and wane over time, military influence is particularly amenable to examination within the case studies that follow this chapter. When the military-civilian divide in a state is weak or nonexistent, homeland irredentist states pursue more aggressive foreign policies toward kin states. The results of interactive tests suggest that military influence is particularly important given the existence of a "discontent" diaspora residing in a relatively politically repressive or economic underdeveloped state.

Two economic control variables uniquely associated with homeland dispute initiation involve recent economic growth and higher levels of global trade (economic growth is a much stronger result). Although not the primary focus of this analysis, these results suggest that economic modernization and nationalist politics may be integrally related. Alternately, the results may simply indicate that states undergoing periods of economic stagnation may find themselves concentrating on internal problems to the exclusion of foreign policy issues (however, if this were so, it is hard to imagine why the effect would not be similar for nontransborder dyads). Either way, the results indicate that nationalist-driven foreign policies do not arise due to the preferences of homeland leaders to divert attention from economic problems at home. Nationalistically oriented aggression is, in fact, related to the presence of relative economic growth.

Last, several of the same factors affecting other states affect the foreign policies of homeland states in irredentist-type dyads. While the presence of a narrow selectorate may influence conflict initiation to some degree, this effect is actually weaker in the irredentist context than in nontransborder dyads. Economic and strategic considerations play a role in dispute initiation, although there is little evidence suggesting that leaders employ nationalist rhetoric as a pretext for pursuing such instrumental preferences. In addition to economic and strategic considerations, homeland states are also influenced by questions of military feasibility. Like all states with potentially aggressive preferences, leaders of homeland states have little stomach for embarking on policies doomed to failure, no matter the domestic consequences of inaction.

Conclusion

The preceding discussion section reviewed many of the findings of this chapter. However, with an eye toward applying the empirical findings to the case studies that follow, a quick recapitulation of the findings is listed. In terms of the demographic-normative hypotheses and econometric models, it was shown that:

1. Dyads with irredentist and contending government-type demographic patterns are associated with higher levels of intradyadic hostility when compared with other contiguous dyads. This relationship exists not only during the Cold War period (1951–1991), but during the post–Cold War period (1992–2001) as well.
2. Irredentist-type dyads witnessing diaspora rebellion are particularly prone to conflict.
3. Territorial disputes are associated with irredentist-type and contending government dyads, with relative polity levels representing an insignificant factor. Regime change disputes are associated with contending government-type demographics as well as a lack of joint democracy. Policy-type disputes are only significantly related to questions of joint democracy and are not found to be strongly related to demographic considerations.

While the theory discussed in chapter 3 suggested a connection between the existence of competing norms and ethnonational demographics, this relationship is not directly assessed in this chapter. The case studies that follow will examine in greater depth the relationship between international norms and state preference in irredentist situations. In terms of the domestic irredentist hypotheses, it was shown that:

1. Diaspora rebellion increases the likelihood of dispute initiation by homelands states. In the presence of such rebellion, most other factors seem to have only marginal influence on the level of aggression pursued by a homeland state.

Even military feasibility seems particularly irrelevant when military influence is coupled with diaspora rebellion, suggesting perhaps a greater potential for military-influenced leadership to overestimate homeland capabilities during crises.

2. High levels of military influence over foreign policy in homeland states in irredentist-type dyads increases the likelihood of dispute initiation by homeland states. This is particularly evident in the presence of a "discontent" diaspora residing in a relatively repressive or economic undeveloped state.
3. Positive economic growth is positively associated with homeland dispute initiation, suggesting a possible connection between modernization and more nationalist foreign policies.
4. Considerations of strategic and economic territorial rivalry as well as the military feasibility of aggression are factors associated with higher levels of dispute initiation in all dyads, including irredentist-types ones.

APPENDIX 5.1 Operationalization of Variables

Kin Uprising (RELEVANT): Simply interacting MINMAJ and UPETHNIC does not directly address the theoretical proposition that minority groups engaged in armed rebellion will draw nearby like-ethnic majority states into increased international disputes, requiring two further coding restrictions. First, the variable is restricted such that an uprising must actually take place in the "minority" half of the dyad. Second, the group that has rebelled must be of the same ethnic group as the majority state in the dyad. This variable is used in the undirected dyad models and the directed dyad affective models to assess hypotheses 1N, 1D, and is involved in the interactive processes underlying hypotheses 6D–9D.

Ethnic Uprising (UPETHNIC): The UPETHNIC variable is coded from the Uppsala Armed Conflict dataset (v. 1.0), which lists all armed uprisings within states that were responsible for at least 25 battle-related deaths. Deciphering which uprisings are full or partly ethnic in nature is fairly straightforward—usually an ethnically based armed group will include some ethnic or territorial label in their name. For questionable groups, the Minorities at Risk dataset was consulted in order to determine whether an ethnic group was engaged in rebellion against their government during the period of the uprising.[19] In the undirected dyad models, the variable is coded "1" if one state had an ethnic uprising the previous year and "2" if both states witnessed one. This variable is only used in the undirected dyad models to assess hypothesis 4N.

Selectorate Size (SELECT): Although the degree of state democracy versus autocracy is considered a control variable in table 5.1, undirected regression (where the presence or absence of joint democracy is assessed), it is theorized to be a key factor in determining the final foreign policy outcomes in homeland states in irredentist dyads. Under the assumption that selectorate size and the presence or absence of democracy are related, this variable draws from the Polity IV dataset, which codes each state government according to its level of democracy and authoritarianism (ranging from -10 for the most extreme authoritarian states, to $+10$ for the most democratic). Newer versions of the Polity IV dataset also provide interpolated DEMAUTLO values in cases of regime transition and anarchy. These values are utilized in this study in order to mitigate the effect of systematically eliminating dyads associated with weak states.

The variable is reclassified into a dichotomous variable which suggests either the presence or absence of a narrow selectorate, which is assumed to exist for Polity scores under −6. While such a dichotomy may seem ad hoc, the variable is operationalized as such with the understanding that the relevant theoretical factor affecting a leader's foreign policy behavior is the ability to isolate him or her from the consequences of foreign policy failure. Even within the somewhat autocratic states that would be represented in the Polity database around the numeral 0, a variety of audience groups may still exist that would be in a position to punish executives for foreign policy failure.[20] Thus, the value is dichotomized to be 1 in the case of a narrow selectorate (*low values* of Polity) and 0 in cases in which the selectorate is not considered narrow. This variable is used to assess hypothesis 4D and is involved in the interactive processes underlying hypotheses 6D–9D.

Military (MILITARY): This variable is intended to indicate whether a state's military can be expected to be influential in a state's policy decisions. MILITARY is coded 1 if one of two criteria is met: (1) if a government is headed directly by a military leader or primarily through military leaders (military-civilian type) or (2) if a military coup has been successfully attempted during the previous five years. The first criterion includes situations in which the role of military leaders in policy-making is clear and direct. The second criterion represents situations in which military rule no longer exists—but its potential return provides a powerful coercive influence over policy. The two criteria are combined due to the fact that many recent coups will result in the continued presence of direct military rule—cases which add no explanatory power to the model because military government is already coded. By combining the variables, I create one single variable that encompasses both direct military leadership plus instances when militaries turned power over to civilian regimes following a coup. The presence of a coup over the last five years and the type of government (REGIME-type) are coded in Banks' (2002) cross-national dataset. This variable assesses hypothesis 4D and is involved in the interactive processes underlying hypotheses 6D–9D.

Diaspora Discontent (DISCONT): One would expect that the economic and political grievances of national kin would foster louder calls for self-determination and provide homeland audiences with affective motivations for interventionist activity on behalf of kin abroad. This variable assesses the relative wealth and political freedom in kin states with homeland states. If a kin state is either poorer or more politically repressive than a homeland state, than the variable is coded as a 1, otherwise as a 0. Economic comparisons are assessed by comparing the average GDP per capita (constant 1996 U.S dollars) of homeland states to kin states based on data found in Gleditsch (2002). Political repression is compared utilizing the Polity variable found in the Polity IV dataset. This variable is used to assess hypothesis 2D and is involved in the interactive processes underlying hypotheses 6D–9D.

Military Feasibility (FEASIBLE): Military feasibility is based on three factors contained in the Correlates of War capabilities index. The first, most direct, indicator of military capability reflects the total number of soldiers in a state's military.[21] The second and third indicators consider a country's population and energy production, which are considered to proxy the human and industrial resources within a state that represent a greater or lesser ability to mobilize for conflict. The three factors are normalized so that they represent similar measurements (essentially transformed so they contain the same number of digits, so that one factor does not tend to subsume another) and added together.

A survey of the dataset suggests that in most cases, the composite measure seems to comport to reality in a sensible manner (for instance, the United States, Soviet Union, and China have roughly equal capabilities in the final years of the Cold War). However, recognizing that this "objective" measure will not conform entirely to reality (as is the case with any purported objective measure of power) and the fact that *perceived* capabilities are the basis of executive decision making, I adopt a fairly loose coding of what is considered a militarily "feasible" opportunity for military aggressive behavior. Within the data, military feasibility is coded as a 1 as long as a homeland state has at least one-fifth the measured capabilities of the kin state within a dyad. Otherwise, the variable is coded as a 0. This variable is used to assess hypothesis 5D and is involved in the interactive processes underlying hypotheses 6D–9D.

Control Variables

Peace Years (PYMID, PYFAT): Pooled time-series datasets require special methods to mitigate serial correlation due to the fact that the behavior of particular observations (dyad-years in this case) is strongly related to the behavior of those observations in preceding or following years. Perhaps the most popular method in international relations for enhancing the temporal independence of observations is through the use of a "peace-years" variable, which controls for unobserved variation in dyadic behavior attributable to the past behavior of the dependent variable. The peace-years variable measures the length of time since a dyad experienced a MID (PYMID) or an Fatal MID (PYFAT). Using such a method closely approximates the results one would obtain utilizing a survival model (Beck, Katz, and Tucker 1998). Adding a variable indicating how many years a dyad has remained at peace since it entered the dataset is the simplest way of modeling the effect of long stretches of war or peace on conflict propensity.

Regional Control Variables: The models utilize regional control variables as a method for mitigating spatial dependence among dyads. Spatial dependence is a phenomenon which suggests that the "neighborhood" within which a dyad exists plays a role in conditioning that dyad's behavior. The use of regional control variables helps control unobservable causal influences that are attributable to a dyad's geographic location and the behavior of regional neighbors. The regional controls employed include: the Americas, Europe, Africa, the Middle East (and North Africa), and Asia. The "benchmark" variable, against which these regions are compared codes states that are split between different regions.[22] The results from regional variables have little theoretical significance for this work, and are thus not reported with the results.

Alliances (ALLIES): Common state interests, possibly coupled with affective normative ties, may lead states to join in common defense alliances. The presence of alliance ties between states within a dyad can be expected to provide a powerful disincentive to conflict. ALLIES is a dichotomous variable coded 0 if no alliance exists and 1 if the states in a dyad are formally allied. The measurement is derived from alliance data compiled as part of the Correlates of War project (Singer and Small, 1993).

Capability-Ratio (CAP): The importance of maintaining a balance of military capabilities is a key realist concept. This variable assesses the capabilities of a state based upon the same formula used to determine military feasibility (manpower + population + energy) derived from the Correlates of War capabilities index (version 2.1). Unlike the FEASIBLE variable, this variable is continuous rather than dichotomized. This variable is utilized exclusively in the undirected dyad models.

Democracy-Autocracy (DEMAUTLO): The independent variable DEMAUTLO represents the classic "polity" variable employed by democratic peace scholars to measure regime type in a state. I draw from the Polity IV dataset, which codes each state government according to its level of democracy and authoritarianism (ranging from -10 for the most extreme authoritarian states, to $+10$ for the most democratic). The DEMAUTLO score represents the lower of the two polity scores in the dyad (the "less constrained" state) in the undirected dyad models in which it is employed.

Trade Dependence (DEPENDLO): Another cornerstone of liberal theory promotes the value of economic interdependence in fostering peaceful relations between states. The DEPENDLO variable examines bilateral commerce within a dyad by dividing total trade (exports plus imports) with a dyadic partner by the GDP of each state. Assuming that the state with the lower trade dependency is the lesser constrained of the two, the variable indicates the level of dependency for the lesser dependent state in the undirected dyad models. In the instrumental directed dyad model, the level of trade of a particular state with its dyadic partner is represented. Trade data derives from Gleditsch (2002). In the relatively few dyad-years in which trade data is not available, a value is derived that represents the average of the last and next years of available data.[23]

Interaction Terms (UPETHNIC × MAJMAJ and UPETHNIC × MINMIN): Two interaction terms are utilized to examine the specific effects of ethnic rebellion within two of the three different types of dyads. Dyads are coded non-zero only if they experienced ethnic rebellion the previous year and fit either the category of MAJMAJ or MINMIN. These variables are only used in the undirected dyad models.

Ethnic Heterogeneity (EHET): This variable assesses whether ethnic heterogeneity in a state mutes state aggression. Marshall (1997) suggests that states may have a power difficult time marshalling resources to project power abroad in ethnically fractionalized states. In terms of conflict initiation by homeland states, Marshall's theory suggests that large minority groups in states controlled by a majority population of a different group may not wish to see their power further diluted by the prospect of an increase in the size of the majority group. Furthermore, leaders may be reluctant to set a precedent for forceful territorial change in fear that it might lend itself to minority secessionist desires at home. Ethnic heterogeneity also represents a useful control variable in undirected dyads due to the fact that bordering states are more likely to share ethnic groups when those states are more ethnically heterogeneous.

The variable EHET is drawn from Vanhanen's (1999) ethnic heterogeneity dataset. As a composite index of race, language, and religion, it is the most appropriate measurement for this study due to its inclusive definition of ethnicity. The measurement ranges from 0 (North Korea) to 177 (Suriname). The coded variable represents the higher value of the two states in a dyad in the undirected dyad models, and simply the coding for a particular homeland state in the directed dyad instrumental model.

Economic or Strategic Territorial Claim (ECONHUTH; STRATHUTH): Leaders may use nationalist issues as justifications for aggression that is intended, at least part, to garner economic power or strategic advantage for the state. The incentive to acquire territories of strategic value is straightforward in terms of realist/neorealist reasoning. Such acquisitions will increase the power and security of a state by allowing for future power projection abroad or by establishing a more defensible geographical periphery that would enhance future state defense. The domestic political implications for leaders acquiring strategic territory are unclear, but one might expect that general political approval among domestic audiences would increase due to perceptions that state leadership was carrying out a successful foreign policy and security agenda. Furthermore, the more secure a state's geographical position, the less threat outside powers represent to a leader's position.

Huth (1996: 52) offers two major reasons why the economic value of territory also provides incentives for foreign policy revisionism. First, the acquisition and development of such resources would benefit certain sectors of the domestic economy, creating additional political support for the leader. Second, income generated through the export of acquired resources would generate future state revenue, which could be used to support domestic programs and defense needs. In addition, one might expect the procurement of additional economic resources to be particularly appealing when a leader's support is based upon a narrow group, or "selectorate," which may trade political support for private gain (Bueno de Mesquita, *et al*, 2002).

These variables are derived from data utilized in Huth (1996) and Huth and Allee (2002).[24] The variables are coded 1 if a given state claims a strategically or economically valuable piece of territory within a bordering area of its dyadic partner. According to Huth (1996: 256–257) strategic value is coded 1 when territory is near major shipping lanes, would provide an outlet to the sea for a landlocked country, contains military bases or threatens military bases of the claimant, could be used to establish a second front against the target state, or blocks a principal route of attack that would be used against a target in a conflict. Economic value is determined by the presence or absence of valuable minerals, fossil fuels, or other natural resources.

3-year GDP change (GDP3): Diversionary theory suggests that leaders use foreign policy initiatives, particular conflict, in a manner such as to deflect attention from domestic problems. Due to the emergence of an "out-group" threat to the nation, leaders seek to create internal domestic solidarity through a "rally around the flag effect" when their popularity sags (Simmel 1955; Coser 1956). Gelpi (1997) suggests the effect is particularly acute in democracies, whereby autocracies may suppress domestic discontent directly. Heldt (1999) finds little association between government-type and diversionary tactics, but he also suggests that such tactics may be employed when international structural opportunities arise. Others argue that high levels of domestic turmoil tend to cause "encapsulation" effects, whereby leadership is less likely to become involved in foreign disputes due to their weak position at home (Hazlewood 1975: 225; also see Salmore and Salmore 1973).[25]

This variable assumes that recent economic success or failure should have a strong correlation to public support of state leadership. Thus, this variable measures the change in GDP that a state has experienced over the preceding three years under the assumption that a finding associating GDP decline with aggressive foreign behavior would support diversionary theories while an association between economic decline and reduced aggression would tend to support the encapsulation theory. GDP data is derived from Gleditsch (2002).

Bilateral Trade and Global Trade (BITRADE; OPEN): These variables are used to examine whether states are restrained in their revisionist behavior through direct bilateral trade ties or through susceptibility to global trade sanctions that may result from aggressive behavior.

Ambrosio (2001) argues that the degree of permissiveness displayed by the international community vis-à-vis particular irredentist situations is *the* primary factor determining the likelihood of militant irredentism. As Huth (1996: 111) points out, however, domestic incentives can often override a perceived lack of international support. While perhaps not representing the same degree of constraint as relative military power might, international constraints lead not only to perceptions that the citizens of a homeland state will pay a price not only for failing in any aggressive endeavors, but also for succeeding.

One form of international constraint lies in the threat that military aggression poses to international trade.. It is now standard liberal international relations theory that economic interdependence "gives each party a stake in the economic well-being of the other—and in avoiding militarized disputes" (Russett and Oneal 2001: 129). Thus, levels of trade among partners within a dyad as well as a homeland state's overall openness to the global economy may affect the propensity of a homeland state to initiate a conflict with a kin state. These variables are monadic indicators of a state's trade/GDP with its dyadic partner (BITRADE) and with the world as a whole (also divided by GDP). This data is derived from Gleditsch (2002).

Large Uprising (UPBIGK): When assessing instrumental opportunities for aggression, one would expect that larger insurrections in target states would lead to greater state vulnerability. This variable eliminates civil conflicts found in the

Uppsala database that are considered "minor" (less than 1,000 deaths in course of a conflict). While there may be affective reasons for greater homeland aggression resulting from minor uprisings in kin states, the instrumental military implications are likely to be less significant. Thus, this more restricted view of uprisings (not necessarily ethnic ones, however) is utilized to assess whether homeland states systematically avail themselves of opportunities resulting from the weakened security status of kin states that are confronting domestic strife.

APPENDIX 5.2

EXPANDED METHODOLOGICAL DISCUSSION

The variables described in Appendix A are used in the construction of the following generalized logit models designed to test the effects of hypotheses 1N–7N and 1D–5D:

Normative-Demographic Model

Prob (MID, FATAL, TERRMID, POLMID, or GOVMID = 1) = $1/\{1 + \exp{-[\beta_0 + \beta_1 \text{MAJMAJ} + \beta_2 \text{MINMA} + \beta_3 \text{MINMIN} + \beta_4 \text{UPETHNIC} + \beta_5 \text{RELEVANT} + \beta_6(\text{UPETHNIC} + \text{MAJMAJ}) + \beta_7(\text{UPETHNIC} + \text{MINMIN}) + \beta_8 \text{EHET} + \beta_9 \text{ALLIED} + \beta_{10} \text{CAP} + \beta_{11} \text{DEMAUTLO} + \beta_{12} \text{DEPENDLO} + \beta_{13} \text{PYMID} \text{ or } \beta_{13} \text{PYFAT} + \beta_{14\ldots 18} \text{ REGIONAL controls } or\ \beta_{14} \text{RGDPPC}]\}$

Homeland Dispute Initiation Irredentist Model
(restricted to dyads that are characterized as MINMAJ)

Prob (MID or FATAL = 1) = $1/[1 + \exp{-(\beta_0 + \beta_1 \text{ RELEVANT} + \beta_2 \text{DISCONT} + \beta_3 \text{MILITARY} + \beta_4 \text{SELECT} + \beta_5 \text{FEASIBLE} + \beta_6 \text{HUTHECON} + \beta_7 \text{HUTHSTRAT} + \beta_8 \text{UPBIGK} + \beta_9 \text{GDP3} + \beta_{10} \text{BITRADE} + \beta_{11} \text{OPEN} + \beta_{12} \text{PYMID} \text{ or } \beta_{13} \text{PYFAT} + \beta_{13\ldots 17}}$ REGIONAL controls or $\beta_6 \text{RGDPPC})$

The models are more specifically analyzed utilizing population-averaged (or marginal) logit models using generalized estimating equations.[26] As a population-averaged model, the General Estimating Equation (GEE) "models . . . the average response over the subpopulation that shares a common value X" (Diggle, et al. 1994 quoted in Zorn 2001: 474), rather than examining case specific trends. This is particularly useful for pooled time-series data, where the object is to establish patterns among subgroups over the entire period, rather than to track temporal changes in specific variables. Since the key demographic variables employed in this study do not fluctuate within dyadic clusters, the implicit assumption is that (all other factors being equal) a minority-majority dyad, such as India-Pakistan, or a majority-majority dyad, such as North and South Korea, will not have a different conflict propensity in 1985 than they did in 1955. The GEE approach is appropriate because the goal is to show whether or not dyads with certain demographic characteristics (i.e., possessing transborder ethnic groups) differ systematically from dyads lacking those characteristics. In his recent article Zorn (2001: 475), provides an example of why a population-averaged model, such as the GEE, is more appropriate for the type of research conducted in this study.

If one were interested in, say, the effect of democratization on the propensity for a particular nation or pair of nations to go to war, then the conditional approach would be more appropriate. If, instead we wished to assess the general propensity of autocracies and democracies to engage in interstate conflict, a marginal approach (such as the GEE) would be called for.[27]

Each equation utilizes Huber robust standard errors. These standard errors are further adjusted for dyadic clustering, which, along with the utilization of a peace-years variable, mitigates the lack of statistical independence within among the dyad-years.[28] All independent variables are lagged one year in order to assure that they represent values that are assessed as temporally prior to the outbreak of a dispute that might occur during the same year.

Contiguous Dyads as the Basis of Analysis

Only contiguous dyads are included in the analysis. The criterion for contiguity is the standard condition that two states either share a border or are connected by a relatively small stretch of water (under 200 miles). In addition, any state adjacent to a colonial holding of another state is considered contiguous with the home country.

The sample is restricted to contiguous dyads for several reasons. Since a prime cause of the escalation of ethnic demographics into international conflict is hypothesized as involving border disputes—whether they are public intergovernmental disagreements or whether they are incidental spillover effects from otherwise internal conflict—it is borders themselves that are generally at issue. Second, while only a handful of major powers are able to project themselves militarily over long distances,[29] "politically relevant dyad" datasets are characterized by a disproportionately large number of noncontiguous dyads composed of at least one major power (approaching two-thirds, usually). Although one may control for such effects utilizing a variable indicating contiguity, including major powers within the framework of this study would pose large analytical and theoretical problems. Due to the myriad of overlapping identities that characterize identities within the large "civic" democracies of the United States, France, and Great Britain, it is difficult to code politically salient ethnic groups within these states.[30] If, for instance, one were to code Americans of African descent as an African "diaspora," one would seemingly have to do the same with the tens of millions of Americans of Irish ancestry—even though their influence on U.S. policy toward Ireland (and Northern Ireland) has been marginal (Guelke, 1996) due to the fact that few Americans would hold their Irish-ness to be a primary identity. Theoretically, considering that the Irish ancestral population in the United States is a minority, one would also expect the Republic of Ireland to view regions of the United States (e.g., Massachusetts) in a similar fashion as it does Northern Ireland—an absurd proposition due to the factor of distance, the lack of any true territorial referents, and the nature of overlapping identities within the United States.

Furthermore, while some self-identified minority ethnic groups residing in major powers might wield some influence on foreign policy, the salience of the regional issues with which they are concerned will not be as high for most of the population. Such influence might lead to greater attention and diplomatic or financial support for one country or another, but, unless the major power has an accompanying strategic interest, it is unlikely to bear the potential costs of military confrontation. Carment and James (1995) note that, while occasionally attempting to use ethnic conflict to their advantage, superpowers often went to great lengths to help manage ethnonationalist disputes and prevent their international escalation. The interests, nature, and capabilities of the major powers were qualitatively different from much of the rest of the world, which continued to be as, or more, concerned with age-old ethnic nationalism as it was with geopolitics or Cold war ideology.

Interactive Analysis—Simplification through the use of a Classification Tree

The second part of the empirical analysis examines factors associated with dispute initiation by homeland states in irredentist-type dyads. In addition to examining such factors separately, it is desirable to examine how they relate interactively. Simply including all the possible combinations of interactions within a standard regression model, however, causes two major statistical problems. The lesser of these problems concerns the difficulty involved in analyzing an "inefficient" regression equation given the presence of 32 variable combinations and only slightly less than 2000 cases. The presence of numerous variable combinations that contain only a small number of observations, in particular, prevents the convergence of statistical estimates. Since many of these combinations yield little explanatory power, modeling is facilitated by narrowing the field to the more relevant variables.

The larger of the statistical problems associated with including numerous interaction terms within a standard regression model involves the issue of multicollinearity. If several interactions involving a particular variable are analyzed simultaneously with that variable, a higher degree of multicollinearity may occur if the interaction primarily takes one value. For instance, if only 10 percent of dyad-years characterized by military influence are also characterized by diaspora discontent, then analyzing military influence (coded as a 1) simultaneously with an interactive variable that is similarly coded as a 1 in the 90 percent of cases characterized as military influence/no discontent causes an extremely high degree of multicollinearity. Multiply this problem by the five potential variables used in each interactive combination, and the difficulty of including the interactions in a standard regression becomes clear.

I simplify the interactive analysis of decision-making outcomes creating a classification tree that examines different combinations of variables. Classification trees represent the division of ordinal or (in this case) dichotomous variables into subtrees and terminal nodes that represent combinations of the variables.[31]

Utilizing tree-modeling software (found in the program *SPLUS*, version 6.2), a classification tree is constructed and "pruned." The construction and pruning of the tree model organizes the variables efficiently so that certain variable combinations end in terminal nodes when further divisions yield little improvement for the overall model. The two major conditions causing a tree to end in a terminal node are: (1) that further division of a variable would result in less than 20 cases in the a subsequent node, which is deemed to small for further statistical estimation, and (2) cross-tabulated analysis suggests high numbers of false predictions for further nodes, indicating that adding further variables to a combination would have little influence.

The resulting terminal nodes each represent a series of dichotomous variables that are coded 1 during particular dyad-years that represent a particular combination of key variables and 0 otherwise. For instance, the United Kingdom-Ireland dyads during the 1960s represent the variable combination: No Uprising, No Discontent, No Military Influence, No Narrow Selectorate, and No Military Feasibility. The terminal node variable representing this combination of factors would be coded 1 during the 1960s for the United Kingdom-Ireland dyads, while all the other variables representing other combinations would be coded 0 for these dyads. The variables that are included in the subsequent regression model are, thus, similar to those indicating geographic region—that is, for each case one variable combination (representing a single interactive variable) will be coded as a 1, and all other variable combinations are coded as zeroes.

APPENDIX 5.3 Specific Codification of Transborder Variables

	Minority-Majority Dyads	
Ethnic Group	**Majority State**	**Minority State**
Haitian black	Haiti	Dominican Republic
American Indian	Bolivia	Peru
		Paraguay
		Chile
		Argentina
Latin (Spanish descent)	Mexico	United States
Latin (Spanish descent)	Cuba	United States
Latin (Spanish descent)	Panama	United States
Irish (N. Ireland Catholic)	Ireland	Great Britain
Dutch/Flemish	Netherlands	Belgium
French/Walloon	France	Belgium
French/Swiss	France	Switzerland
French	France	Luxembourg
Italian/Swiss	Italian	Switzerland
Hungarian	Hungary	Yugoslavia
		Romania
		Czechoslovakia
		Slovakia
Albanian	Albania	Yugoslavia
		Macedonia
Greek	Greece	Albania
Turk	Turkey	Cyprus
Turk	Turkey	Bulgaria
Swede	Sweden	Finland

Continued

APPENDIX 5.3 Continued

Minority-Majority Dyads

Ethnic Group	Majority State	Minority State
Finnish	Finland	Sweden
Hausa	Niger	Nigeria
Mande	Mali	Cote d'Ivoire
Arab	Libya	Chad
Hutu	Burundi	Zaire
Hutu	Rwanda	Zaire
		Uganda
Somali	Somalia	Kenya
		Ethiopia
Arab	Saudi Arabia	Israel
Arab	Egypt	Israel
Arab	Iraq	Iran
Arab	Syria	Israel
Arab	Lebanon	Israel
Arab	Jordan	Israel
Arab	Sudan	Chad
Farsi (-speaking peoples)	Iran	Afghanistan
Chinese	China	Vietnam (DRV)
Hindu	India	Pakistan
Muslim	Pakistan	India
Bengali	Bangladesh	India
Malay	Malaysia	Thailand
		Singapore
		Indonesia
Vietnamese	Vietnam & North and South Vietnam	Cambodia
Papuan	Papua New Guinea	Indonesia
Sotho	Lesotho	South Africa
Tswana	Botswana	South Africa
Polish	Poland	Lithuania
Slovak	Slovakia	Czech Republic
Croatian	Croatia	Yugoslavia
		Bosnia
Serb	Yogoslavia	Croatia
		Bosnia
Slav	Ukraine	Moldova
Russian	Russia	Estonia
		Latvia
		Lithuania
		Ukraine
		Belarus
		Kazakhstan
Belarusian	Belarus	Latvia
Armenian	Armenia	Azerbaijan

Continued

APPENDIX 5.3 Continued

	Minority-Majority Dyads	
Ethnic Group	Majority State	Minority State
Azeri	Azerbaijan	Armenia ("ethnically cleansed" by 1993)
		Georgia
		Iran
Turkmen	Turkmenistan	Iran
		Afghanistan
Tajik	Tajikistan	Afghanistan
		Uzbekistan
Uzbek	Uzbekistan	Afghanistan
		Turkmenistan
		Tajikistan
		Kyrgyzstan
Kazakh	Kazakhstan	Turkmenistan
		Uzbekistan

	Majority-Majority Dyads	
Ethnic Group	Majority State	Majority State
English-speaking	United States	Canada
Latino (Spanish descent)	Guatemala	Honduras
		El Salvador
		Mexico
Latino (Spanish descent)	Costa Rica	Panama
		Nicaragua
Latino (Spanish descent)	Columbia	Venezuela
		Panama
Latino (Spanish descent)	Peru	Chile
		Ecuador
Latino (Spanish descent)	Argentina	Paraguay
		Chile
		Uruguay
German	Germany (&GFR)	Austria
		Switzerland
	West Germany	East Germany
Greek	Greece	Cyprus
Fang	Gabon	Equatorial Guinea
Arab	Algeria	Morocco
		Tunisia
		Libya
Arab	Libya	Tunisia
		Egypt
		Sudan
Arab	Egypt	Sudan

Continued

APPENDIX 5.3 Continued

Majority-Majority Dyads

Ethnic Group	Majority State	Majority State
Arab	Iraq	Syria
		Jordan
		Kuwait
		Saudi Arabia
Arab	Syria	Jordan
		Lebanon
Arab	Saudi Arabia	Jordan
		Oman
		Yemen
		Bahrain
		Egypt
		UAE
Arab	North Yemen	South Yemen
Shi'ite	Iran	Iraq
Chinese	China	Taiwan
Korean	North Korea	South Korea
Vietnamese	N. Vietnam	S. Vietnam
Malay	Malaysia	Brunei
Romanian	Romania	Moldova

Minority-Minority Dyads

Ethnic Group	Minority State	Minority State
American Indian	United States	Canada
		Mexico
American Indian	Mexico	United States
		Guatemala
American Indian	Honduras	Guatemala
		El Salvador
Black	Panama	Costa Rica
		Columbia
American Indian, Black	Venezuela	Columbia
		Brazil
Black	Ecuador	Brazil
American Indian	Ecuador	Peru
American Indian	Argentina	Paraguay
		Chile
Basque/Roma	France	Spain
Roma	France	Italy
Roma	Hungary	Czechoslovakia
		Slovakai
		Croatia
		Yugoslavia
		Romania

Continued

APPENDIX 5.3 Continued

	Minority-Minority Dyads	
Ethnic Group	**Minority State**	**Minority State**
Roma	Greece	Bulgaria
		Turkey
Azeri/Kurd	USSR	Iran
Tajik/Uzbek	USSR	Afghanistan
Buriat	USSR	Mongolia
Mande/Susu	Guinea	Guinea-Bissau
Tuareg/djerema-songhai	Mali	Niger
Fulani	Mali	Guinea
		Burkina Faso
Pulaar	Senegal	Guinea
Yoruba	Benin	Nigeria
Mande	Cote d'Ivoire	Guinea
Mossi-dagomba	Ghana	Burkina Faso
Ewe	Ghana	Togo
Sara	Chad	Central African Republic
Bakongo	Congo	Zaire
Bakongo	Congo	Angola
Tutsi	Zaire	Burundi
		Rwanda
Bankongo/Cabinda	Zaire	Angola
Lunda/Yeke	Zaire	Zambia
Fulani, Mandinka	Guinea-Bissau	Senegal
Fulani, Wolof	Gambia	Senegal
Fulani	Benin	Burkina Faso
Aja-Gbe	Benin	Togo
Fulani, Yoruba	Benin	Nigeria
Fulani	Niger	Cameroon
Dan	Cote d' Ivoire	Liberia
Kisi, Kpelle	Guinea	Liberia
Dagaara, Frafra	Burkina Faso	Ghana
Gourmachema	Burkina Faso	Togo
Ndau	Mozambique	Zimbabwe
Nyanja, Tumbuka	Zambia	Malawi
Urdu (speaking)	India	Pakistan
Rendille-borana/Somali	Kenya	Ethiopia
Tutsi	Rwanda	Burundi
Afar	Djibouti	Ethiopia
		Eritrea
Afar	Ethiopia	Eritrea
White	South Africa	Zimbabwe
		Namibia
San Bushmen	Namibia	Botswana
Berber	Algeria	Morocco
		Tunisia

Continued

APPENDIX 5.3 Continued

	Minority–Minority Dyads	
Ethnic Group	Minority State	Minority State
Kurd	Iran	Turkey
		Iraq
Kurd	Iraq	Turkey
		Syria
Kurd	Turkey	Syria
Baluchi	Iran	Pakistan
South Asian worker	UAE	Oman
Tamil	India	Sri Lanka
Hill tribe	Thailand	Myanmar (Burma)
Chinese	Malaysia	Singapore
		Indonesia
Chinese	Indonesia	Singapore
Albanian	Yugoslavia	Macedonia
Muslim	Yugoslavia	Bosnia
Russian	Ukraine	Moldova
Russian	Latvia	Estonia
		Lithuania
Russian	Belarus	Lituania
		Ukraine
Russian	Turkmenistan	Kazakhstan
Russian	Tajikistan	Uzbekistan
Russian	Krgyzstan	Uzbekistan
Armenian	Georgia	Azerbaijan
Uzbek	Afghanistan	Turkmenistan
		Tajikistan
Tajik	Uzbekistan	Afghanistan
		Turkmenistan

APPENDIX 5.4 Classification Tree

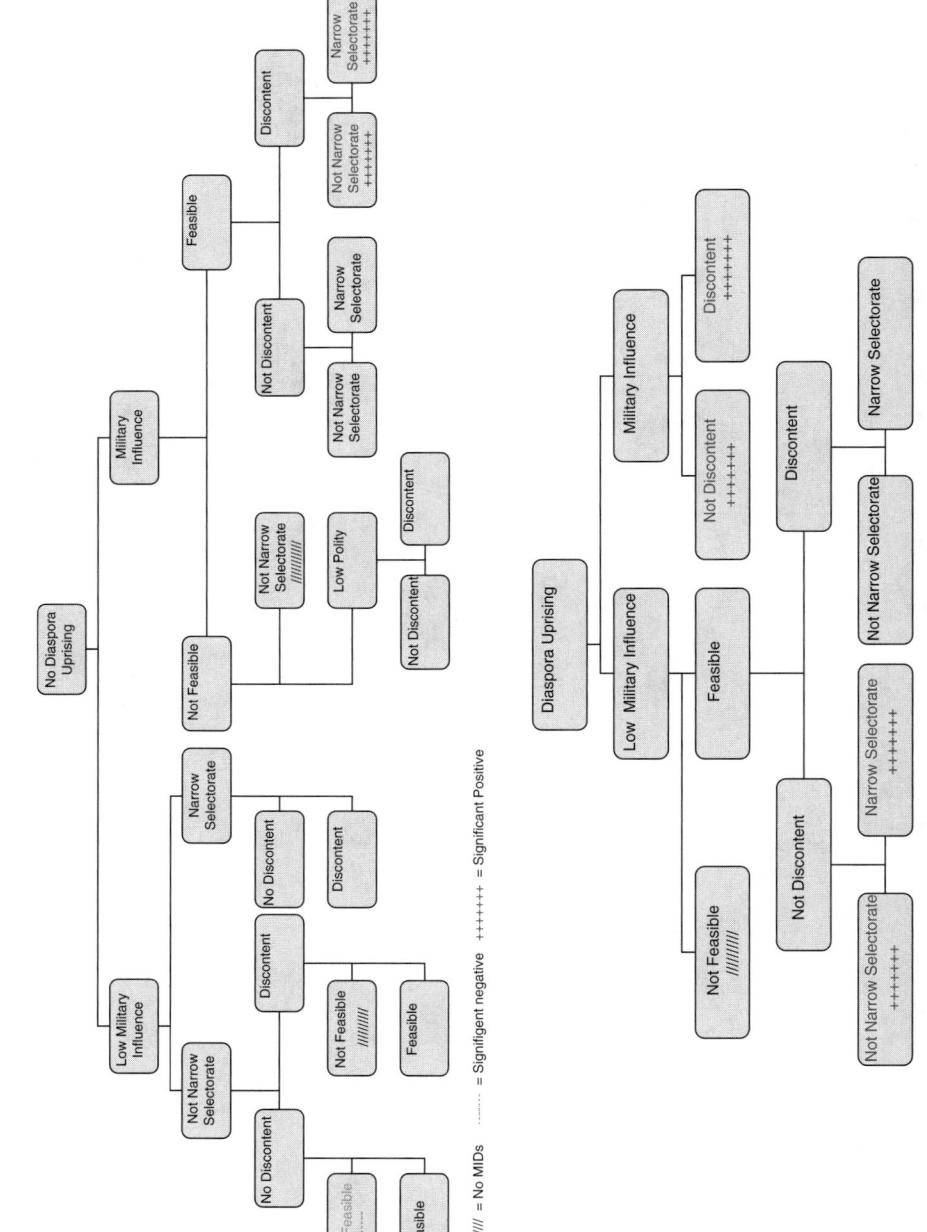

PART II

INTRODUCTION TO CASE STUDIES

The theory and findings of the first part of this work represent the basis of the case studies that follow. The case studies analyze irredentist-type situations that have occurred over the past century and suggest how the presence or absence of conflictual norms affects long-term bilateral relations between states and how issues and structures within irredentist-type homeland affect shorter-term foreign policy agendas. The three main findings to be examined in the context of the case studies are that: (1) the presence of irredentist-type demographics will cause long term bilateral instability due to normative conflict that leads to mutual distrust; (2) military influence over policy will lead to higher levels of conflict initiation by homeland states, particularly if a diaspora is viewed as discontented; and (3) diaspora rebellion will increase both bilateral dispute rates and unilateral dispute initiation.

The first two studies will involve a focused comparison of the relations among three states, and the underlying dynamics involved in these relations. I disaggregate each of these triads into three sets of the bilateral relations, which I examine in turn. The bilateral relations of these states are characterized by alternate values of the key explanatory demographic variable (MINMAJ, or the presence or absence of an "irredentist-type situation") discussed earlier. I choose cases by including states that are as similar as possible in respect to geographical region, general economic development level, and other "fixed" factors not involving demographics that might influence relations over a long period.

In addition to analyzing the bilateral relations between the three states involved in the case studies, I also examine variations in foreign policy outcomes related to an irredentist homeland state in each dyad. The following table summarizes the major findings concerning dispute initiation by irredentist-type states.

Of the factors, Military Influence, Diaspora uprising and the interaction of Military Influence-Discontent-Feasibility are the most theoretically central factors in this work. I will address the surprisingly significant economic growth variable in respect to the cases as well.

The first set of trilateral relations will analyze Somalia-Kenya-Ethiopia. The case study examines the root causes of conflict by examining conflicting (Somalia-Kenya and Somalia-Ethiopia) and complimentary (Kenya-Ethiopia) interpretations and

Factor	MID significance	FATAL significance
Military Influence	p < .01	p < .05
Diaspora uprising	p < .01	p < .05
Economic Growth (3 years)	p < .01	p < .01
Military Feasibility	p < .05	not significant
Strategically valuable territorial claim	p < .01	p < .05
Economically valuable territorial claim	p < .01	p < .01
Military Influence + Discontent + Feasible (interactive model)	p < .01	not applicable

employment of international norms of territorial integrity and self-determination brought about by the presence of a divided Somali nation. Furthermore, the study focuses particularly on the role of nationalist rebellion among Somali diaspora and military rule in Somalia in producing greater or lesser levels of aggression in Somali foreign policy behavior.

The second case study involves relations among Pakistan, India, and China. The general state of relations between these countries closely parallels those of the first case in that one dyad was highly conflictual (Pakistan-India, as compared to Somalia-Ethiopia); one mutually suspicious (China-India, as compared to Somalia-Kenya); and a one quite cordial, despite large ideological differences (Pakistan-China, as compared to Ethiopia-Kenya). Once again, I examine the general roots of conflict and the differences in the "baseline" levels of enmity existing among these three states. Only one of the pairs, Pakistan and India, shares significant transborder national populations. The two other pairs, India-China and Pakistan-China do not share such groups, and offer a basis of comparison with the nationalist-type politicking and instability that has existed between India and Pakistan. The focus on domestic politics then turns to Pakistan, with a particular eye toward understanding the role of military influence in foreign policy decision making.

To summarize, the first two case studies involve these trilateral relations:

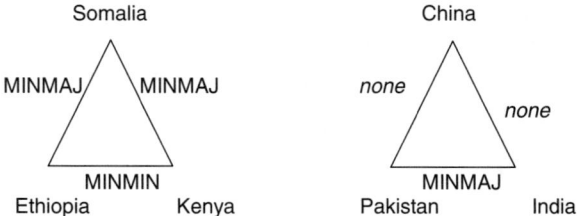

The third case will examine bilateral relations between Greece and Turkey throughout much of the twentieth century. This case merits particular attention due to the fact that a variable of primary interest in this study—namely, the MINMAJ variable, actually changes values for these two states. Until the mid-1920s, both states were home to large minorities of the other ethnic group. Due to ethnic cleansing as well as more orderly population exchanges during the 1920s, the transborder minorities were greatly reduced within each state. As would be hypothesized from this work, three decades of peaceful relations ensued after the mitigation of the transborder nationality issue. However, during the 1950s and after, the independence of Cyprus introduced a new and powerful destabilizing influence on the bilateral relations of these states. I will argue that the Cyprus issue represented the reemergence of the transborder national question—this time by "proxy" given the presence of Greek and Turkish diaspora groups that reside on the island.

CHAPTER 6

SOMALIA, ETHIOPIA, AND KENYA

Contrary to popular perceptions, the colonial powers did not demarcate sub-Saharan African state boundaries with a blatant disregard for the ethnonational tribal boundaries of its inhabitants. African boundaries, for the most part, did not divide large nations—rather, many small ethnic groups where bound together in larger states. This fact has complicated domestic politics, but has not necessarily had a major destabilizing effect on international relations in the region. Due largely to the relatively small number of transborder (not including transborder minority) demographic situations, relations amongst African states have been, until recent years, more peaceful than most global regions. Figure 6.1 displays the relative number of MID and fatal MIDS that have occurred within each global region among the dyads included in this study (divided by total regional dyads). The (sub-Saharan) Africa region, as displayed in figure 6.1, represents all the African dyads except those involving Somalia, which accounts for 23 of 153 regional MIDS and 17 of 54 fatal MIDS. Figure 6.1 indicates that Africa was one of the most peaceful areas of the world during the Cold War, at least in terms of interstate relations. One major exception to the pattern of relatively peaceful coexistence, however, involved one of the very few irredentist situations in the region—namely, the relations between Somalia and its neighbors that have been home to large Somali diaspora.[1]

This chapter is divided into two parts that largely reflect the structure of the earlier empirical analysis. The major reasons for *bilateral* hostility within dyads that contain potential irredentist conflicts involve threat perceptions to states and nations created by conflicting international norms of national self-determination and state sovereignty. The first part of this case study will examine the normatively conflictual elements of the relationships between Somalia and its neighbors, Ethiopia and Kenya, as well as the relationship of the more normatively congruent policies of Kenya and Ethiopia toward one another. I examine the role played by irredentist demographics in the Somalia-Ethiopia and Somalia-Kenya dyads, and how such demographics ultimately affected these dyads differently than the Kenya-Ethiopia dyad, where no such demographic pattern exists. As ideological polar opposites from the fall of the Selassie regime onward, one would expect, from a

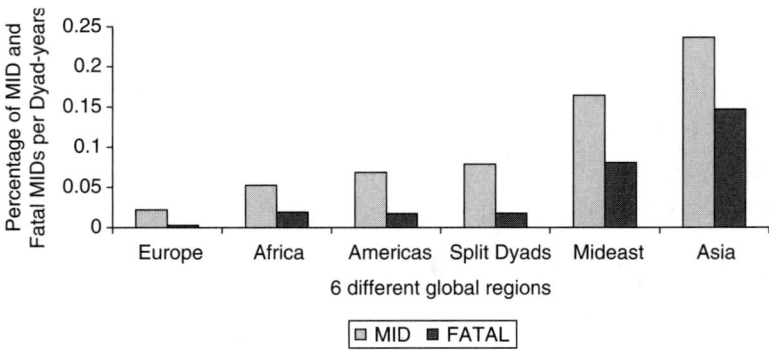

Figure 6.1 Percentage of MID and Fatal MIDs per Dyad-years in Global Regions

Cold War perspective, that Kenya and Ethiopia would have represented the hostile dyad among these three states. As will be described, however, irredentist nationalism trumped political ideology as the major factor determining the course of international relations between these three states.

The second part of this chapter will analyze, with respect to the Somali case, the factors derived from the earlier empirical analysis that were found to be related to rates of dispute initiation by irredentist-type homeland states. Although, due to the irredentist situation facing Somali leaders, one would expect foreign policy to be more aggressive overall than most other states, the level of foreign aggression undertaken by Somali leaders differed in scale during different time periods.

International Norms, Societal Pressures, and Irredentist-Type Demographics

The following section details the bilateral relations between Somalia and Ethiopia, Somalia and Kenya, and Ethiopia and Kenya. Of particular interest is how the interaction between the political norms of territorial integrity and national self-determination played out in the political arena, and how it influenced the course of events throughout the period 1960–1990. In essence, when we are examining the systemic interplay of events among these states, we are analyzing how the presence or absence of irredentist minorities affected expectations and subsequent initiations of conflicts between these states.

Utilizing the systemic regression model displayed in chapter 5 (table 5.1),[2] table 6.1 shows how many disputes are predicted by the systemic regression model versus the actual number of disputes within these dyads over the period 1960–1990.

Table 6.1 reflects how the predicted ordinal relationship of dispute propensities is similar to that found in reality. However, whereas predictions for the Somalia-Kenya dyad are very close to reality, the systemic model greatly underestimates the number of MIDs and fatal MIDs in the Somalia-Ethiopia dyad. Clearly, factors were involved in the Somalia-Ethiopia relationship that caused the relationship to

Table 6.1 Predicted versus Actual MIDs and Fatal MIDs in Dyads

	MID-actual	MID-predicted	FATAL-actual	FATAL-predicted
Somalia-Ethiopia	65%	24%	48%	11%
Somalia-Kenya	11%	12%	7%	7%
Ethiopia-Kenya	0%	7%	0%	3%

be particularly violent, even for an irredentist-type relationship. The difference in conflict levels between Somalia and Ethiopia versus Somalia and Kenya is an important issue that is explored in greater detail later. As predicted, however, both of these dyads are more violent than the Ethiopia-Kenya dyad—even though Ethiopia and Kenya would normally have been expected to be major rivals (after the mid-1970s) in the context of the Cold War divide.

At the heart of hostility between Somalia and its neighbors lies the presence of contending, largely incompatible ideological norms, which alternately stress the value of self-determination versus that of territorial integrity and noninterference. Often, public pressures weigh on executive decision makers, causing them to selectively promote diaspora self-determination, even if such policies threaten traditional international norms. States, such as Somalia, which pursue aggressive foreign policies designed to promote self-determination of diaspora groups abroad are by nature revisionist in comparison to those states that are more responsive to other, more inherently status quo norms. However, states targeted by nationalist foreign policies can be expected to engage in their own forms of defense aggression directed at homeland states due to suspicions arising from the potentially nationalist motivations of homeland state leadership.

The next section begins by giving a brief overview of the development of Somali nationalism in the period before independence in 1960. The drive to obtain independence for territories divided between different colonial powers later morphed into Somali foreign policies that pressed for the realization of self-determination for Somali regions assigned to other African states during the decolonization process.

The Roots of Somali Nationalism

Like most national movements, Somali nationalism in the Horn of Africa predates the establishment of the Somali state. However, despite its later prominent role in domestic politics, a sense of nationhood and its accompanying nationalist drive occurred relatively late in the history of the Somali "ethnic" group. Somalis, although united by linguistic ties and a common Islamic religion, were strongly divided along tribal, one might even say ethnic,[3] lines—the dominant cultural, social, and political cleavage until the post–Second World War period. Despite uprisings against the British rule in 1893, 1898, 1901, 1913, and 1916, it is "doubtful that Somali resistance was undertaken with any clear goals in mind" (Turton 1972:125), while tribal (and intratribal) divides led various factions to side both for and against imperialist powers.[4] This is not to say that no sense of nationalist solidarity (particularly based along religious lines) existed among certain elites in the early part of the century—only that this nascent nationalism did not translate into any sense of mass political nationalism or a sense of national obligation.

Along with Ethiopia, British forces recovered Somalia from Italian occupation in 1941. The modern Somali nationalist movement began in 1943 with the establishment of the Somali Youth Club (SYC)—later renamed the Somali Youth League (SYL). British administrators, who saw the emergence of Somali lobbying groups as a powerful hedge against Italian- national groups opposed to the presence of the British, supported the emergence of the SYC/SYL.

The SYC/SYL expanded rapidly, and, by the end of the 1940s, had opened offices in all of the four main British occupied territories—traditional British Somaliland (in the north), Italian Somalia (on the Indian Ocean), the Northern Frontier District (later part of Kenya), and the Ogaden[5] region. The SYL's stated objectives were to unify all Somali territories; to create opportunities for universal education; to develop the Somali language by instituting a common written language; to oppose the restoration of Italian rule (Lewis 1963:149). Another avowed goal of the SYL was to supplant clan-based individual identities with a wider Somali-based national identity. Nationalist leaders viewed clanism as a primary factor that had "facilitated the partition of their people by foreign powers" (Lewis 1980: 167), and, thus, sought to diminish clan identity in order to maximize the prospects of national unity.

One goal of the SYL agenda was frustrated when the Ogaden region was granted to Ethiopia in 1948—although a British military presence remained. In 1949, insult was added to injury for the SYL when the UN General Assembly voted for an Italian trusteeship in Southern Somaliland. Thus, coupled with French control of "French Somaliland" (Djibouti), Somalis were again divided into five different regions amongst four different foreign powers.

The finalization of the trusteeship arrangement, and the prospect of eventual independence, muted Somali nationalism to some degree in the 1950s. However, in a sign of things to come, the biggest source of nationalist anger revolved around the final abandonment of the Ogaden region by the British in 1954, a scenario that was to be repeated in the Kenyan Northern Frontier District (NFD) in Somalia's postindependence period.

Although the evacuation of the Ogaden stirred nationalist sentiment in the other Somali territories, the pressing tasks surrounding the impending independence of British Somaliland and the Italian trusteeship in southern Somalia hindered potentially violent manifestations of nationalism among Somalis while necessitating continued cooperation with the British. The SYL government led by Abdullah Issa[6] that came to power in 1956 in (Italian) Somalia was more immediately concerned with economic and social affairs than with the Ogaden situation (Lewis 1980: 156–157).

British Somaliland became independent on June 26, 1960, and Somalia followed suit on July 1, 1960. Having concluded agreements with the Italian and British governments on the matter, both governments quickly agreed to unite into a common state. Within a week, a single Republic of Somalia was formed from the former colonial territories. A new national assembly quickly approved the first administration, headed by Aden Abdullah Osman as president and Abdul Rashid Ali Shermarke as prime minister.

The International Context

While Somali foreign policy was notably more militant in regard to Ethiopia than it was to Kenya, many of the same international principles were at stake in both these relationships. Of particular interest are the opposing principles cited by the antagonists in these disputes to justify their positions. Conflicting normative rhetoric, not surprisingly, revolved around competing interpretations and citations of international agreements such as those included within the Organization of African Unity (OAU) and UN charters.

As described in chapter 2, the UN charter and the Universal Declaration for Human Rights both recognize self-determination as a desirable goal. Although the right of self-determination came to be commonly understood as principally associated with anticolonial efforts, the very definition of anticolonial was also open to interpretation. This was particularly relevant in the case of Ethiopia, which Somali leaders always argued represented an imperialist state every bit as much as the European powers of the region.. Unlike other African states, Ethiopia had never been colonized itself (except for its brief occupation by Italy during the Second World War), and had instead steadily expanded its own "Empire" by conquering numerous other ethnic groups in the region.

The OAU charter, in particular, provided plenty of rhetorical fodder for Ethiopian and Kenyan leaders eager to paint Somali leadership as aggressors. While Somali leaders frequently pointed to provisions proclaiming the "the inalienable right of all people to control their own destiny" or the need to "fight against neo-colonialism in all its forms," such calls were rarely received by the OAU or its member-states as legitimate. Provisions frequently invoked by Ethiopian and Kenyan authorities were mainly found in Article III of the OAU charter, which laid out the principles of the OAU including: "respect for the sovereignty and territorial integrity of each state"; "non-interference in the affairs of States"; "Unreserved condemnation of . . . subversive activities on the part of neighboring states" (Article III). Much of the following discussion reveals how the contours of the relationships between Somalia and its neighbors can be seen as driven by the contrary international ideals of self-determination and territorial integrity, and how the clash of norms led to long-term diplomatic acrimony and, ultimately, to the clash of armed forces in Ethiopia.

The last point that should be emphasized before examining the specifics of the relationships between the states involved concerns the nature of Somali irredentism in each case. Often referred to as a "classic" case of irredentism, it is important to note that Somalia never actually laid direct territorial claims to the territory of its neighbors. Instead, Somalia always advocated the right of national diaspora to decide freely whether to remain part of the states into which they had been absorbed. It seems rather clear that support of secession was conducted with the expectation that voluntary merger with the Republic of Somalia would follow.

Pursuing this *secessionist-merger* outcome was clearly the preferred strategy of each Somali administration.

Somalia, Kenya, and the Minority Somalis of the North Eastern Province

Kenyan and Somali relations were generally characterized by instability bred by the presence of a significant Somali diaspora in the North Eastern Province of Kenya (NEP), formally the Northern Frontier District (NFD) before Kenyan Independence. The period of greatest hostility occurred in the immediate wake of Kenyan independence, when Somali rebel activity, public nationalist pressure, and, ultimately, Somali rhetoric pressing for greater self-determination in the NEP were at the peak. Answering to Somali militancy, Kenyan leadership consistently invoked the principle of territorial integrity when addressing both the international community and Somali leadership directly. Appeals to Somali leadership and the international community by Kenyan leaders stressing norms of territorial integrity were loudest during the rebellion of Somali diaspora in the 1960s and during the high points of Somalia-Ethiopian tension during the 1970s. Bilateral distrust characterized much of the rest of the period covered in this case. This distrust declined during the 1980s, however, as Somali domestic nationalist pressures on leadership waned in the face of increasing tribal divisions and strife at home.

Since international normative pressures advocating the abandonment of Somali policies of interference and subversion toward its neighbors was strong throughout this period, the main factor affecting general direction of Mogadishu's policies was the degree of societal pressures placed upon executives during different periods. In the case of Kenya, nationalist advocacy from "the street" waxed and waned during four distinct periods, as summarized by table 6.2.

The tensest period in Somali–Kenyan relations occurred during the mid-1960s. Beginning in 1963 with the approach of Kenyan independence, increasingly vocal demands for the independence of Somalis in the NFD were given wide publicity in the Republic of Somalia (Lewis 1961: 154) and fueled the flames of domestic nationalism. Despite continuing calls from Mogadishu for Ethiopia to relinquish the Ogaden, the Kenyan NFD became the first diplomatic focal point for the Osman-Shermarke administration. Somali representatives of the NFD made their preferences clearly

Table 6.2 Somali Nationalism and Relations with Kenya

Period	Societal Pressure	Main Conditioning Factor	Policy Outcome
1964–1967	Strong	Diaspora Rebellion	Aggressive Diplomacy
1967–1969	Medium	Loss of rebel legitimacy	Détente
1970–1982 approx.	Medium	Status quo irredentist situation[1]	Mutual distrust
1982–1991 approx.	Absent	Fracturing of Somali society	Rapprochement

Note:
1. By "status quo" irredentist situation, I am referring to the hypothesized state of "foreign policy indeterminacy" that is expected to occur when a irredentist situation exists in the absence of rebellion.

known when they brought up the issue of potential secession at major conference meetings that were convened to draft a Kenyan constitution. The British government turned down requests for a UN plebiscite, but agreed to a fact-finding mission in order to determine the state of public opinion in the region. The final British report suggested that 80 percent of the population of the NFD could be characterized as pro-Somali. Nevertheless, the British government withdrew any hint of support for any preindependence territorial changes in March 1963. The Somali government subsequently terminated diplomatic relations with Britain, and nationalist rioting broke out throughout both the NFD and the Somali Republic (Lewis 1980: 156).

What had been a spirited and sometimes tense debate between Somali representatives and leaders of the main Kenyan parties devolved into an increasingly hostile exchange of recriminations. The Kenyan delegation formally submitted to the African Summit Conference in May 1963 a memorandum on the NFD issue which stated empathetically that: "We in Kenya shall not give up even one inch of our country to the Somali tribalists, and that is final" (Hoskyns 1969:39). At the same summit, Somali president Aden Abdullah Osman, citing both norms of self-determination while emphasizing the importance of recognizing Somalis as a national, rather than tribal or ethnic group argued that

> [t]hose who oppose the reunification of the Somali territories attempt to portray the Somali people's desire for unity as a form of tribalism. Such opponents use every means at their disposal to rank the Somali people as an ordinary tribe without any rights to nationhood. The Somali people are a nation in every sense of the word. (p. 32)

Events occurring within the NFD magnified the irredentist pressures facing Somali leaders. The emergence of a Somali-based rebellion signaled the preferences of radical Somalis in the region. It also reflected the overlapping nature of secessionist movements and irredentism. With the regional rebellion taking place, Somali leaders were able to extend their arguments beyond irredentist territorial claims, and point to a desire within Kenya for self-determination by Somalis.

When Kenya came into being in 1963, the Kenyan government countered the growing Somali rhetoric of self-determination by repeatedly and specifically citing the importance of territorial integrity norms. At the 1963 summit meeting of independent African states held shortly before Kenyan independence, Kenyan representatives argued specifically in favor of the "territorial integrity of all states," adopting an implicitly racial argument, that "the principal of self-determination has relevance [only] where foreign domination is at issue" (Hoskyns 1969: 39).

In addition to rhetoric stressing the importance of territorial integrity, the Kenyan government also stressed the importance of the idea of Pan-Africanism, which entailed the sublimation of ethnic and national identity to a common regional identity. Such appeals to African unity were particularly powerful in the early, more idealistic, days following the founding of the OAU. Kenyatta stressed both the norm of territorial integrity and the ideal of Pan-Africanism in a memorandum to the OAU conference of 1963:

> . . . seeking to create new African nations on the basis of tribal or religious identities is a sin against Pan-Africa and a most dangerous weapon for destroying African solidarity.

> The Somalis are Africans. Those who live in Kenya are Kenya Africans . . . if every territory to which people of the Somali tribe migrate is to become part of the Republic of Somalia, in accordance to Pan-Somalism and the policy of creating Greater Somalia, then the concept of territorial integrity of any other state becomes meaningless. (Hoskyns 1969: 37)

A new Somali prime minister, Abdirizaj Haji Hussein, was elected in 1964. Hussein was widely considered the voice of Somali hawks, and the nationalist rhetoric under the Osman-Hussein government was particularly hostile (Sauldie 1987: 26).

The presence of Somali rebellion in Kenya heavily influenced the Republic's foreign policy. Although what was later termed the *shifta* rebellion by Kenyan leaders—with the word *shifta* denoting banditry—was a low-level and poorly documented civil conflict, Somali rebels destabilized the NEP during the middle part of the decade and only faded to a scattered guerilla movement in the latter part (Laitin and Samatar 1987: 135). In the end, however, Somali policy makers refused to support a policy of ethnonational "rescue" by supplying Somali rebels in Kenya with significant arms.

Like the previous civilian administration, the so-called hawkish Osman-Hussein government chose a path of aggressive diplomacy over a course of aggressive militancy. The delicate tightrope walk undertaken by the Osman-Hussein government witnessed Somalia raising its irredentist claims internationally, without overtly breaching international norms. At the same time, the push for greater self-determination by domestic audiences was placated to some degree by the administration's tough rhetoric, although even during this period members of the Somali National Assembly attempted to remove the government with a no-confidence on the grounds that it "lacked courage" (Lewis 1980: 156).

International normative restraints on aggressive Somali behavior during this period were evident, as meetings of both the OAU and the Nonaligned Movement in 1964 reaffirmed their support for existing African borders and Kenyan claims to territorial integrity and state sovereignty. Somali delegates fought against these motions, while the Somali National Assembly passed a motion rejecting outright the resolutions of the conferences stating that

> [b]oth our peoples and territories have been unjustly and brutally partitioned, and they are being denied the basic an inalienable right to self-determination . . . Neither walls nor weapons can ever permanently separate a family or nation. (Adar 1994: 108)

Somali prime minister Hussein argued that the preexisting borders were a legacy of colonial influence and charged that while "no other part of the colonial legacy" had gone unquestioned at the conference, "it appears that members at the conference are prepared to accept the artificial political frontiers" (pp. 106–107).

By early 1966, relations between Kenya and Somali had hit their nadir, with a Kenyan spokesman declaring that Kenya had adopted a "war footing" with Somalia (Hoskyns 1969: xi). In the wake of failed talks that had taken place in Arusha in December 1965, the emergency security zone that had been established on the Kenyan border with Somalia was widened from five to fifteen miles.

Nevertheless, the battle between Kenya and Somalia remained one of words and never escalated into any serious armed conflict.

After July 1967, Somali diplomacy became more conciliatory after a new government led by former prime minister Shermarke (as president) and Mohamed Ibrahim Egal (as prime minister) replaced the Osman-Hussein government. Somalia and Kenya agreed on a framework proposal at the September 1967 Kinshasa OAU summit for future negotiations. The resultant joint declaration stated that both governments would: (1) respect each other's territorial integrity; (2) resolve future disputes peaceably; (3) ensure peace and security on their mutual border; and (4) refrain from conducting hostile propaganda campaigns against one another through mass media outlets (Adar 1994: 117).

Based on the framework agreement, Egal met with Kenyan president Jomo Kenyatta in October and signed the Arusha Memorandum of Understanding—which paved the way for a quick "normalization" of relations between the two states. The new détente led to the restoration of trade ties, the lifting of the state of emergency in the NEP, and an amnesty for all *shifta* guerillas—the remainder of which mostly disbanded. Somali leaders never again pursued a policy of sustained hostility toward Kenya in the wake of the new relationship.

The Egal-Shermarke government was willing to undertake its diplomatic initiatives because domestic views regarding events in the NEP were gradually softening. Widespread demonstrations and support for *shifta* rebels had largely dissipated as Somali rebels turned to questionable tactics after being largely defeated by the mid-1960s. In particular, *shifta* tactics aimed at those allegedly collaborating with the Kenyan government alienated Somalis within the region and the Republic. The murder of a well-known regional clan leader, Omar Shuria, attracted particular attention, with major Somali parties in the region offering a joint condemnation. Increased condemnation by mainstream Somali parties of the *shifta* rebels reflected the subsiding of nationalist pressures within the Somali Republic.

Nevertheless, the perception of the Egal-Shermarke regime that a new foreign policy track could be undertaken without major public backlash was overly optimistic, as the government's policies still alienated many segments of Somali society. Although the National Assembly subsequently supported the Shermarke-Egal administration with a vote of confidence, the government experienced "bitter opposition from those who saw the Arusha memorandum as a sellout" (Farer 1979: 108). With relations with Kenya on the mend, the administration also reestablished diplomatic contacts with Great Britain and attempted to strike a more pro-Western attitude in order to "balance the impression inevitably conveyed by the Somali Republic's increasing military dependence on the USSR" (Lewis 1980: 203). However, as Egal sought improved relations with the West, the Soviet Union began holding back expected military aid. The nationalistically-oriented Somali military thus witnessed two blows—one to the Pan-Somali national cause and one to its own growing power, which was threatened by Egal's pro-Western policies.

In October 1969, President Shermarke was assassinated by one of his guards. The military, led by General Siad Barre, took advantage of the ensuing disorder, launched a coup and assumed power several days later. While the perceived corruption and nepotism of civilian authorities was the primary justification of the move by military leaders, Lefebvre (1991: 50) suggests that because Shermarke and Egal

> seemed to be backing away from the Ogaden issue and striking a deal with Ethiopia by tacitly renouncing Mogadishu's irredentist claim on the region, Shermarke was assassinated, and a new and perceptually more nationalistic military-led government took control.

The Arusha memorandum, however, put the NEP issue to rest in a manner such that Barre's military government had no desire to reopen the issue and increase public expectations. Furthermore, because the agreement had been signed under the civilian government of Shermarke-Egal, Barre could dissociate himself from the lingering sentiments that Arusha had represented a sell-out of the nationalist cause. The impact of the peace pact and its effect on Somali resistance in the NEP was of great importance, however, as much for its role in raising tensions with Ethiopia as it had in lowering tensions with Kenya. With the NEP issue settled, at least temporarily, the nationalist aspirations of Somali leadership and domestic audiences, particularly the military, were free to focus almost exclusively on the Ogaden issue—even more so after the question of French Somalia[7] was settled in the mid-1970s (Laitin and Samatar 1987: 141).

Nevertheless, Kenyan leaders still feared that Somali revisionism would once again turn in their direction—a view backed by a former high-ranking Somali official who suggests that Barre "naively believed, that after he [defeated] Ethiopia, he would then be able to focus his martial attention to Kenya" (Dualeh 1994: 86). The 1970s were to be characterized by mistrust and suspicion between the two states, which contrasted both with the near-war state of affairs of the mid-1960s as well as the previous period of détente. Projecting a sense of indeterminacy in his foreign policy statements, Barre wove a series of mixed messages within his public speeches that alternately assuaged and worried Kenyan observers, who were comforted by Barre's continued emphasis on peaceful negotiations, but threatened by frequent allusions to the right of self-determination for all Somalis. When Barre spoke of the necessity of knowing "our friends from our enemies," listing his friends as all forces against "imperialism, colonialism, and neo-colonialism" (Barre 1971: 87), the implication was not lost that the "enemies" might be thought to include those supporting the remnants of colonialism (Kenya) or were perceived colonial powers themselves (Ethiopia). At the same time, Barre would assert that "Somalia will not nurture hatred for its African brothers, Somalia wants to regain what has been taken from it, through peaceful means; it does not gain anything from the gun" (p. 36).

While Kenyan authorities understandably nursed continued suspicions toward their Somali neighbors, it became increasingly obvious that Somali attention had turned toward Ethiopia when the military government emerged from the diplomatic shell that characterized its early foreign policy. As will be discussed in greater depth in the section dealing with Ethiopian-Kenyan relations, Kenya offered strong diplomatic support to Ethiopia during the period of greatest Somali militarism.

As early as the OAU conference of 1973, Kenya's vice president declared:

> Kenya cannot be party to opening up issues concerning territorial claims against sister states. Kenya . . . cannot and shall not recognize or even consider boundary claims by any African country against its sister country. (quoted in Adar 1994: 177)

Nevertheless, trying to "lighten his load of enemies" Barre repeatedly assured the Kenyans that Somalia had no plans to reinitiate support of dissidents in the NEP (Laitin and Samatar 1987: 140).

When open wartime hostilities erupted between Somalia and Ethiopia in 1977, Somali-Kenya relations declined. Fearful of contagion effects, Kenyan authorities increased security in the NEP while largely terminating trade with Somalia (Sauldie 1987: 53). Relations hit "rock bottom" in November 1978 when Kenyan authorities charged that Somalia was "recruiting Somalis in the NFD to fight against Ethiopia 'and eventually against Kenya itself' " (Legum and Lee 1979: 82). Only two months later, a border clash apparently took place between Kenya and Somalia near Ethiopian territory, one in which Kenyan authorities claimed 23 Kenyans had been killed. The next month, as the war wound down in February 1978, Kenyan planes forced an Egyptian airliner carrying a clandestine arm shipment to Somalia to land in Nairobi. The subsequent withdrawal of Somali forces from Ethiopia was greeted with "great relief" in Kenya (p. 82).

The years immediately following the war in the Ogaden were marked by continued tension between Kenyan officials and a Somali government that remained angered by Kenya's support of Ethiopia during the conflict. However, from the beginning of 1981 until the end of the decade, relations steadily improved between the two states. A combination of factors contributed to the improvement in relations, including: (1) the ideological reorientation of Somalia away from the socialist camp; (2) the diminishment of Somali military capacity and subsequent inability to pose a threat to its neighbors; (3) the clear preference of the Somali population of the NEP to remain part of a now economically vibrant Kenyan state, which will be discussed in the next section; and (4) the eruption of civil strife in Somalia, which prompted Barre to seek outside pledges of support or, at the very least, nonintervention. Furthermore, *the fracturing of the Somali nation and descent into tribalism that characterized the 1980s brought a final and decisive end to the nationalist pressures within society* that had constrained Somali executives from pursuing more conciliatory foreign policies.

In June 1981, President Barre and President Moi (of Kenya) met and signed a major cooperation agreement intended to further normalize relations. During the next year, a general of Somali descent in the Kenyan army played a major role in putting down an attempted coup against the Moi government, an event that subsequently led to public expressions of goodwill by the government toward Somali Kenyans, and, as a result, better relations with Somalia (Laitin and Samatar 1987: 150). By the end of 1984, Somali had agreed to disavow any further claims to Kenyan territory.

Somali-Kenyan relations, never as severely strained as those between Somalia and Ethiopia, mended more quickly in the 1980s. In 1985, Barre stated that "with the exception of [Kenya's relationship with] Ethiopia, we greatly value the good relations which exist between Somalia and Kenya" (Adar 1994: 193). By the end of the decade, Kenyan views had shifted far enough in a favorable direction that there is plausible evidence suggesting that the Kenyan government supplied the Somali government with arms in the late 1980s for use against the growing Somali insurgency (Woodward 1996: 161–162).

Summary—Kenyan-Somali Relations
Somali-Kenyan relations can be divided roughly into four eras. High levels of bilateral hostility and tension characterized the first era, stretching from Kenyan independence to 1967. This period witnessed widespread public pressures on Somali leadership to pursue hawkish policies toward Kenya, and anti-Kenyan demonstrations were commonplace. Seeking to balance the need to accommodate strong nationalist impulses emanating from domestic audiences with a desire to avoid transgressing international norms, the civilian governments of the period pursued aggressive diplomatic postures that focused on the concept of "self-determination," while resisting the urge to challenge the situation militarily.

A brief period of détente characterized the second era of Somali-Kenyan relations occurred between 1967 and 1969. The decline of *shifta* legitimacy in the view of regional parties in the NEP and within the republic correlated with a decline of nationalist pressures within Somali society, which presented a perceived window of political opportunity for the Egal administration to pursue more accommodating policies.

Kenya ceased to be a primary focus of Somali foreign policy designs during the 1970s. Nevertheless, Siad Barre's public statements alternately assuaged and aggravated relations with Kenya. This era represented a classic case of foreign policy indeterminacy breeding mistrust under conditions of transborder nationality. Although Somali criticism of Kenya was muted during this period, Kenyan leadership observed Somali actions warily as Somali leaders continued to pursue irredentist designs toward the Ogaden region of Ethiopia.

The last era I examined was characterized by warming relations during the 1980s. It is unlikely that this process would have been possible a decade earlier, when Somali nationalism played a major role in unifying the Somali public around common foreign and domestic causes. As the domestic consensus shattered in the wake of civil strife in Somalia, however, Barre was freer to pursue conciliatory policies toward its neighbors due to the diminished public saliency of nationalist issues abroad. In this sense, nationalism as a societal norm largely vanished during the 1980s, allowing the Somali government to pursue a process that culminated in the permanent abandonment of Somali claims to Kenyan territory in 1984.

Somalia, Ethiopia, and the Minority Somalis of the Ogaden

An "instinctive animosity" colored relations between Somalia and Ethiopia to a degree that exceeded the level of distrust between Somalia and Kenya (Legum and Lee 1979: 82). Even the European powers were rarely viewed with such fear and loathing among Somalis as the Ethiopian Empire. One of the primary arguments employed by Somalis during the decolonization period was that Ethiopia, which had remained independent throughout almost all of its history, was an imperial power equivalent to the Western imperial powers in the region—and that its territorial holdings should be granted freedom in a similar manner as those in the region that had been colonized by the whites. Its proximity to its territorial acquisitions, as well as the racial undertones that the international self-determination debate had taken on, however, meant that Ethiopia was not generally viewed by the international community in the same way as other colonial powers in the region.

Unlike Somali views toward Kenya and its control of the NEP, there were two forces in particular that intensified the hold of nationalism toward the Ethiopian enemy on Somali public consciousness. The first, as mentioned earlier, was the fact that tribal ties to Ogaden Somalis were stronger than tribal ties to Somalis in the NEP. The second factor involves the role that religion has played in both Ethiopian and Somali identity. In essence, "typical" ethnonational nationalism is reinforced by what might be described as a mini "clash of civilizations" between predominately Christian Ethiopia and Islamic Somalia. Since the 1897 transfer of the Ogaden region to Ethiopian control Somalis have regarded the Christian "encroachers" as the prime regional threat to Somali territory and culture. As explained by Lewis (1961: 269):

> Somali nationalist aims tend to be associated with the ideal of Muslim solidarity opposed to Christian government. This aspect of Christian influence in inspiring nationalist aspirations is particularly strong in what Somali regard as the imperialist policies of the Ethiopian government.

Similarly, the Selassie regime in Ethiopia referred to their empire as a "Christian island" and the prospect of "Muslim encirclement" meant that fears of Somali revisionism simply reinforced a preexisting siege mentality in Ethiopia (Legum and Lee 1979: 3). Although the religious dimension of the rivalry diminished after the rise of socialist rule in Ethiopia, the contribution it had made to Somali-Ethiopian enmity was long term.

While pointing frequently to "territorial integrity" norms, as did Kenyan leaders, the views of Ethiopian leaders, particularly under the Selassie regime, was somewhat more complicated. Ethiopian leaders justified the existence of their multiethnic state, including Somali-inhabited regions, on principles of historical continuity. Although dropped in the 1960s, Selassie frequently called, in the precolonial period, for the incorporation of the entirety of Somalia into Ethiopia. Following Ethiopia's liberation from Italian control in 1941, Selassie spoke of the need to restore "the independence of my country including Eritrea and Benadir (Somalia)" (Neuberger 1986: 46). As late as the 1963 OAU conference, Ethiopia's prime minister declared:

> Ethiopia has always existed in history for centuries as an independent state and as a nation for more than 3,000 years. That is a fact. The second fact is that the historical

frontiers of Ethiopia stretch from the Red Sea to the Indian Ocean, including all the territory between them. Third fact: there is no record in history either of a Somali state or a Somali nation. (Hoskyns 1969: 34)

Although no longer countering Somali claims to Ethiopian territory with counterclaims to Somalia, Ethiopian leadership under Mengistu continued to defend its control of the Ogaden with a measure of historical argumentation. At the OAU summit of 1977, Mengistu dismissed Somali calls for self-determination in the Ogaden as "historical fiction" (Sauldie 1987: 12).

While Ethiopia was accused by Somali leadership of representing an African imperialist state, Ethiopia countered by drawing a thick line between European colonialists and their state. According to Ethiopian authorities, the Ethiopian empire had offered "staunch political and military resistance to colonialism" while Somali tribal chiefs had remained "indifferent and quiet while they were being sold cheaply" (Healy 1983: 106). During the early 1960s, the Ethiopian government suggested a racially-oriented "coming home" for not just Ogaden Somalis, but for all Somalis:

> In view of the abject misery of the Eritrean and Somali populations under the fifty years of Italian occupation which forced them to suffer the indignity of being treated legally as an inferior race in their own country . . . it cannot be suggested that their lot would be worse under the regime of their Ethiopian brothers . . . To provide for such a return would be merely to recognize the realities of the existing historical and other ties which bind them integrally to Ethiopia. (quoted in Healy 1983: 98)

Thus, the Ethiopian government countered growing Somali irredentism with rhetoric suggesting that cultural bonds and race constituted the national ties binding all Somalis, not just those in the Ogaden, to a central Ethiopian state.

In addition to the arguments presented earlier, Ethiopian authorities made appeals to territorial sovereignty similar to those of Kenyan leaders. Appeals to norms of territorial integrity and noninterference were particularly favorite rhetoric of the socialist regime, which tended to distance itself somewhat from the historical-cultural appeals of the Selassie government. However, claims based on the sanctity of colonial borders placed the Ethiopian government in a dilemma due to its continued claim to Eritrea, which had a different colonial history and yet been forcibly annexed in 1962. While the Mengistu regime insisted on the sanctity of colonial borders in the Ogaden while denying them in Eritrea, it argued the question in the context of Marxist-Leninism. While supporting "progressive" self-determination, the regime argued that the question of self-determination need be assessed case by case according to whether or not a particular instance "promotes or retards, strengthens or weakens, advances or modernizes the revolutionary struggler of the proletariat" (Neuberger 1986: 115). None of the ethnonationalist uprisings in Ethiopia met these conditions in the eyes of the Ethiopian leadership.

Although usually at a high level, public interest in the Ogaden issue varied in a manner similar to issues associated with Kenya. Roughly, speaking, one can divide the degree of public pressure on Somali leadership into three eras (this is reflected in table 6.3).

Table 6.3 Somali Nationalism and Relations with Ethiopia

Period	Societal Pressure	Main Conditioning Factor	Policy Outcome
1964–1967	Medium	Status quo irredentist situation	Aggressive Diplomacy
1967–1969	Medium	Status quo irredentist situation	Détente
1970–1974	Medium	Status quo irredentist situation	Mixed Messages
1974–1982 approx.	High	Diaspora rebellion	Conflict
1982–1991 approx.	Absent	Fracturing of domestic society	Rapprochement

Public nationalism in regard to the Ogaden issue was rather moderate from independence until 1974, much higher between 1974 and 1982, and lowest after approximately 1982.

The attitude of Somali leadership toward the Ogaden question was similar, although more strongly felt, than the issue of Kenyans in the NEP. In describing the unification of Somaliland and Somalia during 1962, SYL Prime Minister Abdirashid 'Ali Shermarke foreshadowed future Somali foreign policy aims and their justification:

> This was not an act of "colonialism" or "expansionism" or "annexation." It was a positive contribution to peace unity in Africa and was made possible by the application of the principle of the right to self-determination. (quoted in Lewis 1963:151)

Somali politicians also pursued a course of aggressive diplomacy toward Ethiopia, rarely missing an opportunity to call for the self-determination of Ogaden Somalis within international forums. Somali nationalism ran particularly high in the wake of independence, and even before the public focus shifted to the Kenyan separatists, the presence of the sizeable Somali population in Ethiopia commanded public attention. Public nationalist pressures, coupled with a poorly demarcated border, promoted aggressive frontier policing that sometimes spilled over into "accidental" border clashes.

During this period, Somali and Ethiopian military units fought a series of skirmishes along their common, ill-defined border. A "major armed clash" between state militaries took place in 1961 in the wake of an abortive coup attempt against Haile Selassie (Selassie 1980: 105). In late 1963 the Ethiopian government alleged incursions by Somali regular troops, while, in February 1964, according to the Somali government Ethiopian military aircraft attacked Somali villages (Castagno 1964: 187). Following the alleged aircraft attack, fierce clashes erupted along the border, resulting in a death toll that perhaps reached into the hundreds (*Africa Digest*, April 1964 quoted in Hoskyns 1969: 48). UN Secretary U Thant was brought in to mediate, resulting in a temporary reduction in tensions.

By the mid-1960s, Somali policies toward Ethiopia were roughly similar as those directed at Kenya, even though public opinion focused more on Kenya at the time. As was the case in Kenya, the Ogaden region was home to disorganized armed groups that seemed to pose more of an annoyance than a threat to the regime.[8] These groups received material support, although hopes for rebel victory in the region were limited. Unlike the issue of Somalis in the NEP, insurgency in the Ogaden did not provoke a surge of nationalist sentiment at home during the 1960s. This is largely due to the fact that the rebellion in the Ogaden, which comprised several ethnic groups, was not primarily associated with Somali rebels.

The bilateral enmity between the two states thawed during the Egal tenure. In the OAU summit held in September 1967, Somali and Ethiopian delegates engaged in several "encouraging exchanges" (Lewis 1980: 203) leading to an eventual "modus vivendi" between Emperor Haile Selassie and Somalia's prime minister Egal (p. 52). By September 1968 Somalia and Ethiopia agreed on establishing commercial air and telecommunications links and the state of emergency that had existed in the Ogaden was lifted (Rinehart 1982: 32).

As was described earlier, the takeover by the Barre military government resulted in an inward turn in priorities as the new government consolidated power. By the time of the OAU summit of 1974, however, Somali leaders had clearly adopted a policy of increasing antagonism toward Ethiopian authorities. Somali calls for reexamination of the Ogaden issue during the 1973 OAU summit in Addis Ababa had led to the appointment of a special OAU mediation committee, which had little to report a year later. In the wake of "hot words" that were exchanged between President Barre and Emperor Selassie, as well as the presence of provocative pamphlets circulated by a group calling itself the United Liberation Front of Western Somalia, Emperor Selassie "left the [1974] summit in anger" (Sauldie 1987: 34). The renewed vigor of Ogaden dissidents, coupled with the overthrow of Selassie a mere three months after the summit, marked the beginning of a long march to war by Somali leaders.

Societal pressures on the Barre government during this period became more and more intense. In an indication of how widespread nationalist impulses were in Somali society during this period, "now famous Somali songs" ridiculing the Barre regime's inaction in Ethiopia began to be heard (Selassie 1980: 110). Nevertheless, a lack of replacement parts, widespread drought, and continued international pressure fostered a sense of caution on the part Barre's government, despite the direct pressure applied by military advisors advocating a more decisive stance on Ethiopia. Subsequent events, however, were to place even more pressure on the government to intervene militarily on behalf of insurgents in the Ogaden.

As Somalia's military grew in strength (due to an upswing in Soviet aid), Ethiopia seemed on the brink of collapse. The overthrow of Selassie facilitated rebellion not only in the Ogaden, but also across much of the multiethnic country. At one point in the mid-1970s, 10 of the country's 14 provinces were engaged in armed rebellion against the central government (Lefebvre 1991: 35). By the end of 1976, it was widely reported that Somalia was providing substantial material support to the Western Somali Liberation Front (WSLF), as well as other rebel groups associated with other ethnic minorities. Earlier in the year, Ethiopia had informed several Arab states that Somalia was engaged in a "war of subversion" in anticipation of a full-scale war (Sauldie 1987: 43). With WSLF rebels scoring increasingly large victories in the Ogaden, the situation was "slipping out of hand with the passing of each day" (p. 47).

By July, the Somali government had committed to a "full-scale invasion," albeit with many regular troops "thinly disguised" as WSLF rebels (Henze 1985:55) out of a desire to avoid antagonizing the international community. In September, the Somali forces achieved their deepest penetration into Ethiopian territory, capturing the major town of Jijiga. However, the offensive been to bog down as waves of Ethiopian militia flocked to the area, in a surprising show of patriotic solidarity in the face of the invasion.

In November 1977, increasingly disillusioned Somali leaders attempted a desperate ploy to garner domestic and international support by canceling Somalia's 1971 Treaty of Friendship and Cooperation with the Soviet Union. The move turned out to be counterproductive, however, as the Soviet Union used the occasion to throw its full support behind the Ethiopian regime. At the same time, widespread international perceptions of Somali aggression meant support from other sources turned out to be limited. Saudi Arabia and Iran were the only states that pledged to support Somalia, but only in the case that Ethiopia would attempt to overrun the country's borders as the tide of battle turned.

The threat to Somalia itself became reality in early 1978, after the Ethiopian army, heavily supported by Russian resources and Cuban troops, smashed and routed the Somali forces in the Ogaden. On March 9, 1978 Barre announced the withdrawal of all Somali regular forces in Ethiopia—even though, recognizing international sensitivities, he had always denied the existence of such troops in the first place (Henze 1985: 56). Just as the Soviet Union had played a role in restraining Somali aggression during the mid-1970s, Soviet pressure on Ethiopia subsequently played an important part in preventing an invasion of the Republic itself.

The loss of the war brought Barre's legitimacy and political survival into question, and the very clanism that he had sought to eliminate in the early years of military rule began to emerge again. Shortly after the conflict, a "civil war" broke out within the armed forces, in April 1978, when officers of the Majeerten clan (Barre belonged to the Darod clan) attempted to overthrow the government (Laitin and Samatar 1987: 92). Although the coup failed, its clan-based nature strongly foreshadowed events to come.

The early 1980s represented the last gasp of Somali irredentist designs. At the beginning of the period the Republic's military was in shambles; by the end of the period the state itself was beginning to collapse. What followed in the wake of the war was a return to the status quo in terms of Somali policy toward Ethiopia. With the Somali military in disarray and the Ethiopian military stronger than ever, policy reverted from outright aggression to more discrete forms of subversion. At the same time, Ethiopia embarked on a policy to subvert the Somali state by supporting new dissident groups that sprung up in the aftermath of the failed war and seizing on growing clan divisions.

By the end of 1981, however, the Ogaden issue was rapidly declining in relative importance to the Somali leadership. Mogadishu's concerns "had been diverted from pursuing irredentist claims in the Ogaden to waging a counterinsurgency campaign inside Somalia to ensure the survival of an authoritarian regime" (Lefebvre 1991: 236). The "shoe was on the other foot" as Ethiopia pursued a strategy within Somalia of supporting a growing rebel movement known as the Somalia Salvation Front (renamed the Somali Salvation Democratic Front, or SSDF, in October 1981) a group most associated with the Majeerteen clan. A group associated with the Isaaq clan, known as the Somali National Movement

(SNM), also attracted support from Ethiopia and grew in strength throughout much of the 1980s.

In June 1982, Somali and Ethiopian forces engaged in their last major clash. Somali forces accompanying WSLF rebels attacked Ethiopian forces in the Ogaden. In retaliation, as many as 9,000 Ethiopian troops moved to support the SSDF in occupying two border towns in Somalia. The Ethiopian move sparked an emergency airlift of military supplies by the United States to the Somali government, a measure which helped dissuade the Ethiopian military from taking any further action.

Barre's regime weakened even further in 1986, following a car accident which severely injured the president. The accident set off a power struggle among "assorted factions" within the government, and almost led to the disintegration of central authority (Laitin and Samatar 1987: 168). Although Barre recovered from the accident, he faced a domestic situation that was increasingly spiraling out of control and reducing Somalia to a certain "beggar" status on the international front—especially vis-à-vis Ethiopia. As was the case with Kenya, the fracturing of the domestic consensus in Somalia lent itself to similar policies, as rapprochement was unlikely to inflame nationalism given Somalia's chaotic internal situation.

Barre eventually had little choice but to abandon any further claims to Ethiopian territory in exchange for a cessation of Ethiopian support to rebels in Somalia. In February 1988, a formal peace accord was signed between Barre and Mengistu, within which Barre allowed for a formal demarcation of the border; a renunciation of further claims in the Ogaden; and opening of formal diplomatic relations—receiving in exchange only a pledge to evict SNM bases from Ethiopian territory. The Ethiopian government won the decades-long battle with Somalia over the Ogaden by engaging in subversive tactics similar to those long pursued by Somali leadership in Ethiopia. Hussein Ali Dualeh writes that, following the agreement, Barre confided in him, "Mengistu Haile Mariam personally defeated me because he had the Isaaq and the SNM support. I have only one objective now, to seek vengeance against the Isaaq" (Dualeh 1994: 115).

Barre proceeded to undertake a series of brutal measures against the Isaaq population of northern Somalia. However, Barre's repression did little to stem the tide of rebellion, and probably encouraged it. By 1990, members of the Hawiye clan had revolted as well, forming a major rebel group known as the United Somali Congress (USC), which brought the fighting to the central and southern parts of the country. Barre's fate was thus largely sealed, and he was ousted from power on January 26, 1991.

Somalia further disintegrated into the collapsed state that it largely remains—its irredentist designs of the past long forgotten by most. Only the renewal and strengthening of a common Somali identity, promoted through a stress on common language, religion, or history, will result in the revitalization of the Somali nation-state. Such a renewal, however, may bring renewed claims to regions inhabited by Somali diaspora within the borders of Somalia's neighbors within the Horn of Africa.

Summary—Ethiopia-Somali Relations
Relations between Ethiopia and Somalia were poisonous from the start—and only became worse through the following decades. Public nationalist pressures on

leadership during the 1970s were much higher than that of the 1960s, facilitating the full-scale conflict with Ethiopia. This is not to say that domestic audiences ignored the Somali diaspora of Ethiopia during the 1960s. On the contrary, civilian leaders were obliged to maintain an aggressive diplomatic posture throughout much of the 1960s in order to placate domestic audiences. When the Egal government failed to pursue aggressive policies toward Kenya and Ethiopia during the late 1960s, widespread public discontent erupted. By the 1980s, however, the domestic situation in Somalia had deteriorated to the degree that nationalist projects abroad had faded from public imagination, providing the Barre government an opportunity to work toward solving outstanding disputes.

The ascension of a communist regime in Ethiopia, rather than soothing relations in the name of international socialist solidarity, instead presented Somalia an opportunity to take advantage of Ethiopian instability. The war clearly signaled the lengths to which Somalia would go in realizing its irredentist (or secessionist-merger) ambitions, and the message was not lost on Ethiopian leadership. What followed was the period of "duel subversion" pursued in the early 1980s as each state leadership attempted to undermine the position of the other through the support of rebel insurgents. The bilateral enmity came to full fruition in the 1980s, as Somalia's territorial desires where countered by Ethiopian strategies designed to promote a regime change in Mogadishu.

Ironically, the success of insurgent movements in both countries ultimately led their rapprochement in the late 1980s. Mutual interest trumped mutual antagonism when the very existence of both regimes came into question, as confrontation rather rapidly shifted toward conciliation. In the end, it was too late for both governments, however, as both Mengistu and Barre met similar fates in 1991.

Ethiopian and Kenya—Unlikely Cold War allies

Given the presence of a common rival with common claims on national territory, it is hardly surprising that Ethiopia and Kenya sought to maintain a close relationship with one another throughout the period covered by this case study. The two countries signed a mutual defense treaty in 1964 that was renewed in 1980 and then in 1987. Not surprisingly, the provisions of the agreement displayed the clear "concern for respect for the principle of territorial integrity" (Adar 1994: 143). While the closeness of their relationship during the 1960s and early 1970s should come as little surprise given both states' ties to the United States and mutual antipathy toward the Soviet Union, the fact that the relationship continued practically undisturbed once Ethiopia adopted a hard communist line is a tribute to the power of interest over ideology.

The primary factor explaining this close relationship was the mutual threat presented by Somali calls for national self-determination. The threat concerned both the prospect of outright Somali militarism and the "contagious" spread of native Somali rebellion at the encouragement of Mogadishu. Since neither state shared any significant national group with the other,[9] they did not view one another as a threat and viewed their mutual border as inviolable.

Without the presence of a mutual threat, one would have expected relations between the two states to be warm during the Selassie regime and cold during the

Mengistu years—but largely comparable to other pairs of states. The Somali factor and its effect on Ethiopian-Kenyan relations, however, displayed how regional relations during the Cold War often failed to meet the expectations of geopolitically minded analysts due to the role played by local nationalist politics.

The rapidity with which Kenya and Ethiopia signed their mutual defense treaty in the wake of Kenyan independence indicates how strongly Kenya, in particular, viewed the threat to its frontier. While the treaty itself was kept secret,[10] Kenya and Ethiopia, led by prominent leaders in the anticolonial movement,[11] provided strong diplomatic support for one another throughout. During the Ethiopian-Somali border dispute in 1964, a Kenyan representative declared to the Council of Ministers that Kenya would have assisted Ethiopia in the battle "if the Ethiopian government had asked for assistance" (Hoskyns 1969: 60). In cultivating Ethiopian support in the NEP dispute—support which was quickly forthcoming—Kenyan diplomats stressed the historical appeals preferred by Selassie by claiming that the region had historically belonged to the Oromo—the largest national group in Ethiopia (Adar 1994: 58–59).

Relations between Ethiopia and Kenya were uneventful throughout the late 1960s and early 1970s as Somali governments alternately sought détente (Shermarke-Egal) and relative isolation (Barre's early years). With the shift in Somalia's military government toward greater assertiveness in 1974, Ethiopia and Kenya once again grew closer with a common cause—both governments firmly criticizing the events of the 1974 OAU summit. After the highpoint of instability following the overthrow of Selassie in Ethiopia ended, Kenya was the first black African state to ally itself openly with the Ethiopian government (Legum and Lee 1979: 58–59). Early in the Ogaden conflict, Ethiopia and Kenya issued a joint statement condemning Somalia's "brazen and naked aggression" (Lewis 1980: 234). During the war, Kenya's Ministry of Foreign Affairs openly admitted its assistance to Ethiopia, stating, "Kenya gave Ethiopia material support and if the Ethiopians now required transport including trucks and tanks, Kenya was ready to supply them" (Adar 1994: 155). At the conclusion of the war, President Moi of Kenya, hosting Mengistu at a dinner declared:

> The excellent relations that exist between Ethiopia and Kenya started long before Kenya's independence. It is founded on geographical, historical and political realities . . . We are concerned that inter-African wars based on territorial claims must be avoided at all costs. (p. 34)

Even though Somali-Kenyan relations warmed more quickly during the 1980s than relations between Somalia and Ethiopia, Kenya and Ethiopia maintained both strong relations and a common front toward Somalia. As late as 1987, Kenya and Ethiopia issued a joint statement criticizing Somalia's threat to territorial integrity norms in the region, indicating a lingering sense of distrust of Somali intentions despite recent moves toward détente. Although Somali's military impotence became increasingly clear quickly after the Ogaden War, continued Somali subversive activities in the Ogaden were not only a concrete threat to Ethiopia, but also one perceived in Kenya. With the eventual collapse of the Somali government, Ethiopia and Kenya no longer faced the common threat that once existed.

Relations to this day, however, have remained warm, largely due to the fact that the two states, like most African neighbors, face many more threats from within stemming from heterogeneous ethnonational demographics than they face with one another in the absence of transborder nationalism.

Domestic Influences on Somali Dispute Initiation

Factors Hypothesized to Affect Varying Levels of Somali Militant Revisionism

Although Somalis in general have always held widespread irredentist grievances regarding territories inhabited by Somalis governed by other states, these grievances were addressed differently under different leadership and different circumstances. In this section, I examine the effect, on Somali foreign policy outcomes, of variables that were found in chapter 5 to significantly influence dispute initiation by homeland irredentist states. Table 6.5 illustrates the correlation of three of the four major variables hypothesized to relate to homeland state aggression and the initiation of fatal MIDs by Somalia against Ethiopia and Kenya. Although no one variable can alone be said to relate to conflict initiation, the chart below suggests an additive effect. Overall, the presence of diaspora rebellion, military rule, and military feasibility all seem to enhance the potential for MID initiation.

Table 6.4 only reveals so much information, however, without a more detailed assessment of the variables that may be involved in influencing Somali policies. As the most important causal influence on Somali dispute initiation, variations in *militant activities among Somali diaspora* were clearly responsible for many of the changes in Somali policy during the period examined. As I argued in the earlier parts of this work, the clear signals sent by self-determination-seeking diaspora during periods of rebellion create strong audience costs at home, creating a crisis-type situation which is largely sufficient to spark aggressive foreign policies regardless of domestic structure. During periods of insurgency in the NEP and the Ogaden,

Table 6.4 Somali Decision-making Factors and Fatal MID Initiation

COUNTRY	Period	FATAL MID %	Diaspora Rebellion	Military Influence	Feasible
Ethiopia	61–69	33%	no	no	no
	70–72	0%	no	yes	no
	73–74	50%	no	yes	yes
	75–85	100%	yes	yes	yes
	86–91	0%	no	no	no
Kenya	64–69	17%	yes	no	yes
	70–91	10%	no	yes	yes

FATAL MID% = percentage of years during period witnessing MID initiation by Somalia.

Note:
Several questionable database codings, such as the lack of rebellion in Kenya during the sixties, have been altered for the above table based on the more detailed findings of the case study.

Somali governments, both under parliamentary and military rule, provided "subversive" aid to insurgents. More than any other factor, the presence of diaspora insurgency seemed to be the most necessary condition for aggressive Somali diplomatic and military postures. In the brief period when little or no diaspora rebellion took place, during the early 1970s, Somali government priorities turned inward and Somali revisionism was at its lowest ebb of the entire 30 year period covered by this study. However, unlike the civilian government of the 1960s, the Somali military government supported rebels in the Ogaden to such an extent that they were drawn into open warfare.

A major finding of the empirical sections of this work concerns the role of *military influence* in foreign policy decision making in irredentist situations. Military influence over policy in Somalia grew initially under parliamentary government, but burst forth under the military government of the 1970s, only to recede after the shattering defeat sustained at the hands of Ethiopia in 1978. The rise of military decision making should be viewed as more than simply a reflection of the policies of Barre. Rather, it is clear that Barre was, himself, subject to the influence of other military leaders from "below." Two important manifestations of military influence were the growth of militant nationalist preferences in foreign policy formulation and the growth of Somali military capabilities—largely a result of the desire of military leaders to divert funds to their own power base. Unlike civilian authorities confronting rebellion in the Kenyan NEP during the 1960s, the military government under Barre escalated its dispute with Ethiopia to full-scale war when rebellion broke out there.

I also examine the *combination of military influence and diaspora discontent*, as proxied by relative economic and political conditions. Ethiopia as a whole, and certainly the Ogaden region as well, was relatively poorer than Somalia throughout the case, and governed under the rule of a series of repressive Ethiopian leaders. Relatively poor economic and political conditions in this region contributed to high levels of nationalism among the diaspora Somalis within Ethiopia—leading not only to discontent during the period of military rule, but also outright rebellion.

In comparison, relations between Somalia and Kenya noticeably improved throughout the 1970s because of the decline in discontent among the Somali diaspora in Kenya. Increasingly, the Kenyan diaspora signaled a lack of desire for any change in the status quo or any increase in "self-determination." The NFD was a largely neglected region at the onset of the case study. However, unlike Ethiopia's, the Kenyan economy, which started off at roughly the same level of economic development as Somalia, grew at a more consistent pace throughout much of the period covered by the case study. At the same time, the political system of Kenya was relatively more open and inclusive than Somalia's (also in contrast to Ethiopia). These factors played a role in muting the discontent of its Somali minority, which largely abandoned violent resistance by the early 1970s. As figure 6.2 shows, the state of the Kenyan economy was, overall, one of growth, while the Somali economy tended to decline over the decades.

Of particular importance is the period in the early 1970s, when Somali irredentism within the NEP largely subsided during an era of rapid economic growth. This coincided with the rise of military leaders in Somalia, who were, as a result of the muted nationalism among Somalis in the NEP, not eager to pursue Somali

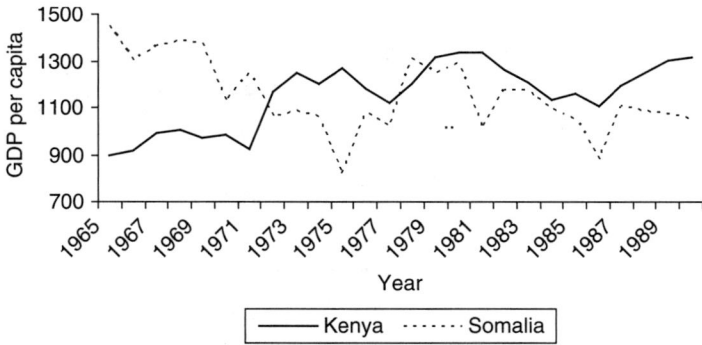

Figure 6.2 GDP per capita (in Real 1996 U.S. Dollars)—Kenya and Somalia

irredentist claims against Kenya. The idea that Kenyan Somalis were relatively advantaged in comparison to their Ethiopian counterparts is seconded by Laitin and Samatar (1987:136), who suggest:

> ... the Somalis of the northeastern province have not been subject to the same degree of humiliation as have the Somalis in the Ogaden. Many Somalis in Kenya feel they can become Kenyan citizens and gain from their citizenship. In the Ogaden most Somalis feel that under Ethiopian suzerainty Somalis get little but retribution.

The degree of economic vibrancy, as proxied by *GDP growth*, was a control variable found in the empirical analysis to be associated with varying levels of dispute initiation. When assessing this variable, the Somali case becomes somewhat complicated due to widely fluctuating periods of economic growth and decline. Figure 6.3 shows Somali GDP per capita alongside arrows indicating years within which Somalia initiated MIDs against its neighbors.

While there is no clear relationship between MID initiation and economic growth overall, the period leading up to the Somali-Ethiopia war is intriguing. During this period, the Somali military regime focused on a variety of modernization programs that it coupled with strong appeals to Somali unity intended to mobilize the populace for domestic works projects. One such modernization effort included the introduction of the first Somali written script in history. According to Lewis (1980: 236), nationalist sentiments were "stimulated to an unforeseen degree by Somali literacy," and were manifested as public pressure on Somali leadership during the mid-1970s. During the years immediately before the war, as figure 6.3 indicates, the Somali economy had also turned the corner from years of drought in the earlier 1970s and witnessed the highest growth rates recorded in this study. Thus, while the relationship between economic growth and MIDs is unclear, the evidence lends some credibility to the idea that economic modernization can be an important precursor to war waged on nationalist grounds.

Several variables were found to relate not only to irredentist conflicts, but also to conflicts in general as well. The first such variable concerns the role of *military feasibility*—and particularly the constraint posed by a lack thereof. As has been

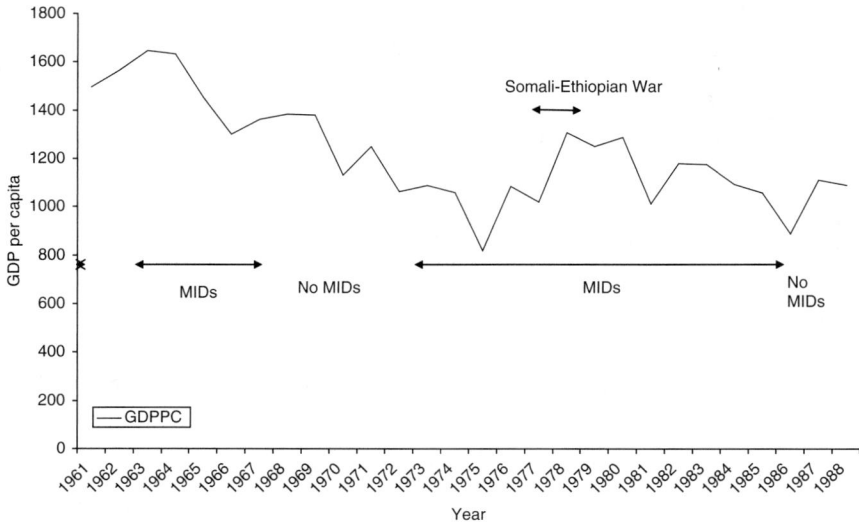

Figure 6.3 Somali GDP per capita (in Real 1996 U.S. Dollars) and MIDs Initiated

noted, this is a straightforward concept based on the idea that a state that faces overwhelming military retaliation from another state will be less likely to embark on aggressive policies toward that state. The initiation of MIDs are considered "feasible" as long as a kin state is less than five times more "capable" than a homeland state (in this case, Somalia). Using this criterion, aggression by Somalia toward Kenya was always "feasible" during the period covered in this study. On the other hand, military threats and aggression by Somalia against Ethiopia did not achieve feasibility until 1972 (see figure 6.4), after which there was less than a five-to-one ratio of capabilities between the two states until the end of the decade. The fact that Somalia leadership nevertheless initiated numerous MIDs against Ethiopia before 1972 is testament to the high level of domestic nationalist pressures faced by Somali executives during the 1960s.

Of the variables affecting states in general, two are largely static throughout the study. The first is *strategic territorial claims*, which were found to have an effect on MID initiation levels across cases. While Huth's (1996) data codes both the Ogaden and NEP regions to be strategically insignificant throughout all years, this coding seems misleading in respect to the Ogaden, in particular. According to Farer (1979: 124), "Somalia's acquisition of Ethiopia's southern provinces promised to alter permanently the Horn's indigenous balance of power." The long-term strategic worth of the region likely intensified the preference of Somali leadership to detach the Ogaden from Ethiopia.

The second variable indicates important *economic territorial claims* on disputed territory by homeland states. However, while the lack of any major economic resources in the NEP seems clear, the situation is less clear-cut in the Ogaden. While the existence of large-scale gas and oil deposits in the region has never been proven, Tenneco, a U.S. company, discovered potential evidence of such deposits

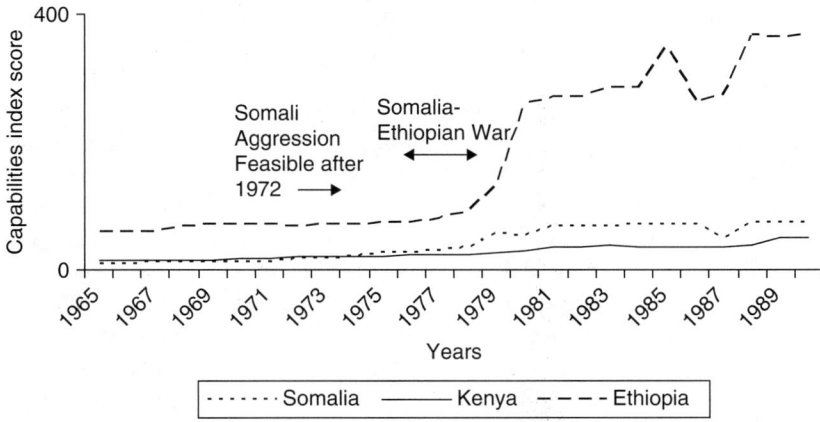

Figure 6.4   Somalia–Kenya–Ethiopia Capabilities

in the Ogaden in 1972. A year later, the company began drilling, and, by doing so, added an additional instrumental incentive to preexisting Somali claims on the region. According to Farer (1979: 118), "the spirit of détente, conjured into existence by [Somali leaders in the late 1960s] Egal and Shermarke, had begun to whither from the moment Tenneco first arrived in the area." While Somali leadership never mentioned economic motivations as a factor in Somalia's future militant revisionism, it is certainly possible that the discovery of potentially valuable resources in the Ogaden[12] figured in calculations of potential gain when decisions were made regarding the scope of intervention upon which Somalia was to embark in Ethiopia. Although Farer seems to overstate the importance of the suspected reserves, which have still to this today not been proven, the discoveries of the early 1970s may have provided an extra incentive for war half a decade later.

Why Ethiopia and Not Kenya? Civilian Versus Military Government

Thus far, this case study has described how societal nationalist pressures on Somali executives differed during different periods, depending upon events both in Somali-occupied lands in Kenya and Ethiopia as well as events within Somalia itself. During the 1960s, Somali politicians adopted aggressive diplomatic postures toward both Ethiopia and Kenya. During the 1970s, an initially quasi-isolationist military government turned hostile toward Ethiopia by the middle of the decade, but largely accepted the territorial status quo with regard to Kenya. As Somali society fractured during the 1980s, societal interest in Somalia's relations with its neighbors greatly declined, making rapprochement not only a less politically dangerous strategy for Barre's regime, but a sensible one designed to reduce outside interference in internal affairs.

Two major questions that remain, however, are:

1. Why did the uprising in the Ogaden during the 1970s lead to war, but not the uprising in Kenya during the 1960s?

2. Why were Somali irredentist designs on the NEP in Kenya so readily abandoned, while the Ogaden issue remained so salient?

In order to answer these questions, it is useful to consider several of the factors in conflict initiation. First, it is clear that diaspora uprising was the main underlying factor affecting the policies adopted by Somali leadership toward its neighbors. Not surprisingly, relations with Kenya were particularly poor during the mid-1960s when the *shifta* rebellion took place. Similarly, poor relations with Ethiopia became explosive during the period of WSLF rebellion during the 1970s and early 1980s.

Although not central to the variables discussed, cultural reasons explaining differing Somali policies toward Ethiopia and Kenya were clearly important. Somali rivalry with the centuries-old Ethiopian state was a more deeply engrained part of Somali culture than rivalry with the newborn state of Kenya. This rivalry also took on messianic undertones, as the Ethiopia state claimed to represent East African Christianity while Somalia projected itself as a key player in the Islamic world. Clan linkages between Somalis in the Republic and the Somali populations of Ethiopia were also much stronger than those between clans in Somalia and Kenya.

Cultural explanations aside, many of the variables utilized to explain conflict initiation by homeland states also seem relevant to the case as well. The most important structural correlate of war presented in the early models suggests that a military dominated government will be more conflictual than civilian-based rule.

In the case of Somalia's foreign policy, the military government under Barre approached growing rebellion in the Ogaden much differently than Somalia's government approached rebellion in the NEP. Unlike the civilian government of the 1960s, which attempted negotiations with Kenya at the height of tension in 1965 and sought to press its disputes diplomatically through numerous international forums, the military government under Barre was consistently escalatory in its approach to Ethiopia—and was hindered from taking action against its neighbor sooner only by severe drought conditions occurring in the middle of the decade.

In addition, the level of aid provided by the civilian regime to NEP insurgents was much smaller than that provided by the military regime to insurgents in the Ogaden. While aid from Somalia is unlikely to have affected the *existence* of insurgency, it likely affected the *level* of insurgency. Insurgency in the Ogaden rose to such a level that it was perceived to have a viable chance of success. This presented the Somali a rare window of military opportunity that proved too tempting to pass up. On the other hand, the civilian authorities of the 1960s resisted the urge to supply *shifta* rebels with large amounts of material and training, which helped prevent the uprising from growing beyond the stage of scattered guerilla warfare. According to Lewis (1980: 200), the early civilian authorities consciously avoided escalating disputes with Kenya (and Ethiopia) in an effort to prevent nationalist considerations from derailing other priorities of the Somali state:

> Clearly vital though the Pan-Somali issue was to Somali national sentiments, it could not be allowed to override the Republic's other interests . . . success in attract[ing] substantial aid . . . vindicated the government's policy of not allowing the Pan-Somali dispute to affect the Republic's general position.

Overall, the civilian authorities, while pursuing an aggressive diplomatic front, tended to focus more on the domestic problems associated with independence than on military aggression abroad. While a focus on domestic affairs also characterized the policies of the military government in its early years, Barre's military regime quickly fell prey to the extremist impulses of nationalism in Somali society.

Finally, the military control over policy influenced the material capabilities of the Somali armed forces, as the military government obtained and spent higher amounts strengthening those capabilities than earlier civilian authorities. Soviet material support for the Somali military had led to the empowerment of an assertive political actor, an actor that had become the chief policy maker in Somalia. Due to the pro-Western stances of the Shermarke-Egal administration, many suggest that the Soviets helped engineer the overthrow of civilian authorities (Laitin and Samatar 1987: 79; Dualeh 1994: 66). The adoption by the new military government of "scientific socialism," meant a closer alliance with the USSR, and opened the floodgate of military aid during the ensuing years.

The Somali military grew quickly during the early 1970s. By 1974, the Somali armed forces, while smaller in manpower, were equivalent to Ethiopia's in aircraft, tanks, and other sophisticated weaponry (Henze 1985: 52). According to Samatar (1988: 128), Somalia's "close embrace" of the Soviet Union, resulted in "the growth and dominance of a military culture in the political economy." Military rule provided the opportunity for Somali leaders to arm the Somali state to a degree far beyond what normally would have been expected of a state of such limited resources.

The large-scale armament program initiated by the Somali government during this period continued until the outbreak of hostilities between Somalia and Ethiopia. The Soviet-funded armament program, already at high levels, accelerated even more after 1974. Between 1974 and 1977, the Soviets sharply increased sales to Somalia, selling US$ 300 million in weapons during this period (Hensel 1985:53). Although by some measures the Ethiopian military seemed stronger than the Somali military, the Somali military was better trained and better equipped. Thus, in comparison to the civilian authorities of the previous decade, military governance led to an increase in capabilities for both the insurgent movement and the Somali military itself—each factor fostering the perception that the eventual invasion of the Ogaden region might yield success.

At the same time, however, Somali capabilities of the 1960s largely matched those of Kenya and, yet, a large-scale military confrontation did not ensue. Thus, we should not only look at the role of military governance in creating a force capable of challenging Ethiopia, but also the different preferences that led to its willingness to do so. As has been asserted, military-influenced decision-making tends to be more nationalist-oriented than civilian decision making—a factor that, unlike the desire to divert increased funds to the military, actively sets military governance in irredentist situations apart from situations within which nationalism plays less of a role. As was noted earlier, civilian authorities during the 1960s, while pursuing an aggressive pattern of diplomacy pressing for Somali diaspora "self-determination," also tempered foreign policy belligerence with a high degree of restraint in order to assure continued international support for internal development. In other words, despite public pressures, the civilian regime's general priorities placed internal development over the pursuance of nationalist objectives abroad.

For the military government, on the other hand, nationalist politics went hand in hand with development, as appeals to Somali pride were essential in mobilizing the public for a series of "modernization" efforts. Nationalism, more so than "scientific socialism," became the chief ideology propounded by the military government, and also represented the guiding principle of elite decision making. However, inward appeals to Somali unity easily morphed into calls for Pan-Somalism in foreign affairs. Even though Barre himself began to display renewed interest in the national struggle during the mid-1970s, it was not merely his preferences, but also the preferences of the military officials below him that drove the march to war. Many reports suggest that a reluctant Barre was increasingly "pressured by his general staff to plan for the liberation of the Ogaden" (Laitin and Samatar 1987: 141) and facing growing calls to action from military leaders "below" (Farer 1979: 126; Selassie 1980: 111; Woodward 1996: 127). The growing perception that a military attack on Ethiopia was possible dovetailed with nationalist military preferences that such an attack was desirable, despite the potential international repercussions that would even be associated with success.

The course pursued in Somalia's relationships with Ethiopia was in stark contrast to those pursued toward Kenya during the 1970s. A large part of this is due to the fact that Kenyan Somalis no longer seemed desirous of self-determination as they had in the mid-1960s. The improvement of conditions for Somalis in Kenya coincided with the incidence of military rule in Somalia. This work has suggested that military-influenced decision-making tends to breed conflict initiation more frequently when foreign diaspora reside in states that are poorer or more politically repressive than the homeland state. Neither condition characterized Kenya at the time. In the absence of a Kenyan diaspora desirous of liberation, the position of the military government toward Kenya remained rather passive. In the end, the only MID initiated against Kenya during the 1970s was "incidental," in that it involved the violation of Kenyan territory only in the context of the conflict with Ethiopia. Thus, in contrast to efforts on behalf of the highly nationalist diaspora in Ethiopia, claims to Kenya were never really pursued after 1970.

Conclusion

This chapter was divided into two parts. First, I explored the roots of the conflict between Somalia and its neighbors, Ethiopia and Kenya, and why good relations existed between Ethiopia and Kenya despite strong ideological differences. The clash between norms of self-determination and norms stressing territorial integrity defined regional politics in the Horn of Africa more than the clash of Cold War ideologies.

Although always present, bilateral enmity between Somalia and its neighbors rose and fell during the period examined. The translation of public pressure into aggressive diplomacy was evident during the 1960s, when diaspora rebellion in Kenya occurred. Similarly, public pressure on Siad Barre was extreme during the period before the initiation of major hostilities with Ethiopia during the 1970s.

During other periods not witnessing rebellion, such as Ethiopia during the 1960s and Kenya during the 1970s, relations were tense, but not explosive as they were during times of diaspora rebellion. When the internal situation in Somalia fractured into clanism during the 1980s, public attention largely turned away from foreign affairs, enabling Somali leadership to pursue reconciliation with Ethiopia and Kenya.

As a basis of comparison, this chapter also examined relations between Ethiopia and Kenya. Unlike relations involving Somalia, relations between Ethiopia and Kenya were not beholden to any dispute involving a transborder group. While, within the context of the Cold War rivalry, one would have expected relations between the two states to be tense after the rise of a communist regime in Ethiopia, this was not the case. The comparatively peaceful nature of Kenyan-Ethiopia relations reflects the fact that societal pressures on executives agitating for foreign policy aggression are clearly more responsive to issues of nationalism than more abstract issues of political and economic ideology.

Despite the fact that the underlying normative issues were similar in Somalia's disputes with its neighbors, it must also be noted that relations with Ethiopia were far more conflictual than those with Kenya. It would seem that the baseline probability of conflict between Ethiopia and Somalia was higher overall due to the presence of many unmeasured factors, including: enmity derived from a long history of dispute during the colonial era; religious differences that overlapped ethnic differences; and closer affiliations between Somali clans and Ethiopian diaspora.

The second part of the study examined factors influencing the degree of aggressive behavior displayed in Somali foreign policy. Part of the utility of the case study approach is teasing out the finer contextual points that are not readily apparent through large-n empirical approaches. In the case of Somali-Kenyan relations, I described how Somali policy was quite aggressive during the mid-1960s, due in part to the presence of Somali rebellion in Kenya. As the *shifta* uprising subsided and the apparent acceptance of the status quo among Kenyan Somalis increased, Somali policy toward Kenya warmed considerably. The lack of a "discontented" Somali minority in Kenya during the years of military government in Somalia translated into Mogadishu largely abandoning its claim to Kenyan territory.

The factors underlying Somali policies toward Ethiopia are a bit more difficult to tease out. Somali rebellion in Ethiopia was prevalent through most of the period, making it difficult to assess how relations between Somalia and Ethiopia would have taken shape in the absence of such rebellion. During the lull in rebellion that took place in the early 1970s, tensions between Ethiopia and Somala ebbed, but this may have been as much a consequence of the domestic consolidation process of the military government and the previously established détente agreements as it was due to lack of rebellion.

Diaspora rebellion creates such strong audience costs that other factors may be overridden in importance, at least as far as the initiation of militarized disputes is concerned. During years coded as experiencing diaspora rebellion in Ethiopia, 100 percent also witnessed the initiation of a militarized dispute by Somalia—clearly indicating the role of ethnonational "rescue" policies in influencing international relations.

However, when rebellion in the Ogaden was coupled with a military dictatorship in Mogadishu, the government pursued a course of escalation that led to open warfare. In contrast, while rebellion during the 1960s that occurred in Kenya and Ethiopia received a measure of diplomatic and material support from civilian authorities in Mogadishu, many of the insurgents, particularly in Kenya, were disappointed that more aid was not forthcoming. While the conclusion remains tentative, the case of Somali policy seems to affirm the escalatory tendencies of military influenced governments in irredentist-type disputes. These escalatory tendencies seem both a preference of military governments in irredentist disputes as well as a consequence of policies that serve to inflame diaspora rebellion to the point at which military governments are then drawn into disputes. Although not analyzed empirically in the earlier statistical analysis, I will investigate the relationship between military government and the initiation of full-scale war further in the next case study.

CHAPTER 7

INDIA, PAKISTAN, AND CHINA

The relations between India and its neighbors have been contentious since the withdrawal of the British from the subcontinent in 1947. India has fought three major wars against Pakistan and one against China. Dozens of smaller scale militarized disputes have occurred between India and its neighbors as well. Fundamentally different factors have led to India's historically poor relations with Pakistan and China. India's difficulties with Pakistan have revolved around the irredentist-type Kashmir dispute, resulting in high levels of bilateral enmity and the constant threat of war. India's relations with China, on the other hand, have resembled more of a mini–Cold War, characterized by tense relations but only rare instances of military confrontation over the past several decades. A comparison of Pakistani-India enmity with Sino-Indian rivalry illustrates the fact that nationalist-based disputes tend to breed conflict to a degree unmatched by those based on *realpolitik*-type factors.

Politics in both India and Pakistan involve multiple identities, with language, region, and local culture competing with religion as alternate sources of allegiance. While identities overlapping the dominant religious affiliation of the majority populations of both states have had important implications for domestic affairs in these countries, religious differences lie at the heart of the conflict between these two states. The existence of Pakistan is predicated on the idea that Hindus and Muslims represent separate nations (Brines 1968: 29), and Pakistan's nationalist-oriented foreign policies are derived from that state's Islamic identity (Jalalzai 2000: 39). In contrast, India has attempted, at least in principle, to avoid reference to religious differences in its policies. This fact helps explain why the focal point of conflict has revolved around Pakistan's irredentist claims to Kashmir rather than India's concern for the Hindu minority of Pakistan.[1]

As with the previous chapter, I divide this chapter into two major parts. The first part examines the differing conceptions of legitimate rule that have traditionally guided the foreign policies of India and Pakistan, and why the existence of normative incongruence has created instability and distrust for decades. At the same time, I examine the interactions between China and these two states in order to juxtapose the different nature of the relationships involved when basic normative issues are not at stake. The period examined during this chapter is longer than that of the previous chapter, primarily spanning the era from the independence of India and Pakistan in 1947 to 1991, and briefly noting the period since 1991.

The second part of this chapter will analyze, with respect to Pakistan, the factors derived from the earlier empirical analysis that were found to be related to rates of dispute initiation by irredentist-type homeland states. As with the earlier Somali case, the level of aggression displayed by Pakistani government differs during different periods. Of particular interest are the differences in policies adopted by Pakistan's leaders under military rule during the 1960s and 1980s, in comparison to those adopted by civilian leaders during much of the 1950s and 1970s. Due to the fact that rebellion in Kashmir was largely nonexistent until the late 1980s, the role of military influence on government decision making can more easily be assessed than was the case in the previous chapter examining Somalia's policies.

This case offers several contrasts to the earlier case examining the relations of Somalia with its neighbors. In the case of Somalia, variations in societal nationalist pressures on Somali executives accounted for a degree of variation in foreign policy decision-making outcomes. However, international pressures tended to weigh heavily against Somali aggression throughout, as international audiences generalized sympathized with Kenyan and Ethiopian rhetoric emphasizing Somali transgressions of international norms.

With the case of the Indo-Pakistani dispute, however, societal pressures within Pakistan were relatively consistent. However, international constraints were less consistent than in the Somali case, as the international community, which was initially tolerant of Pakistani aggression, gradually adopted a more balanced approach to the region. Nevertheless, to this day, the international community is rarely united in its opposition to Pakistan's activities in Indian-occupied Kashmir, allowing Pakistan greater leeway to pursue aggression than most other states holding outstanding irredentist grievances.

International Norms in Transborder Versus Nontransborder Situations

As in the previous chapter, it is useful to begin by reviewing the results of the bilateral regression model displayed in chapter 5 (table 5.1). The following chart shows how many disputes are predicted by the normative-demographic model versus the actual number of disputes within these dyads over the period 1951–1991.

The predictions arrived at from earlier econometric analysis and applied to the dyads in this case study are, as reflected in table 7.1, quite close to the actual course of events in the cases of India-China and Pakistan-China. The model, however,

Table 7.1   Predicted versus Actual Bilateral MIDs and FATAL MIDs in Dyads

	MID-actual	*MID-predicted*	*FATAL-actual*	*FATAL-predicted*
India-Pakistan	66%	76%	44%	78%
India-China	39%	33%	18%	18%
Pakistan-China	6%	11%	6%	5%

slightly overestimates the number of MIDS and moderately overestimates the number of fatal MIDs.[2] One reason the model overestimates MID probabilities is that the model considers both India and Pakistan as potentially irredentist homeland states due to the presence of a significant minority of Hindus within Pakistan. As has been noted, however, India has traditionally pursued foreign and domestic policies that deliberately downplay religious and ethnic differences—a policy which lends itself to a certain distancing from the Hindu diaspora in Pakistan. The following section, explores more deeply the roots of the important distinctions between Pakistani policies focusing on ethnoreligious identity and those of India, which seek to downplay communal distinctions.

Nationalism and Self-Determination versus "Secular Nationalism" and Sovereignty

The division of territories resulting from decolonization sowed the seeds of future conflict between India and Pakistan. Unlike other cases such as within the Horn of Africa, however, the division of territories between India and Pakistan was not imposed from above by the unilateral decree of an imperial power or powers. Rather, British officials guided a process by which accession to either India or Pakistan would be determined by local rulers, recommending only that it would be in the best interest of such states to observe the principles of geographical contiguity and to pay due regard to the religion of the majority of their citizens (Varshney 1991: 1007).

The Independence of India Act, which granted formal independence to India and Pakistan on August 15, 1947, entrusted hundreds of rulers within "prince states" to decide the fate of their territories. While partition sparked widespread Hindu-Muslim rioting that cost hundreds of thousands of lives, the legal process of accession proceeded in a fairly orderly manner. Three cases, in particular, however, were highly contentious. Rulers in Hyderabad, a Hindu majority state with a Muslim ruler, and Kashmir, a Muslim majority state with a Hindu ruler both initially opted for independence, while the ruler of Janagarh, a Muslim who ruled a Hindu majority, opted for accession to Pakistan. Both Hyderabad and Janagarh, which were surrounded by Indian territory were invaded by and annexed to India in 1948.[3] Geography was not as merciful to the people of Kashmir, who, unlike the people of Hyderabad and Janagarh, reside in a territory adjoining both Pakistan and India—which has facilitated the ability of both states to pursue their claims through force.

Stipulations within the Independence of India Act calling for partition were not equally supported by Indian and Pakistan leaders of the time. The very ideological underpinning of the agreement supported the dominant Muslim contention, for which the "father of Pakistan," Mohammed Ali Jinnah, had long fought—namely, that two separate nations existed on the subcontinent. This proposition, however, was rejected by the major Indian leaders of the time including Mahatma Gandhi and Jawaharlal Nehru, both of whom opposed the idea of government division based on ethnic or religious differences. Kashmir became a permanent symbol of the disagreement concerning the very legitimacy of partition based on religious identity.

The dispute over Kashmir, then, is one of clashing ideologies, or, more specifically, clashing norms concerning legitimate governance. On the one hand, for Pakistanis "the creation of their nation through Islamic idealism will be incomplete as long as Muslim Kashmir . . . remains unabsorbed" (Brines 1968: 51). In achieving this goal, Pakistani leaders have "appealed to moral law and mobilized the principle of self-determination" (Choudhury 1971: 69) in order to justify diplomatic, subversive, and outright military action designed to "liberate" the region from Indian control.

On the other hand, Indian leaders have retained control over Kashmir due in part to the idea that "Kashmir is symbolic of secular nationalism and state-building and the possibility of a Muslim-majority area choosing to live and prosper within a Hindu-majority country" (Ganguly and Bajpai 1994: 402). Once again, harkening back to the very principle of partition in the first place "many Indians . . . believed that the creation of Pakistan was a rape of Mother India and that the loss of Kashmir would be a further unacceptable violation" (Brines 1968: 7). From a more practical point of view, allowing Kashmiris to decide their own fate via plebiscite would also raise concerns of both "an internal domino effect" whereby other regions of multi-ethnic India might demand similar treatment as well lead to "a Hindu backlash against Muslim communities" (Ganguly and Bajpai: 414).

Many scholars would not describe what the Indian government refers to as "secular nationalism" as nationalism at all. Rather, the Indian commitment to liberal values and, particularly, allegiance to the Indian state, much more closely reflects the idea of "patriotism," a loyalty that is often in fundamental conflict with nationalist sentiments—as is the case in Kashmir where Kashmiri nationalists reject the power and influence of the Indian state. In this sense, the liberal concept of "secular nationalism" is bound to a legalistic interpretation of original consent, a line of argumentation Indian leaders have utilized at various points, as will be discussed, to argue against a more organic concept of self-determination.

The legalistic position of Indian governments also lends itself directly to the norms of territorial integrity and sovereignty that I have discussed at length in this work. Placing state authority as the primary source of legitimate rule over populations inherently means a strong emphasis on the demarcation of the boundaries of that authority as determined by the treaties among states represented in international law. Indian emphasis on legalistic interpretations of territory, coupled with the traditional liberal focus on individual rather than group rights, translates into less support for Hindu minorities in Pakistan than one might normally expect from a "homeland" state, but greater intransigence on the issue of autonomy or self-determination for minorities within India's borders.

However, self-determination offers both a moral and, to a weaker degree, legal, challenge to Indian interpretations of state sovereignty. The legal dimension of the challenge stems not only from international resolutions citing self-determination as a "right," but also from specific UN resolutions that call for a plebiscite to be held in Kashmir in order to assess the desires of its population. While India has denied the validity of early UN resolutions for several decades, the legitimacy accorded to the Pakistani position by the international community has only dimmed, not disappeared, in the intervening years.

The following section offers, in detail, the historical development of the normative dispute between India and Pakistan. By understanding the basic ideological incompatibility of the positions of the two sides, and how differing normative understandings have facilitated conflict and mistrust, basic insights may be gleaned as to why the bilateral relations between the two states have tended to be much more violent than those between most states.

The Violent Divorce—Muslim Nationalism, Partition, and Communal Strife

Like many nationalist movements, the roots of Muslim nationalism in the subcontinent are today imagined to run deeper in history than was actually the case. While Muslims certainly understood themselves as a separate identity group than the Hindu majority of India since the very introduction of Islam over a thousand years ago, there existed no movement for greater political autonomy until the twentieth century. The Muslim League, the first Muslim-based advocacy group, was founded in 1906. However, the party varied widely in its positions in the ensuing decades, at times adopting very similar positions as the Indian National Congress, the primary "secular nationalist" party of the time (and until today).

In 1935, Muhammad Ali Jinnah took control of the Muslim League, and began to advocate greater Muslim separatism. Although receiving little support among Muslims during provincial election in 1937, the group began to attract mass public support in 1940, shortly after the outbreak of the Second World War. As Indian agitation for independence grew, many Muslims increasingly feared trading British rule for Hindu rule, which gave greater impetus to Islamic-based nationalism. At a conference in Lahore in March 1940, Jinnah formally declared for the first time "Hindus and Muslims were two nations by any definition or test of a nation" (Choudhury 1988: 7).

Jinnah and the Muslim League were to achieve their nationalist goals with the announcement of the Independence of India act on June 2, 1947. However, what had begun as a negotiated process between British authorities, secular Indians, and the Muslim League resulted in massive Hindu-Indian violence and dislocation during the coming years. The road to both partition and communal violence had clearly begun by August 1946, when widespread rioting broke out in Calcutta, necessitating the arrival of six British divisions to quell the bloodshed. The Calcutta violence between Hindus and Muslims was unprecedented in its scale, but only the beginning of a process through which violence spread throughout much of the subcontinent.

The rioting that broke out in Calcutta occurred as a result of efforts by Muslim nationalists calling for a nationwide strike of Muslims to press for an Islamic state to be created upon independence for Britain. This nationwide strike, labeled Direct Action Day was sparked by frustration on the part of the Muslim League, which failed to achieve an acceptable compromise with the Indian National Congress Party over the conditions for the subcontinent's independence. Although largely intended as an act of peaceful civil disobedience, the violence that ensued and spread in the wake of Direct Action Day ultimately achieved the desired aim of Muslim nationalists, if not through the desired means, by pressuring British authorities to consider partition as the only viable solution to the rising turmoil within the subcontinent.

The highpoint of intercommunal violence occurred during the summer of 1947. No precise figures exist on the number of people killed in the chaos, with estimates ranging as low as 200,000 and as high as three million (Hasan 2002). As the largely disorganized violence between Muslims and Hindus began to recede in the fall, however, new issues arose that were to lead to organized violence between the states home to the majority populations of these communities. The most important of these issues involved the status of the Kashmir region, which was rooted in the normatively based clash between Pakistani preferences for the self-determination of the majority-Muslim region and the rejection by Indian leadership of the principle of utilizing religious demographics to determine legitimate governance.

Shortly before independence, an announcement by the Hindu Maharajah of Kashmir, Hari Singh, stated that Kashmir intended to pursue "standstill" agreements with Indian and Pakistan. These agreements suggested, at least in the immediate future, that the Maharajah would not accede to either India or Pakistan. Similar to India's reaction to Hyderabad's policy of nonalignment, the decision of the Maharajah particularly incensed Pakistani leaders, who subsequently pursued a variety of pressure tactics to force accession, including an economic blockade (Park 1952: 265).

Pakistani-Indian Relations—A History of Antipathy

Relative to other regions demarcated by partition, relations between Hindus and Muslims in Kashmir were remarkably peaceful until the summer of 1947. However, when a "peasant revolt" in the western Kashmir region of the Poonch began in July–August 1947, the already heightened nationalist sentiments of many Pakistanis were inflamed further. Despite the fact that the initial revolt had little to do with religious identity (Brines 1968: 69), Pathan[4] tribesman from the neighboring Northwest Frontier Provinces of Pakistan soon began providing material support for the rebellion, interpreting the anti-Maharaja movement as a pro-Muslim jihad. In October 1947, thousands of these tribesmen crossed the border in order to liberate Kashmir by force.

Materially abetted by the Pakistani government,[5] the raiders quickly defeated the state forces of the Maharajah and moved toward the state capital of Srinagar. At this point, the Maharajah sent an emergency plea for assistance to the Indian government and formally agreed to accede to India in exchange for such support. The Indian government responded with an emergency airlift of Indian regular forces, which pushed back the tide of insurgents. By the late spring of 1948, insurgent forces were on the brink of defeat, at which point the Pakistani government decided to intervene directly by sending a large military contingent in order to hold the western areas of Kashmir still under rebel control. The subsequent clash of Indian and Pakistani forces marked the beginning of the first of three interstate wars.

The conflict ended with a ceasefire, drawn up by a special UN Commission sent to investigate the dispute, on December 31, 1948. Under the terms of the ceasefire, the military lines of control[6] were frozen in place, leaving Kashmir divided along a de facto border that separated Pakistani Kashmir (known as Azad Kashmir, or "Free Kashmir" and Indian Kashmir (actually part of the state of Jammu and Kashmir). Further demilitarization was to occur preceding the conduct of a UN supervised plebiscite to determine the whether the people of Kashmir preferred accession to India or Pakistan.[7]

Of particular relevance to international norms is the fact that the international community recognized Kashmir as a "disputed territory," rather than an integral part of either state. This meant that the Line of Control dividing the territory *was never widely recognized as an international border.* Over the years, this fact enabled Pakistan to commit aggression across the ceasefire line with less international backlash than one would associate with the violation of one's state's territory by another.

Despite the bloodshed, the period following the First Kashmir War was hopeful, due to the fact that Pakistan, the United Nations, and even India seemed ready to resolve the issue based on principles of self-determination. Having acceded to the creation of Pakistan despite philosophical opposition to territorial division along religious lines, Indian leaders were initially amenable to one last compromise of the principles of secular nationalism, by allowing a plebiscite to take place.

The early years after partition were a clear victory for Pakistan diplomacy, which "consistently attempted to cancel out the military failures of 1947–48 by enlisting the support of the world behind her 'moral' right to claim all of Kashmir" while encouraging the UN to adopt "uncritical slogans [such as] the term 'self-determination'" (Brines 1968: 85 and 87). As is often the case when the rhetoric of self-determination is employed, Pakistani leaders suggested that they did not wish territorial gain for instrumental reasons. Rather, the welfare of the Kashmiri people was paramount in allowing a plebiscite—a plebiscite that, if conducted fairly, was likely to result in secessionist-merger type outcome, which the international community would find acceptable. The Pakistani representative to the Security Council expressed such an outlook in 1951, arguing:

> It is well known that, although every factor on the basis of which the question of accession should be determined—population, cultural and religious bonds, the flow of trade, the economic situation, communications, the geographical position, strategic considerations—points insistently in the direction the accession of Kashmir to Pakistan, nevertheless we have not asked for the accession of Kashmir to Pakistan on those grounds. We have agreed . . . that the question should be settled through the freely expressed wishes of the people of the state (quoted in *Documents on the Foreign Relations of Pakistan* 1966: 289).

As noted, initially India was receptive to the idea of a plebiscite, despite the widespread belief that the result would not be in India's favor. However, the actual preparations for such a plebiscite never took place due to India's objections to what was perceived as the continued large-scale presence of Pakistani soldiers in Azad Kashmir and an overly aggressive posture by Pakistan in resolving the dispute (along with a variety of other disputes at the time). Nehru's acceptance of the plebiscite in principle, but not in practice, was expressed in a September 1951 letter to the head of the UN Commission on India and Pakistan:

> ... The Government of India not only reaffirms its acceptance of the principle that the question of ... the State of Jammu and Kashmir to India shall be decided though the democratic method of a free and impartial plebiscite under the auspices of the United Nations, but is anxious that the conditions necessary for such a plebiscite should be achieved as quickly as possible (quoted in *Documents on the Foreign Relations of Pakistan* 1966: 303–304).

Nevertheless, the initial conciliatory stance of the Indian government grew increasingly intransigent. Publicly this was explained as a reaction to the continuing hostile stance of the Pakistani government and India's fundamental distrust of Pakistani intentions. Indian decision makers clearly distrusted the intentions of their Pakistani counterparts, who, facing domestic pressures for continued aggressive policies and international pressures advocating compromise, were "placed in a tragically difficult situation in relation both to outside opinion and political opponents at home" ("India and Pakistan" 1951: 139).

The adoption of a Pakistani-U.S. defense pact in 1953 was largely the "last straw" for Indian's government, as the pact was interpreted as not only a betrayal of the idea of nonalignment that was a cornerstone of India's foreign relations, but also an indication that Pakistani leaders intended to build up their state's military capabilities in order to once again attempt a forced solution to the Kashmir issue in the future. According to Nehru in 1954, the Indian state would no longer negotiate the status of Kashmir due to the fact that "the pressure of arms has taken the place of the previous peaceful and cooperative approach" (quoted in *Documents on the Foreign Relations of Pakistan* 1966: 353). Although there were other reasons for Pakistan's military relation with the United States, the Kashmir issue had become the lens through which India interpreted major Pakistani foreign policy decisions.

The earlier amenability of the India government disappeared completely during the period 1953–1963 as the Indian government developed a line of argumentation intended to justify its disavowal of the earlier UN-backed plans for a plebiscite. The harder Indian line not only stressed the continuing aggression of Pakistan and the occupation of Azad Kashmir by Pakistan, but increasingly focused upon the concepts "sovereignty"; the importance of Kashmir to the existence of India as a secular state; and increasingly described Kashmir as an *integral* part of India.

Shortly after the breakdown of negotiations in 1953, elected representatives of the Kashmiri Constituent Assembly, led by Sheikh Mohammed Abdullah, a Muslim favoring integration with India, passed a resolution affirming Kashmir's status as part of India. Attempting to fend off the normative successes of Pakistan at the UN, the resolution was seized upon by Indian leaders as the authoritative expression of "self-determination" by the population of the region. The general support of elected representatives in Kashmir enabled the Indian government to accelerate the political assimilation of the state.

Any hopes for a plebiscite ended in the early 1960s. Upon its initial accession, Kashmir had been granted a special status with a high degree of autonomy under the Indian constitution. In 1964, the Indian parliament passed articles 356 and 357 of the Indian Constitution, which essentially transformed Kashmir into a "normal" Indian state, governed by the same federal rules as other regions. The new measures were symbolically momentous, essentially signaling the preclusion of any further negotiations by India over the now integral state of Jammu and Kashmir. During early 1964, the Indian representative to the Security Council made it clear that India would no longer consider a plebiscite when he announced that:

> We cannot possibly contemplate with equanimity the threat to the integration of our country and the danger to our cherished principle of secularism by the holding of a plebiscite in Kashmir . . . under *no circumstances* can we agree to the holding of a plebiscite in Kashmir (quoted in *Documents on the Foreign Relations of Pakistan* 1966: 381).

The events of 1964 outraged public opinion in Pakistan, leading the Pakistani foreign minister (and future president) Zulfikar Ali Bhutto to write to the president of the Security Council denouncing the "sinister design of the Government of India to obliterate the special status of the State of Jammu and Kashmir" as a "gross breach of the India's commitment to the principles of the resolutions of the United Nations" involving the purge of officials "whose only fault was that they were in some small measure conscious of . . . the right of self-determination" (quoted in *Documents on the Foreign Relations of Pakistan* 1966: 427–428). *The degree of support shown by the international community for the Pakistani cause of Kashmiri "self-determination" provided an important measure of justification for policies of aggression that were subsequently pursued.*

By integrating Kashmir with India and removing the issue from the negotiating table, India essentially froze the status quo situation in place, guaranteeing continued bilateral enmity for decades to come. A frustrated Pakistani leadership turned again to a strategy of forcibly ejecting India from the territory of perceived conationals.

During the spring of 1965, Indian forces attempted to occupy a Pakistani outpost in the Rann of Kutch, a largely unpopulated marshland area bordering on the Arabian Sea. Pakistan responded with military force that was "clearly greater than required by the tactical situation" and rather decisively defeated Indian forces in the area (Brines 1968: 289). According to Feldman (1972: 135), Ayub Khan interpreted the victory as a clear signal that Pakistani soldiers clearly outmatched their Indian counterparts, an impression reinforced by the earlier rout of Indian forces at the hands of the Chinese several years earlier.

The Pakistani plan to seize Kashmir involved two stages. The first stage, codenamed Operation Gibraltar involved an infiltration of approximately 7000 armed guerillas across the border. These guerillas were to take advantage of the perceived discontent and unrest among the local population, and to help fan the flames of rebellion. The anticipated local uprising was to be supported by a second phase, known as Operation Grand Slam, a conventional attack by Pakistani forces intended to cut off the region from the rest of India.

Operation Gibraltar was launched on July 24, 1965. The infiltrators quickly ran into serious problems, lacking both the training and local knowledge of terrain to effectively confront Indian security forces. More important, the infiltrators largely failed in their primary goal, as local Kashmiris not only refused to assist the Mujahadeen, but in many cases aided Indian security forces in the apprehension of the guerillas (Jalalzai 2000: 118). On August 14, Pakistani forces made a series of limited moves across the Line of Control, to which India responded the next day by launching their own limited strikes in Azad Kashmir. This tit-for-tat escalation continued until September 1, when Pakistan struck in force with armored divisions in southern Kashmir, quickly pushing back the Indian forces in the region.

The international community's overall response to the conflict once again demonstrated how weakly international norms of nonaggression and noninterference were being applied to Pakistan. India responded to Pakistani attacks by launching an attack across the international border in the state of Punjab to the south, a move that brought more international condemnation than the Pakistani attack in Kashmir. According to Brines (1968: 333), India's insistence that the Jammu-Kashmir line had represented an inviolable international border was, in the eyes of the international community, a "controversial" defense of the concrete violation of the international border in the Punjab. The Indian attack achieved its desired effect, however, with Pakistan suddenly forced on the defensive. After weeks of intense fighting, the two sides reached a ceasefire on September 22, and again withdrew into their own territories behind the Line of Control.

In the wake of the conflict, Indian and Pakistan signed a Soviet-brokered accord known as the Tashkent Declaration. The accord, which focused on the principle of mutual nonintervention, represented an attempt to normalize relations between India and Pakistan.

However, with continuing Pakistani designs on Kashmir and continuing Indian suspicion of Pakistani intentions, little qualitative change occurred in the relationship between the two states as the Kashmir issue remained unresolved. In 1970, on a visit to the region, Indian prime minister Indira Gandhi reasserted the Indian position that "[t]he accession of Kashmir is part of our history, and history cannot be reversed or changed" (Hasan 1998).

Although Pakistani aggression was muted during the late 1960s, lingering suspicions of Pakistani intentions remained among Indian leadership. Similar to Ethiopia's invasion of Somali territory and support of insurgents within Somalia during the 1980s, lasting mistrust and enmity on the part of the "target" state in the Indo-Pakistani dispute manifested itself during the early 1970s as the internal weakness of Pakistan offered an opportunity for Indian retribution and weakening of the Pakistani state.

During 1971, the military government of Pakistan, under General Yahya Khan, attempted to restore a measure of democracy by conducting elections during the spring to a new National Assembly. The Awami League, representing the voice of Bangladeshi nationalism, won 160 of the 162 seats in East Pakistan (and a majority of seats overall), setting the stage for confrontation with central authorities as negotiations for a new constitution became deadlocked. This deadlock, in turn, led the government of Yahya Khan to postpone the formation of the National Assembly. In response, the Awami League led a general strike in East Pakistan, while inciting growing demonstrations in the region. In turn, Yahya Khan suspended all political activity and outlawed the Awami League at the end of March 1971. In a further effort to quell instability, Yahya Khan ordered the military to arrest the Bangladeshi political elite and eliminate any political unrest. The heavy-handed military crackdown led to massive defections within Bangladeshi units, fostering the rise of armed rebellion that increased throughout 1971.

The Indian government seized upon the crisis in the east quickly. On March 31, 1971, Indira Gandhi announced in parliament that Bangladeshis would receive "wholehearted Indian support" in their efforts and called upon the world community to stop their "decimation" (quoted in Afzal 2001: 443). Diplomatic attacks launched against Pakistan were accompanied by a consummately *realpolitik* diplomatic initiative that led to the signing of the Indo-Soviet Treaty of Friendship in October 1971. The heightened potential for Soviet retaliation against China were China to act against India meant that India had a freer hand to act against Pakistan. After a three-week trip abroad in the fall of 1971 to assess the diplomatic mood of Western leaders, who were in no great hurry to defend the increasingly repressive Pakistani government and its tactics, Indira Gandhi ordered the invasion of East Pakistan on November 22, 1971. On December 3, 1971, Pakistani leadership finally ordered a counterattack in Kashmir, but the situation was irreversible, and little ground was gained in Kashmir. Under heavy diplomatic pressure, the two antagonists agreed to a ceasefire on December 17, 1971 leaving India in possession of the newly "liberated" eastern half of Pakistan. Three days later, Yahya Khan resigned in disgrace and was replaced by Zulfikar Ali Bhutto, who became the first civilian leader of Pakistan in over a decade.

Indian leaders utilized the victory in the 1971 conflict to strengthen their hitherto vulnerable international claim to Kashmir in postwar negotiations. The Simla Accord, similar to the Tashkent Declaration, attempted to set relations between India and Pakistan on a new course. The fear of future Pakistani aggression on the part of India is noticeable in the fact that three of the first six articles mention the value of "territorial integrity." Similarly, provisions of the document explicitly mention mutual respect for noninterference and sovereignty.[8] However, the most important long-term implications of the accord involved clauses that obligated the sides to resolve their disputes "bilaterally." Conscious of early receptiveness of UN bodies to the normative appeals of Pakistan, Indian leaders were to utilize the mantra of "bilateral" talks, as contained in the Simla Accord, as a cornerstone of future diplomatic efforts designed to resist outside pressures on the matter.

Bilateral negotiations on the Kashmir issue, not surprisingly, were largely nonexistent during the ensuing years. Although the remainder of the 1970s was notable for the absence of military conflict (the reason for this will be described later in a section examining internal determinants of Pakistani policies) there was no resolution for continuing India-Pakistani enmity. During the 1980s, Pakistan largely resumed many of its previously aggressive policies, but not to the extent that it had during the 1960s. As has been mentioned earlier, the Simla accord helped create the conditions by which India could claim the matter a "bilateral" dispute, which helped reduce international sympathy and involvement for Pakistan's cause.

The hallmark of military government during the 1980s lay not in outright aggression, as it had in earlier military regimes, but rather in the execution of covert operations within Afghanistan, India, and Kashmir. This is largely a consequence of the loss of international support for Kashmiri "self-determination," and the requisite desire of Pakistani decision makers to limit any potential international backlash that more blatant transgressions in Kashmir would have engendered. Covert operations, including supplying and training militants for cross-border infiltration were conducted by the Pakistani Inter-Service Intelligence (ISI),[9] which was granted a high degree of influence over policymaking during the 1980s.

The relationship continued in a tense stasis until the late 1980s, when rebellion erupted in Kashmir. Not surprisingly, the rhetoric surrounding the insurgency that ensued in Kashmir mirrored that of earlier decades, with Pakistan framing the uprising as a spontaneous revolt by native Kashmiris seeking self-determination. India has criticized the uprising as a manifestation of Pakistani aggression and militant revisionism and repeatedly asserted the indivisibility of the Indian state. Soon after the outbreak of rebellion, the two houses of the Indian parliament met and, in an "unprecedented move" approved a unanimous resolution repeating that Kashmir was an "inalienable" part of the Indian State (Ganguly and Bajpai 1994: 409).

The instability following elections in Kashmir during 1983 were indicative of events to come. Elections in 1987 created even greater instability, with opposition groups claiming wide scale electoral manipulation and fraud on the part of the proIndian National Conference and Congress parties, former rivals which had cooperated heavily during the election. Due in part to the "first past the post" system used in the state, these parties won only 53 percent of the popular vote, but garnered 87 percent of the legislative seats. The sense of disenfranchisement experienced by many supporters of the opposition, led to a large increase in the number of recruits seeking training, organization, and material aid across the border in Pakistan (Ganugly and Bajpai 1994: 405; Widmalm 1997: 1022). By this time, the ISI was well structured and equipped to handle the type of training and support that Kashmiri militants sought, and proceeded to fan the flames of insurgency by doing so. By the time of military leader President Muhammad Zia al-Haq's death in August 1988, the insurgency and ISI support of militant activities was well underway.

According to one eminent scholar on the Kashmir issue, "we may never find out the whole truth about Pakistani involvement," which is to say that the *extent* of Pakistani involvement remains cloaked in the secrecy one would expect to surround such covert activities. Nevertheless, the fact of Pakistani intervention remains unquestioned, even if at times exaggerated by the Indian government.[10] In the end, internal events can be said to have sparked the grievances underlying the outbreak of militancy in the region. However, without the organizational capabilities, training, material support, and safe haven provided by the ISI initially under the military government of President Zia, the insurgency may never have become as widespread.

After the death of Zia, civilian governments under Benazir Bhutto and Nawaz Sharif oversaw the continuation of covert activities in Kashmir. In response to the Pakistani role in supporting insurgent activity in Kashmir, the Indian government massed troops along the Line of Control in the spring of 1990. Although the situation did not escalate to war, the pattern of Pakistani assisted infiltration and border tensions and skirmishes continued throughout the 1990s. Soon after the accession of yet another military government under Pervez Musharraf, the situation escalated into a brief "war" when Indian troops clashed with Pakistani infiltrators in the

Kargil gap region. This situation will be examined in greater depth later when I examine the relationship between military government and conflict.

Summary—Indian-Pakistani Relations

Clearly, the terms of hostility between India and Pakistan changed little during the course of their history. This is because the number one issue coloring their relationship with one another, the irredentist dispute involving Kashmir, remained unresolved from independence up until the present day. The presence of a Muslim majority state ruled by an Indian government lay at the heart of a normative and ideological dispute pitting Pakistani calls for self-determination against the Indian stress on "secular nationalism" and territorial integration. Within this cyclical rivalry, Indian policies were often assertively and aggressively defensive in response to the perceived continuation of Pakistani revisionism, leading to the forced dismemberment of the Pakistani state. The tough line presented by India, on the other hand, contributed to continued Pakistani militarism by cultivating a continuing frustration of the nationalist goals of Pakistani leaders, who resorted to aggressive tactics in many cases due to the perceived lack of progress on the political front.

While the degree of nationalism within Pakistani society can be said to have been fairly constant through the period examined, the real normative story underlying Pakistani-Indian relations involves India's desire to limit the involvement of an international community that was surprisingly muted in its criticisms of Pakistani actions. During the earliest years of the dispute, the UN essentially advocated many of the same positions as Pakistan when it called for self-determination for Kashmiris and the conducting of a regional plebiscite. When Indian subsequently turned away from the holding of a plebiscite, Pakistani leaders perceived international constraints to aggressive action as weak, and felt justified in launching an invasion across the Line of Control in 1965. Later, Indian leaders were able to diminish international involvement in the dispute with the acceptance by both parties of the Simla Accord, which stressed conducting future negotiations exclusively on a bilateral basis.

The existence of a sizeable Muslim population in Kashmir created a high baseline level of bilateral hostility between India and Pakistan. However, during what was largely a consistent state of mistrust and tension, Pakistani policy manifested periodic increases and decreases of aggression associated with changing international and domestic factors, which will addressed in the second half of this chapter. Now I turn to relations between India and China. *Realpolitik* factors conditioned Sino-Indian relations and engendered a certain degree of distrust, but never presented the intractable barriers faced in the Indo-Pakistani relationship.

Chinese-Indian Relations—Realist Rivalry Contrasted to Nationalist Rivalry

While Indian-Pakistani relations were dominated by a regional irredentist situation, Indian-Pakistani relations fell largely in the realm of power politics. As such, the relationship between China and India was marked by consistent rivalry. However, that rivalry never reached the level of instinctive animosity coloring relations between India and Pakistan. Disputes between India and China involved arguments of territory; but not territory that evoked any strong nationalist-type sentiment in either country. Furthermore, what may have appeared as simple border disputes on the surface actually involved strong elements of prestige politicking as both India and China jostled for leadership in the eyes of the Third World.

Some realist scholars might suggest that Indian-Chinese relations should be expected to have been more peaceful than those between India and Pakistan due to the fact that the military capabilities of India and China were more balanced. On the contrary, however, it was the very balance of capabilities that occasioned a more tense state of affairs between India and China than might otherwise have been expected. In comparison to Chinese-Indian relations, Chinese-Pakistani relations were exceedingly warm, despite the fact that China and Pakistan also shared a common border that provoked similar border disagreements in the 1950s and 1960s. Brines (1968: 198) argues the *realpolitik* outlook of Chinese leaders in particular conditioned heightened bilateral instability in the India-China relationship, particularly in view of long-term Chinese Premier Zhou Enlai's outlook that "large powers can grant concessions to smaller ones without losing face, but to do so to a nation of comparable size would be the gravest sign of weakness." Rather than the questions of national preservation and protection that arose in the India-Pakistani disputes, China and India militancy committed lives in the name of issues involving state prestige and pride of place in the Third World movement.

The immediate issues between China and India involved the postcolonial demarcation of the border between China and the northwestern and northeastern borders of India. The northeast sector of the dispute involved the Chinese contention that the McMahon Line, which established a border between Tibet, India, and China, was invalid. According to the Chinese view, the Tibetan representatives to the Simla Conference of 1914, which established the border, were not competent to conclude treaties due to the quasi-independent status of Tibet vis-à-vis China at the time. In the northwest, Chinese claims involved the Aksai Chin region of Kashmir, which the Chinese government considered strategically important in terms of Chinese control of Tibet. Particular after uprisings in Tibet during the late 1950s, the salience of the Aksai Chin claim increased even more so for Chinese leadership.

The Chinese government pressed its "historical and cultural" claims to the border areas throughout the late 1950s and early 1960s, and small-scale skirmishes along the border began to mount. During 1960, a summit conference between Nehru and Zhou Enlai was unsuccessful in resolving the bilateral territorial issues between the two states, and gradual preparation for the upcoming conflict began soon thereafter. In 1961, India adopted a forward military deployment, establishing several bases in the Aksai Chin. The following year China initiated a limited strike across the McMahon Line in September 1962, followed by a full-scale assault across both fronts in October, which quickly overran ill-trained and ill-supplied Indian troops.

On November 21, Beijing declared a unilateral ceasefire and withdrew behind the original borders. Beijing conducted the surprise military attack primarily to gain international prestige, particularly among lesser-developed countries—reflecting how the larger issue of influence in the Third World superseded the specific territorial issues involved. By announcing the unilateral ceasefire, China "had broken off the action at the moment of India's deepest humiliation" (Brines 1968: 195) and "by inflicting a humiliating defeat on India, China sought to show that India was not much of a rival for the leadership of Asia" (Syed 1974: 105).

The border issues between India and China continued throughout the decades, although 1962 represented the only major conflagration concerning the dispute. Nevertheless, bilateral relations remained cool, and a consequence of the 1962 war included "dramatically heightened suspicions of Chinese intentions" on the part of Indian leadership, which came to view subsequent Chinese policy through the "prism" of "humiliation and resentment" (Elkin and Fredericks 1983: 1129).

After the 1962 war, China chose to pursue its diplomatic offensive against India through less direct means by cultivating closer ties with India's gravest enemy, Pakistan.

As the relationship between India and China after 1962 was intimately tied to that of China and Pakistan, we will continue to explore India-Chinese relations in the next section, which focuses on Chinese support for the Pakistani cause in Kashmir.

In terms of the specific bilateral border disputes between China and India, no attempt to address the issue was made for the two decades following the 1962 war. Finally, in December 1981, formal border negotiations between the two states were reinitiated, motivated in part by Indian desires to reduce its dependence on the Soviet Union and achieve greater diplomatic flexibility (Elkin and Fredericks 1983: 113). A series of vice ministerial talks occurred between 1981 and 1987, producing few concrete results but enhancing overall India-Sino relations. In 1987, Rajiv Gandhi instituted a new course in Indian policy by dropping Indian insistence that the normalization of relationships depended on the final resolution of the territorial question (Garver 1996: 325). In response, Beijing noticeably moderated its position in support of Pakistan over the Kashmir issue, a move of no little importance considering mounting tensions in the area at the beginning of the 1990s. After the end of 1988, when Rajiv Gandhi undertook a visit to China, relations between the two states could be characterized as warmer than any period since the mid-1950s (Garver, 1996: 323). A final sign of the new relationship between the two states became evident with the reestablishment of military exchanges between the two countries in the mid-1990s.

Although maintaining a close relationship with Pakistan, China increasingly reached out to India during the 1990s. Although China's continuing relationship with Pakistan will continue to present barriers to warmer relations with India, it is clear that the Chinese-Indian disputes of the past no longer carry the salience that they once did. In *the absence* of an outstanding nationalist conflict, relations between India and China have been "free" to improve. This lies in contrast to the conflict between India and Pakistan, wherein leaders have been constrained by societal nationalist impulses from fundamentally altering the underlying relationship between the two states. While territorial disputes between China and India remain outstanding, border questions have not prevented a gradual improvement in relations between the two states—an outcome much more attainable and stable than a permanent strengthening of Pakistani-Indian ties.

Pakistan-China Relations—Realist Alliance Contrasted to Nationalist Rivalry

This chapter turns now to the topic of Pakistan-China relations, a relationship based heavily around the Kashmir issue and the wedge that it has driven between India and Pakistan. Politics often makes strange bedfellows, and no better example exists than the entente existing between the ideologically and philosophical incongruent states of Pakistan and China since the early 1960s. Even though the two states could hardly have differed more in terms of the dominant principles shaping domestic governance, their interests in the international arena converged due to their mutual antipathy toward India. Just as Pakistan's friendship strengthened China's position within the context of China's *realpolitik*-type rivalry with India, China's goodwill allowed Pakistan to adopt a more aggressive posture in pursuance of that state's nationalist oriented policies toward Kashmir.

Chinese and Pakistani leaders grew increasingly close after it became evident that no plebiscite would take place in Kashmir and after the Soviet Union openly allied itself with the Indian position in 1955. In a 1956 visit to Pakistan, Chinese Premier Zhou Enlai stressed that there were "no conflicts of interest between the countries [and that] ideological differences should not prevent them from strengthening their friendship (Syed 1974: 68). By 1961, when both India and Pakistan faced border disputes with China, Pakistani leader Ayub Khan, in contrast to the Indian position, reached out to Chinese leaders by declaring:

> The Chinese have their ideology, and we have our ideology. They have no faith in our ideology and we have none in their ideology. But we are neighbors and we would like to live as good neighbors. We have no cause to quarrel over our undemarcated border and all we have said is: let us define it and let us see what comes out of it. (quoted in Syed 1974: 84)

As if to further snub India in the wake of its defeat in 1962, China and Pakistan announced in December of that year that they were in "complete agreement" on their common border issues. Shortly before Indo-Pakistani talks the next year, the border agreement between China and Pakistan became official. Because the border agreement turned Pakistani-held areas of Kashmir over to China, an infuriated India government charged that Pakistan had "no *locus standi* to . . . conclude agreements with any country regarding the boundaries of Jammu and Kashmir" (Razvi 1971: 177, emphasis in the original).

China openly came out in support of Pakistan's position on Kashmir in 1964; the year widely considered the beginning of the Chinese-Pakistan "entente" (Garver 1996: 324). Although China's motives were clearly self-interested and had little to do with sympathy for the people of Kashmir, Chinese leaders viewed India's "vulnerability on the question of Kashmiri self-determination" as "a golden opportunity to cement its relations with Pakistan and to discredit India further in the eyes of the Afro-Asian world" (Simon 1967: 180). After 1964, Chinese leaders frequently employed normative appeals based on self-determination to antagonize India, frequently citing earlier "promises" made by India to the United Nations.

Chinese support for Pakistan was unambiguous during the subsequent wars of 1965 and 1971, even if Beijing was unwilling to intervene militarily. By stationing troops along the northeastern border of India in 1965, China effectively prevented India from deploying several divisions to the theater of battle in Kashmir. Although unable to respond as aggressively in 1971, due to the threat of Soviet retaliation in the north, China maintained a singular position throughout both wars, casting India as the "aggressor" and harping on the denial of self-determination in Kashmir.

Although relations were consistently close during the 1970s, small cracks began to appear within the Sino-Pakistani entente during the 1980s as Sino-Indian relations began to warm somewhat. In June 1980, Chinese leader Deng Xiaoping seemed to adopt the longstanding Indian position when he stated that the Kashmir issue was a *bilateral dispute*, although "balanced" this "nod to New Delhi" in December when he stated the desire for the dispute to be resolved "according to relevant United Nations resolutions" (Garver 1996: 327). Nevertheless, the comments marked the beginning of a slow warm-up in Chinese-Indian relations throughout the decade.

By 1990, against the backdrop of renewed conflict in the region, it became clear that Beijing had noticeably moderated its position on Kashmir (Garver 1996: 329). No longer did Beijing allude to the United Nations, assenting to India's "bilateral" position in earnest. Rather than labeling India a guilty party, as it had in the past, the Chinese government responded to the growing Kashmir crisis of the 1990s mainly by expressing a desire for peace (Garver 1996: 332).

Relations between China, India, and Pakistan have become more nuanced than they have in the past. China and India have a warmer relationship than decades past, but the structural considerations of *realpolitik* will likely continue to prevent these rapidly developing, nuclear armed, rivals from completely dispelling their mutual suspicions for some time to come. On the other hand, while losing a measure of support on the Kashmir issue, Pakistan still regards China as a key ally and supporter, while China views Pakistan as an important hedge against future disputes with India. Relations between India and Pakistan are easiest to characterize, and remain based on the mutual suspicion fueled in large part by the unresolved Kashmir dispute.

Domestic Influences on Pakistani Dispute Initiation

Factors Hypothesized to Affect Varying Levels of Pakistani Militant Revisionism

This section, which examines the domestic variables conditioning levels of Pakistani military aggression, differs slightly in structure from the previous chapter's analysis of Somali revisionism. Because many of the relevant variables are theorized to be significant solely within the context of an irredentist dispute, this section exclusively examines Pakistani policies toward India (as opposed the previous chapter which examined Somali relations toward both Kenya and Ethiopia).

The lack of *militant activity among the Muslim "diaspora"* in Kashmir facilitates the examination of the role of military influence over Pakistani foreign policy. The only period witnessing an indigenous uprising in Kashmir was the period 1988–1989 and after. One might also argue that an uprising took place during the period surrounding partition during 1947, when a revolt against local leaders took place in the Poonch. However, most of the subsequent insurgency was not attributable to local forces, but rather to Islamic "jihadists" originating from within Pakistan. The uprising of the late 1980s, was, however, primarily homegrown, and will be discussed later within the extended section that describes the effect of military governance on policy.

Even more clearly than in the Somali case, Pakistani governments characterized by *higher levels of military influence over policy* were associated with higher levels of militarized dispute initiation. Furthermore, the only major war initiated by Pakistan during the period 1951–1991 occurred in 1965 at the high point of military influence over policy. Since military rule characterizes a majority of the years of Pakistani rule covered in this case, it might be even more to the point to note that the years of civilian rule (1951–1957; 1973–1978; 1989–1991) were noticeably more peaceful than those years under military rule. Only the last set of dates, 1989–1991, represented a strong conjunction of civilian rule and Pakistani aggression, but, as will be explained, this is due in part to lingering legacies of the 11 year Zia military regime.

I will also discuss the *combination of military influence and diaspora discontent* within the section discussing the effects of military governance over policy. The highpoint of discontent in Kashmir occurred during the period immediately before Pakistan initiated the war of 1965, as several internal crises sparked a rise in disorganized violence. As will be discussed, this discontent played a major role in the decision by the military government at the time to launch major hostilities against India.

I will briefly discuss the degree to which *the Pakistani economy* rises or declines during each period, but there appears to be little correlation between Pakistani economic growth/decline and foreign policy behavior. Unlike the Somali economy, the Pakistani economy has generally displayed stable macroeconomic growth. While the 1950s experienced several (relatively small) upward and downward swings in economic growth, during the 26 year period from 1965 until 1991, Pakistan only experienced economic decline during five years. At the same time, growth rates generally hovered around a consistent 3–5 percent per year, as displayed in the figure 7.1. Perhaps the main conclusion is that Pakistan was better able to maintain an overall aggressive policy in part due to the lack of major economic crises at home that would have otherwise diverted the energies of the government.

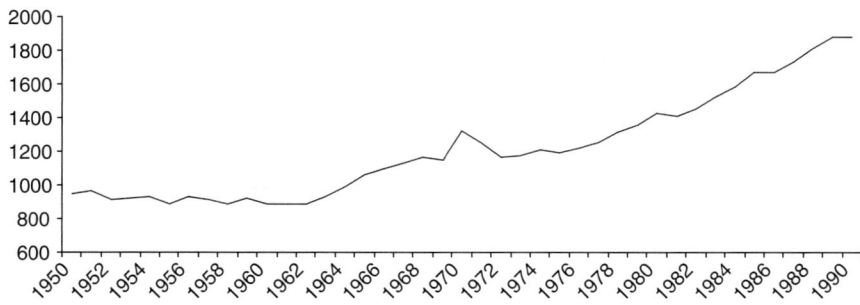

Figure 7.1 Pakistani GDP per capita (in Real 1996 U.S. Dollars)

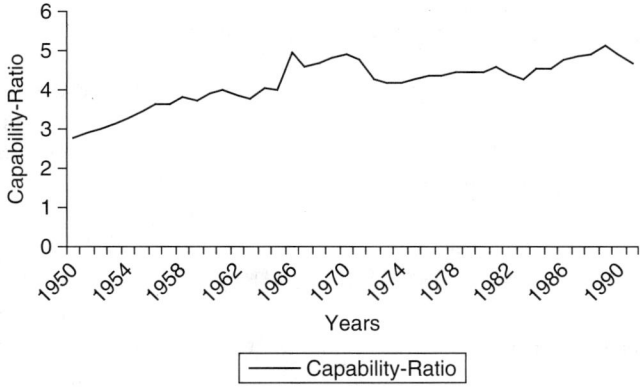

Figure 7.2 Ratio of Indian to Pakistani Capabilities

Finally, the question of *military feasibility* is important in understanding the high level of revisionism directed by Pakistan at India. Pakistan's military capabilities never came close to matching those of India. The impossibility of doing so was recognized by policy makers in Pakistan, however, and the long-term Pakistani strategy revolved around preserving Pakistani capabilities that were strong enough to deter any major Indian attack undertaken in retribution for Pakistani subversion—the very definition of "military feasibility" as employed in this study. Figure 7.2 shows that, after a divergence in capabilities during the early years after independence, Pakistan was largely successful in preventing India from "running away" with a larger gap in military capabilities than what existed during the mid-1960s. Nevertheless, the gap was large enough for India to drive into Pakistan during the 1965 war and to dismember the strategically exposed region of East Pakistan during 1971.

Turning again to the first of the two "static" variables in this study, Kashmir clearly took on additional value to the Pakistani government due to its *strategic importance*. Including both sides of the Line of Control, Kashmir extends to within 30 miles of the Pakistani capital, and borders not only on India, but also on China and Afghanistan, which, at its narrowest separated Kashmir from the Soviet Union by a mere 40 miles (Brines 1968:3). Choudhury (1971: 54) goes so far as to compare Pakistani fears concerning Indian control of Kashmir to that of "Czechoslovakia after Hitler's [conquest] of Austria." The prospect of Pakistani control over all of Kashmir would allow Pakistan to take up strategic positions to the north of India, similarly threatening that state from two different directions.

As far as the *economic importance* of Kashmir is concerned, there is little about Kashmir to distinguish the territory as economically crucial to either India or Pakistan. Certainly, natural resources including timber and the prospect of hydroelectric development separate Kashmir from territories such as the barren Rann of Kutch, over which the two states fought in 1965, but few readily extractable resources exist in the territory. Clearly, many other factors, including strategic value, are of greater importance in promoting conflict over Kashmir than the region's natural resources or contribution to national revenue.

Military versus Civilian Decision Making in Pakistan as a Major Determinant of Foreign Policy Aggression

The Pakistani case is difficult to explain from a normative perspective alone, as the intense nationalist sentiment within Pakistani society did not noticeably change throughout the decades. Several factors, however, do help one understand why Pakistani policies were more or less aggressive during different eras.

Figure 7.3 depicts how the normative-demographic model retroactively predicts the potential a bilateral MID initiation between the dyads involved in this case study throughout the years. Not surprisingly, the line depicting the Pakistani-India dyad is predicted to be generally more conflictual throughout the years due to the presence of irredentist-type demography. Overlaying the Pakistani line, however, are stars depicting the years in which Pakistan actually initiated a dispute. As will be argued, the initiation of military disputes is strongly correlated with the presence of military-based decision making, whereas the periods of peace correlate with the presence of civilian authority.

Schofield (2000) suggests as well that a direct line of causality exists between the presence of militarized decision making and Pakistani dispute behavior during crises.[11] He first notes that under civilian decision making during the 1950s war was largely averted due to the subservient role of the military in the decision-making process. During this period, a high level of instability along the Line of Control accompanied the diplomatic acrimony surrounding the plebiscite issue and the future status of Jammu and Kashmir. According to an article in *The Economist* ("India and Pakistan" 1951: 139) at the time, "The danger of war between India and Pakistan, has, once more, become acute." Similarly, Schofield (2000: 138) describes the summer of 1951 as the summer of the "war scare." In light of an Indian decision to convene the first Kashmiri Constituent Assembly, both countries increased their deployment along the Line of Control and the neighboring Punjab region. In response to heavy public pressure, the Pakistani prime minister, Liaquat Ali Khan, pursued a hard line during the crisis of 1951. Khan, however, never initiated full-scale hostilities against Pakistan, and the crisis had begun to lose steam when Khan was assassinated under mysterious circumstances during the fall of 1951. Unlike the military government that took power at the end of the decade and led the country to war in 1965, the civilian authorities of the early 1950s pursued a

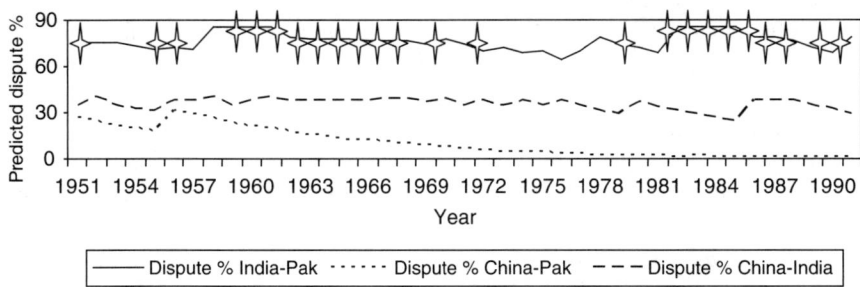

Figure 7.3 Predicted Bilateral Dispute Probabilities and Actual Pakistani Dispute Initiation

sustained policy of aggressive diplomacy toward India, but stepped back from the brink rather than escalating the dispute into full-fledged armed conflict.

Instability accompanying civilian rule helped pave the way for the growth of military influence in policymaking, a process that ended in military takeover in 1958. In a process that mirrored the rise of military government in Somalia, the failures of civilian leadership were accompanied by an enhanced role for the military as a consequence of material assistance provided by a superpower—in this case the United States. As civilian leadership became increasingly paralyzed, an elite composed of high level civil service and military officers increasingly dictated policy (Choudhury 1988: 19). Schofield (2000: 138) sets the date of "significant" military influence over Pakistani policies at approximately 1954, with 1958 representing the culmination of a process through which military leaders exercised increasing control over policy.

President Iskandar Mirza opened the door to military rule when he suspended the democratic processes of Pakistan in response to continued economic and political instability, including rising regional and sectarian opposition to the processes of political centralization, particularly in East Pakistan. Mirza selected Army Chief Ayub Khan as the chief martial law administrator. Khan, in turn, utilized his position to depose Mirza two weeks later, assuming the presidential post for himself.

As was the case in Somalia, domestic factors influenced the rise of military rule more than international factors. According to Akbar (1997:44), the coup was fostered by "a general feeling of political malaise, by a near consensus among the politically aware segments of the population that the politicians had somehow failed in their duty to provide the country with a workable political system." Although the rise to power of military governments generally involves domestic political failures on the part of civilian leadership, the consequences of military leadership on foreign policy formulation within irredentist situations can be profound.

Top generals and bureaucrats dominated political decision making under Ayub Khan. Reminiscent of the decision making in Somalia and Barre, Ayub Khan also relied heavily on informal consultations with an "inner-circle" of fellow military leaders, whose advice was often favored over the more formal decision-making processes. Thus, decisions within the Ayub Khan regime were "insulated from domestic politics," and based primarily on the preferences and views of military officers (Schofield 2000: 139).

At first, it seemed that the accession of Ayub Khan would exacerbate India-Pakistani relations even further. Nehru responded to Ayub Khan's seizure of power by referring to the new regime as a "'naked military dictatorship' without parallel in the 'wide world today'" (Syed 1974: 27). For his part, Ayub Khan shored up his domestic position with threats of "extreme action" against India unless the Kashmir dispute was resolved (Afzal 2001: 297). Nevertheless, during the early years of the Ayub Khan regime, tension over Kashmir was largely deescalated as a result of surprisingly conciliatory policies adopted by Pakistan's military leadership. Particularly impressive was the ability of the Ayub Khan regime to reach agreement on a variety of border issues with India, culminating in the Indus Basin Treaty of 1960, which involved the division of waters from the Indus River Basin for (primarily) irrigation purposes. Furthermore, during this period, Ayub Khan offered, on several occasions, to negotiate a "joint defense" agreement with India—an offer that understandably suspicious Indian authorities ultimately rebuffed.

The brief period of accommodation pursued in the early years of the Ayub Khan administration turned around abruptly in 1962. According to Brines (1968: 226), 1962 marked the year that Ayub Khan "turned his country with increasing vigor towards fierce . . . jingoism," a move that was accompanied by a relentless "hate India" campaign, which was pursued daily through the press.

A series of events may have triggered the turnabout in the military government's policies. First, a series of definitively worded statements by the Indian government suggested the definitive end of negotiations on the Kashmir issue and the rejection of any further possibility of holding a plebiscite. The year 1962 also marked the year war took place between India and China, which presented the Pakistani government an opportunity to solidify its growing relationship with China through a series of diplomatic attacks on India. Also aware of the growing capabilities of the Pakistani military, Ayub Khan may have been laying the groundwork for the future invasion of India, an invasion that was increasingly perceived as militarily feasible.

An unusual incident within Kashmir itself encouraged the new, more aggressive stance of the Pakistani government. As has been discussed, military governments seem particularly likely to engage in hostilities when signs of discontent are present among a diaspora population. On December 27, 1963, a sacred relic, reputedly a hair of the Prophet Mohammed, was stolen from a mosque in Srinagar, prompting widespread rioting and unrest. Although the relic was recovered the following month, demonstrations continued until the spring (Brines 1968: 213). The instability surrounding the incident, seized upon by Pakistani propagandists, also influenced Pakistani leaders, who perceived anti-Indian demonstrations as a clear sign of discontent among Muslims in Kashmir.

In December 1964, the Indian government provided another impetus for war when it initiated the policy of assimilating Kashmir into India at the same constitutional level as other Indian states, stripping the region of the special status it had held earlier. Faced with the prospect of Kashmir becoming even more tightly tied to India, military aggression was increasingly perceived by Pakistani leadership as the only method through which the territory might be "liberated."

The arrest of regional leader Sheik Abdullah in May 1965 further intensified Pakistani perceptions that discontent was growing among Muslims in Kashmir. Once again, widespread antigovernment violence ensued—violence that Brines (1968: 247) describes as "unprecedented in Kashmir's history." According to the Indian government, the instability claimed the lives of 153 members of Indian security forces (Feldman 1972: 143). According to Afzal (2001: 306), Ayub Khan affirmed the go-ahead for an invasion of Kashmir during the same month.

For the first time since independence, it can be said that military rule, diaspora discontent, and military feasibility were all simultaneously present. Although "diaspora discontent" likely did not exist in the sense that locals preferred Pakistani rule to Indian rule, such preferences were attributed by Pakistani leadership to the local population due to the antigovernment demonstrations associated with the Hair of the Prophet incident. The theoretical importance of diaspora discontent lies less with the objective conditions of a diaspora group than with the perception among homeland states that such groups are desirous of liberation. Buoyed by the growing capabilities of the Pakistani army, military leaders in Pakistan saw antigovernment violence as a signal that the Muslims of the region would support an invasion.

At the height of his support among the armed forces, Ayub Khan initiated war against India. Although normally viewed as a cautious man (Afzal 2001: 306), Ayub Khan perceived war to be the only way to resolve the Kashmir issue in the face of growing Indian intransigence. The dearth of diplomatic progress on the issue combined with the widespread perception in military circles that a short window of military opportunity existed combined to exert a high level of political pressure on Ayub Khan to take assertive action in order to "weaken India's resolve and bring her to the conference table" (Afzal 2001: 306). In the end, the military government not only formulated a policy of aggressive warfare, but Ayub Khan himself assumed a dominant role in the strategic planning of the conflict (Schofield 2000: 141).

The Tashkent Declaration that followed the fighting was generally ill received among the Pakistani public, which had been led to believe that victory had been at hand in the 1965 war. Particularly among the armed forces, Ayub Khan lost a great deal of support (Razvi 1971: 1958), and a long downward slide in the legitimacy of the military government had begun. The Tashkent Declaration turned out to be the turning point in the political life of Ayub Khan, who never recovered the status he had enjoyed prior to the 1965 conflict (Akbar 1997: 45). Partly a result of the Tashkent Declaration, a "generally militant attitude" prevailed between the two states for the remainder of the decade (Feldman 1972: 166) as Khan sought to placate those below who viewed the settlement as a sell-out.

The loss of support for Ayub Khan's government was evident in the resignation of Foreign Minister Zulfikar Ali Bhutto (father of later prime minister Benazir Bhutto), who was seen as a chief opponent of the Tashkent Declaration. Following his resignation, Bhutto founded the Pakistan People's Party, which supported a series of student demonstrations beginning in 1968. Violence surrounding the growing demonstrations erupted in early 1969, and within three months Ayub Khan resigned, handing the reigns of power over to the Army Chief of Staff Mohammed Yahya Khan. Khan reinstituted martial law soon thereafter, restoring a measure of political order by the summer. This order, however, would be short-lived, as a growing autonomy movement in East Pakistan began to make itself heard.

Despite his initial resort to martial law, Yahya Khan sought to set Pakistan back on the path to democracy from the onset of his tenure. In the Legal Framework order of March 1970, the conditions for elections for a National Assembly were established. However, as described earlier, the elections that took place quickly degenerated into a separatist rebellion in East Pakistan.

The military government was ill-equipped to handle the civilian separatist forces unleashed during the aborted process of democratization. According to Hayes (1984: 96), "while Yahya's ultimate intention may have been to establish a regime based on democratic principles, he relied almost entirely on the military in the meantime"—thus fostering a more militant posture among separatists in East

Pakistan who felt frustrated in their abilities to work through democratic channels. Similarly Schofield (2000: 142) notes how pressure from within the army isolated Yahya Khan from civil institutions and advisors during a period when their advice was most greatly needed.

India initiated the war of 1971 by providing material support for separatists within, and later invading Bangladesh. Thus, in this case, one cannot hold the military leadership within Pakistani responsible for international aggression. However, it is interesting to note that policies instituted by the military government at the time, and during the past, did contribute to the eventual secession of Bangladesh. According to Awami League leader, Mujibur Rahman, the aggressive policies pursued by Pakistani leadership toward India "served the interests of the military and certain capitalists in West Pakistan" (Hayes 1984: 109). A central point in the platform of the Awami League called for drastic reduction in military expenditures in order to diminish the influence of the military over political policy. Indian leaders also viewed the continuation of military rule in Pakistan with suspicion, believing it would lead to future Pakistani aggression.

Unlike the aftermath of the Tashkent Declaration, however, the "spirit of Simla" took hold for much of the decade, as Bhutto's government turned away from its aggressive stance on the Kashmir issue in order to pursue a series of agreements with India in other areas. Bhutto initiated a policy of greater nonalignment, similar to that advocated by India for decades, and removed Pakistan from the British Commonwealth and SEATO. These moves, although certainly not undertaken to placate India, sent a powerful signal to the Indian government that Pakistan would no longer utilize its relationship with Western powers as a source of financial, military, or diplomatic backing in its efforts to reclaim Kashmir. The warming atmosphere also led to various trade, shipping, travel, and cultural exchange agreements that emerged from the Simla process (Jalalzai 2000: 108). Perhaps most symbolic of Bhutto's desire to depart from the past was his final announcement at the Organization of Islamic States' conference of 1974 that Pakistan would recognize Bangladesh, thus acknowledging the consequences of India's military conquest.

Clearly, the Pakistani government under civilian rule adopted less aggressive policies toward India than past and future military leaders. According to the data utilized for this project, Pakistan did not initiate a single militarized dispute during the past five years of civilian rule (1973–1977)—the only such stretch during the 50 years covered by this study. The civilian regime under Bhutto worked with India to bring about amicable settlements of issues surrounding the 1971 war (prisoner exchanges, recognition of Bangladesh, etc.), while restoring postal and telecommunication links by 1975 and full trade relations in 1976. As foreign minister, Bhutto had gained prominence for his hard-line nationalist rhetoric and promises of a "thousand year war" with India. As prime minister, however, Bhutto, "repeatedly called for an end to the era of confrontation with India" Syed (1974: 190).

Furthermore, Bhutto actively sought to reduce the role of the military in politics through a variety of organizational restructuring measures. Ultimately, however, Bhutto fell short in securing the loyalty of the officer corps, who readily supported a military coup led by Mohammed Zia al-Haq in the aftermath of disputed elections during 1977.

General Zia, or President Zia as he officially preferred to be called after 1978, fanned the flames of Islamic nationalism in order to legitimate military rule. Jalalzai (2000: 108) draws comparison between the former civilian leadership of Bhutto and Zia by suggesting that:

> Bhutto had realized and initiated the process of environment building, necessary for normalization between India and Pakistan . . . With the advent of General Zia, this process came to a halt.

Under Zia, the armed forces would once again "determine all the major aspects of Pakistani foreign policy" (Shah 1997: 216). An early sign that the era of "détente" largely ended with the reassertion of military control over foreign policy occurred in 1978, when Zia's new government refused to renew the landmark trade accord signed three years earlier, instead prohibiting most private industries from dealing with India.

Although his policies were not as overtly aggressive as those of Ayub Khan during the years preceding the 1965 war, Zia pursued covert, low-levels of aggression against India throughout his tenure. Soviet intervention in Afghanistan in December 1979 fostered a sense of Islamic unity and common cause in Pakistan that Zia utilized to his advantage in maintaining power. Without the "outlet" for Islamic militancy in Afghanistan, it is very possible that the same Islamic militants with whom he sought to ally himself would have forced Zia into even more aggressive policies toward India.

Not long after the initial invasion of Afghanistan by the Soviet Union, the United States agreed to provide Afghanistan 3.2 billion U.S. dollars in military aid over five years in exchange for Pakistani assistance in supporting the mujahadeen insurgency against the Soviets. While this aid solidified Pakistan's relations with the United States, turning the country away from its dalliance with nonalignment during Bhutto's administration, the threat from the Soviets in Afghanistan was in fact intensified by Pakistan's stance against Moscow. Fearing the possibility of conflict on two fronts, however, President Zia pursued a "peace offensive" toward India, which was intended to reduce the possibility of future Indian aggression. At the same time, however, Zia's military government began pursuing a variety of covert policies meant to destabilize India from within.

Pakistan's policies during this period were rather duplicitous, with soft diplomacy being coupled with aggressive subversion within India. Dixit (2002: 248), a former Indian diplomat, describes the policies of Pakistan at the time as an "apparent" peace offensive, which masked "covert moves to erode India's unity, influence and strength." A somewhat more objective source, Jalalzai (2000: 108–109), an Afghani, similarly describes the peace offensive as "a strategic move," adopted as part of a "war on all fronts, barring the actual battle front." Part of the peace offensive entailed a "no-war" pact offer by Zia similar to that offered by Ayub Khan during his early tenure. The offer would mainly have benefited Pakistan by dissuading Indian reprisals undertaken in response to Pakistani subversion. The subsequent rejection of the offer by India, however, provided Pakistan a public propaganda victory. Although the diplomatic efforts of the day, culminating in a face to face meeting between Zia and Indira Gandhi in 1982, smoothed bilateral relations to so some degree, it is clear that Zia ultimately pursued such policies in order to shore up Pakistan's short-term position, rather than as an effort to achieve a new understanding with India. The return to the pattern of annual Pakistani initiated MIDs during this period attests to the aggressive nature of covert policies pursued by Pakistan, particularly within Kashmir and the Punjab.

The influence of the military clearly dominated Pakistani policies under Zia. Zia himself led the nationalist charge by stressing Pakistan's Islamic roots, and promoting the idea that "the armed forces bear the sacred responsibility for safeguarding Pakistan's ideological frontiers" (quoted in Jalalzai 2000: 1). Those "ideological frontiers" clearly centered on Kashmir and the desire to extended control over the region in the name of Islamic solidarity. While publicly pursuing peace with India, Zia quietly pursued policies of subversion in Kashmir (and the Punjab) similar to those pursued by Ayub Khan's military regime when Operation Gibraltar was initiated. Unlike Ayub Khan's policies, however, Zia's were much more gradual, and focused on supporting indigenous discontent without the visible presence of large numbers of armed infiltrators.

The legacy of militarized government under Zia influenced the course of events under the Pakistani civilian leadership of the 1990s. First, the strengthening of the ISI through numerous covert operations during the 1980s allowed the military to retain a strong influence over policy—influence that was cloaked in secrecy but very much real. Second, the support given by the Zia administration to the burgeoning insurgency during the late 1980s helped intensify the rebellion to a degree that civilian leaders could not ignore without imperiling their political support.

The Kashmiri Insurgency and the Kargil Gap War

Although this work primarily focuses on events occurring before the early 1990s, some discussion of the Kashmiri insurgency is useful as a basis for continuing the discussion of the earlier chapter concerning the response of civilian and military governments to diaspora rebellion. As has been asserted, the type of government within a homeland state seems largely irrelevant when considering the initiation conflict with a kin state that is home to diaspora rebellion. The civilian governments in Pakistan from the late 1980s into the mid-1990s clearly felt beholden to domestic pressures, and thus maintained policies of controlled aggression against India.

The roots of the Kashmiri uprising can be traced to 1982, when the longtime figure of stability in the region, Sheikh Abdullah, died. Acts of violence marred elections in 1983—violence not been witnessed in previous elections held in 1977. In October 1983, disturbances by adherents to the future militant party Jamaat-e-Islami following an international cricket match ratcheted up tensions in the region. The level of violence in the state was notable increasing in 1984, and "increasing reports of insurgency" were evident by 1985 (Widmalm 1997: 1017).

Although most scholars mark the beginning of the Kashmiri insurgency as 1988 or 1989, it is clear that militant activities had been escalating since the mid-1980s. The insurgency, however, became most visible under the government of Benazir Bhutto, who saw few domestic political alternatives to continuing the policy of support that had existed in the past. The subversive activities of the Zia military government had helped spark a long string of small-scale border clashes with India throughout the 1980s, clashes which escalated during the latter half of the decade and, particularly, in the 1990s. By this point, civilian leaders had become political hostages to the events in Kashmir that had already been set in motion.

Severe military pressure placed on Prime Minister Nawaz Sharif, facilitated the escalation to war that occurred during 1999. Although it was the first time that a civilian administration had initiated a major armed incursion into Kashmir, that administration was strongly influenced by the Pakistani military, led by Pervez Musharraf. Although many of the factors leading to the decision of the military government to send forces into the Kargil remain unknown, Musharraf expressed unwavering support for Kashmiri militancy. As the Director General of Military Operations under the civilian governments of the 1990s, Musharraf personally played a large role in planning the operation and, according to former prime minister Benazir Bhutto, had presented the plan to her with a promise to "put the flag of Pakistan in the Srinagar assembly" (*The India Express*, January 22, 2002). The desire of the Sharif government to bring the conflict to a diplomatic resolution was a central factor in his removal by military coup in October 1999 (BBC News, September 24, 2001).

Despite recent overtures to India, militarized governments in Pakistan have a poor record when it comes to the promotion of sustainable peacemaking efforts. Bhutto, referring to Musharraf's post-9/11 "makeover" as a moderate peacemaker, warned that he might yet represented another military leader whose legacy is one of aggression toward India:

> General Musharraf needs to dwell on the principles of a society that can breed a violence-free generation. Such a challenge can be difficult for a regime which has gone from one crisis to another. Hardly had the noise of guns thundering on the Afghan border died down then arose the thunder of guns between Indo-Pak troops. In jumping from crisis to crisis, Musharraf is fulfilling the legacy that history dons military dictators with. War is always historically avoided under Pakistan's democratic leaders. (*The Indian Express*, January 22, 2002)

Historical developments in both Pakistan and Somalia seem to suggest that military governments—or at least governments strongly beholden to the military—tend to escalate violence to a level that most civilian governments will not, particularly given the presence of diaspora rebellion. Similarly, in the Somali case, the military government of the 1970s brought the country to war during a period of rebellion in Ethiopia, whereas early civilian governments had refused to pursue high levels of aggression when faced with rebellion in Kenya. In the next case study concerning relations between Greece and Turkey, I will again address this connection between military influence over governance and the escalation of irredentist-type interstate disputes to full-scale war.

Conclusion

This chapter was divided into two main parts. The first dealt with the nature of the Indian-Pakistan rivalry as a normative dispute, and compared this irredentist-type situation with that of the Sino-Pakistani and Sino-Indian relationships. Continuing disputes between India and Pakistan, which involved nationalist issues, were shown to be much more conflictual overall than the other bilateral relations examined, which were based on considerations that can best be described as *real*-political.

Nevertheless, even within the India-Pakistan dispute, there was some variation in the explanatory power of norms on bilateral relations. After India successfully framed the Kashmir issue as a "bilateral" affair, thus reducing the influence of an international community that had been surprisingly receptive of Pakistani rhetoric calling for self-determination, Pakistani aggression became less overt.

Although the normative-demographic model suggests that a higher overall baseline of hostility should exist between India and Pakistan in comparison to the other dyads, structural and situational factors best explain variations in Pakistani conflict initiation. In particular, Pakistani policies were most aggressive during periods when military leaders controlled policy, and least aggressive during periods when civilians were in control. The most extreme manifestations of this phenomenon were witnessed in 1965 and 1999, when one military regime, and one democratic regime heavily pressured by military influence initiated large-scale warfare against India. In comparison, the civilian regime of the 1970s under Bhutto pursued a series of goodwill gestures with India, and represented the most peaceful era of Pakistani foreign affairs. Similarly, while not as accommodating as the Bhutto government, the civilian governments of the 1950s and early 1990s were comparatively more restrained in their foreign policy adventures than those governments most influenced by military pressures.

CHAPTER 8

GREECE AND TURKEY

Over recent years, relations between Greece and Turkey have improved in comparison to previous decades. While lingering distrust from their many years of rivalry continues, and disputes over important strategic and economic areas of the Aegean Sea remain, the future of relations between these two states looks comparatively bright in contrast to their often contentious past. In 1999, major earthquakes in both countries resulted in quick responses of aid from the other, setting off a series of goodwill gestures that became known as "seismic détente." A poll taken less than a year later revealed that two out of three Greeks held "friendly and positive sentiments" toward the Turkish people (Purvis 2000). Athens dropped its objection to Turkish candidacy to the European Union in 1999, and has only increased its support of Turkey's membership over the past half decade. How is it possible for such long time adversaries to turn the corner in their relations so quickly, and is it possible for this interstate rivalry to fade away once and for all? This chapter addresses both these question by examining the nature of past Greco-Turkish disputes through the framework of the theories presented thus far in this work.

The design of this case study differs somewhat from the previous two chapters. Unlike the earlier studies, which contrasted relations within dyads characterized by irredentist demographics versus those without, this study focuses primarily on the question of transborder nationality as related to Greece and Turkey and the consequences for interstate peace and conflict. I will also examine the role played by the Cyprus issue.

Within this chapter I will examine periods witnessing different levels of hostility between Greece and Turkey and examine: (1) The role of irredentism in relations between and Greece and the Ottoman Empire (1832–1923); (2) A period when transborder nationalist issues were largely absent between the two states (1923–1954); (3) Greek and Turkish responses to the issue of Cyprus, which involved a somewhat tangled web of different degrees of irredentism and even "contending government" nationalism (between the Greek and Cypriot governments), which has hitherto remained unaddressed within the case studies presented (1954–1974); and (4) an era when issues of transborder nationality largely disappeared as a factor involved in the Greco-Turkish relationship, only to be replaced by a series of clashes over strategic issues that, in time, are expected to decrease in salience as an

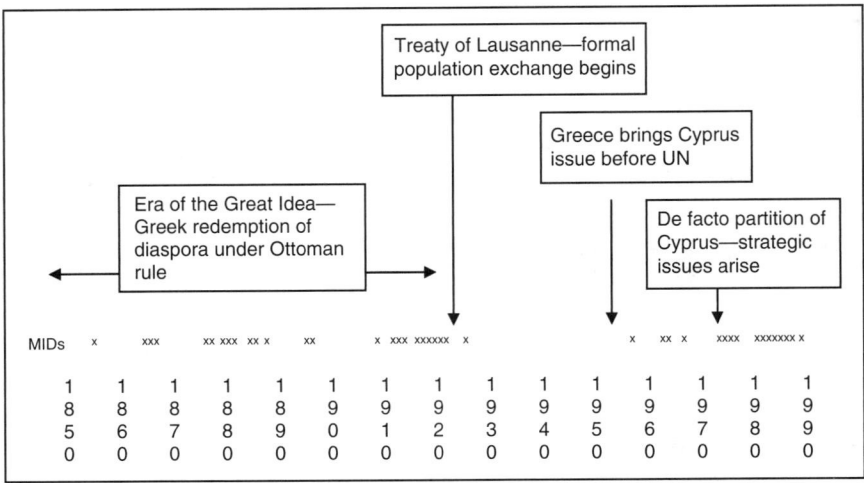

Figure 8.1 Greco-Turkish Bilateral Relations during Different Eras

Note:
The "x" indicates the years in which a militarized interstate dispute (MID) took place.

important source of interstate conflict (1975–till date). Figure 8.1 provides a glimpse of the patterns of interstate disputes between Greece and Turkey, and how the frequency of such disputes varies during the different eras mentioned earlier.

This chapter represents one of the closest representations of a "natural experiment" that can be found in international relations, as transborder nationality rarely appears or disappears as a primary factor influencing interstate affairs between two specific states. The fact that Greece and Turkey experienced periods within which both the presence and near absence of transborder groups, as well as the treatment of those groups, affected the relations between these two states presents a unique "test" of the ideas presented thus far.

The first section of this chapter, similar to the previous case studies, focuses primarily on the role of demographics in conditioning relations between Greece, Turkey, and (to a lesser extent) Cyprus, and how leaders faced varying levels of domestic and international pressures that affected the overall state of interstate conflict. This first section is divided into four major historical periods—each characterized by distinct demographic situations within which the presence or (relative) absence of transborder nationality ultimately affected interstate relations. At the end of each section is a summary of the role of transborder demographics and the role played by domestic and international normative considerations in the period covered.

Following the historical discussion concerning the interplay between demographics, domestic nationalism, and international constraints, I analyze the role of specific domestic and situational factors involved in initiation of irredentist disputes in the second part of this chapter. The three key domestic factors that I examine concerning dispute initiation by Greece and Turkey are (1) the influence of the military over politics; (2) the perceived condition of diaspora groups; and (3) whether or not military aggression is "feasible." Once again, one finds that familiar patterns of military influence and diaspora discontent lead to higher levels of dispute initiation in irredentist situations. Considerations of military feasibility, however, were surprisingly absent during many of the conflicts initiated by Greece, perhaps indicating in part that nationalist considerations often overrode realist rationality in foreign policymaking, particularly during the nineteenth century.

Greece and Turkey: The Rise and Fall of Transborder Nationality

I. *The Era of the "Great Idea"*

Greek Irredentist Designs on the Ottoman Empire in the Nineteenth Century
Just as the dissolution of European empires in Africa and the Subcontinent led to an "incompletely realized" state of independence for Somalia and Pakistan, the withdrawal of Ottoman forces from Greece brought about the birth of a newly independent, and strongly irredentist state. By the finalization of Greek independence in 1832 under the Treaty of Constantinople, Greek irredentist designs on the lands of the Ottoman Empire were already evident. As a point of reference, the Greek War of Independence had been based on the idea that revolutionary activity by Greek populations was to be the chief determinant of the future borders of the state, or, in other words, "Greece would consist of the districts that had taken up or would take up arms against Ottoman rule" (Koliopoulos 1987: 307).[1] The presence of diaspora rebellion became an informal, but powerful, influence that largely determined which territories would become the primary focus of Greek irredentist designs.

What developed over the coming decades among Greek leaders and scholars was a formulation of nationalistic goals that became known as the Great Idea, or *Megali Idea*.

According to Smith (1973: 4), distinct strands of the Great Idea existed, stressing greater or lesser ambitions of how a Greek empire might be carved from Ottoman lands. The more radical ambitions stressed the Byzantine identity of Greeks, and focused on the wholesale collapse of the Ottoman Empire and a revival of a Byzantine-Greek Empire centered on Constantinople. Somewhat less, and eventually dominant, interpretations saw the "progressive redemption" of Greek diaspora through the series of head-on collisions with the Porte that came to pass. The Great Idea was perhaps most famously articulated by Ioannis Kolettis, who declared before the Greek National Assembly in 1844 that

> [t]he Greek kingdom is not the whole of Greece, but only a part, the smallest and poorest part. A native of Greece is not only someone who lives in this kingdom, but also someone who lives in Ioannina, in Thessaly, in Serres, in Adrianople, in Constantinople, in Crete, in Samos, and in any land associated with Greek history or the Greek race. (quoted in Peckham 2000: 85)

What developed during the last half of the nineteenth century was a classic case in which a government, faced with a stronger adversary, engages in, or turns a blind eye to, the systematic subversion of the diaspora-inhabited lands of its stronger neighbor (i.e., secessionist-merger strategies). During this period, small local militias mounted frequent raids into Ottoman lands, ostensibly in the name of Greek liberation, but often with the less noble goal of obtaining plunder in the form of livestock and other portable goods. Nevertheless, "irredentism provided the necessary ideology to justify the plundering raids issuing from the frontier" and over time "the irregular forces came to be regarded as the proper armed forces of the nation, to be kept in reserve for the liberation of unredeemed Greeks across the border" (Koliopoulos 1987: 318 and 7)especially when the international circumstances were ripe.

The normative-demographic model upon which much of this work is based considers public pressures and international constraints to be the two main forces in determining the general course of bilateral relations between states. The course of events in the nineteenth century between Greece and the Ottoman Empire can be viewed through this framework as well, as Greek leaders, having cultivated a sense of nationalism among the public, were ultimately faced with the need to balance the pressures of public nationalism with the ebb and flow of constraints from the international community. During much of the latter half of the century, the Great Powers, particularly Britain and France, sought both to guarantee Greek independence, which they had fought to achieve, as well as disallow "the extension of Greece's frontiers by force of arms at the expense of the Ottoman Empire" (Koliopoulos 1987: 320). Thus, while Greek authorities could attempt to foster instability within the Porte in the hope that members of the Greek diaspora might successfully liberate themselves, international pressures strongly discouraged overt military action by the Greek government during this period.

An opportunity to circumvent international pressures arose, however, during the Crimean War when conflict with Russia distracted France and Britain. According to Woodhouse (1986: 167), the Greeks were "delighted" by this turn of events, and felt that the moment for the realization of the Great Idea had arrived. Despite the remonstrances of these states, Greece committed its regular army against the Ottomans, and was quickly defeated. This defeat led to a temporary waning of nationalism and brought about the temporary suppression of activities by Greek raiders along the border.

Although the Great Idea remained a "grand theme running through . . . this period" (Veremis 2003: 53), the next 30 years presented few opportunities for active aggression against the Ottoman Empire, despite uprisings in both Crete and Thessaly during the late 1860s. No better example of constraints on Greek policy during this period existed than the aborted attempt of Greece to enter the Russo-Turkish War of 1877–1878—a move that was met by threats from Britain to blockade Greek ports. Although the Greek government and public continued to actively and passively support subversive activities in the more rebellious areas of the Ottoman Empire, the overall policy of the Greek government as the turn of the century neared was one in which

> [t]he Greek authorities followed an ambivalent policy which was the result of conflicting pressures: from public opinion, which called for action to liberate the unredeemed Greeks, and from the great powers of Europe, which counseled avoidance of such action on pain of intervention. (Koliopoulos 1987: 218)

Public pressure, however, ultimately overwhelmed international considerations in 1897, when renewed rebellion broke out in Crete. The rebellion in Crete was fomented in part by the influence of the "National Society," or *ethniki Etairia*, an Athens-based group that also worked to renew nationalist sentiment among the Greek public. With nationalist pressures at home at a boiling point, Greek authorities disregarded concerns about international reaction and moved against the Ottoman Empire in support of the Crete separatists. The predictable reaction by the international community, which included a blockade that prevented effective support of the rebels, helped defeat a Greek invasion that seemed to have little hope from the start. The Thirty Days' War made it clear once again that, if the Great Idea were to be furthered, it would have to be under favorable international circumstances. Those opportunities, however, lay only a decade and a half away as the Balkans were to become the scene of the great nationalist wars of the early twentieth century.

The Great Opportunity: The Balkan and First World Wars
In the wake of the defeat of 1897 and subsequent events in Macedonia in the first decade of the twentieth century, the Greek government came under heavy criticism for its impotent stance on the diaspora question. In Macedonia, Greek irregulars battled Bulgarian, Serb, and Ottoman forces for control of the territory, while the Greek state formally distanced itself from the struggle. Seeking to placate Ottoman authorities, while facing a perceived threat from Bulgaria, Greek leaders proclaimed a policy of cooperation with the Porte during this period (Triandafyllidou and Paraskevopoulou 2002: 81). Disenchantment with the state was such that the idea of Greeks as a "stateless nation" became a slogan of government opponents of the time.

The government returned to a path of irredentist nationalism in 1909 when a bloodless revolt, known as the Goudhi coup, led by military officers under the banner of the "Military League," paved the way for the ascension of the pro-expansionist Cretan politician, Eleftherious Venizelos. While the League itself disbanded quickly, Venizelos, its civilian political leader, subsequently won the backing of the Greek public and was overwhelmingly elected prime minister in elections held in 1910 and 1912. Military intervention in politics, later supported by a strong public mandate, led to the adoption of strong nationalist preferences in Greece's foreign policy.

The first opportunity for the realization of Greek territorial ambition took place in 1912, when, as a result of deft diplomacy, Venizelos managed to secure an alliance with Bulgaria and Serbia (and later Montenegro) that was clearly aimed at the Ottoman Empire. In October 1912, Montenegro declared war on Turkey, and Serbia and Bulgaria followed suit. Greece declared war on the Ottomans soon thereafter. Unable to act and restrain such a broad alliance of states, the Great Powers stood by as the Balkan League quickly overran the Ottoman army. This First Balkan War was followed a mere three months later by the Second Balkan War, wherein an alliance of the former allies, along with the Ottoman Empire, defeated Bulgaria and divided up that state's spoils of the previous conflict. For the Greeks, this meant, most importantly of all, securing possession of southern

Macedonia and the long sought after island of Crete. Nevertheless, the irredentist desires of many within the Greek polity had not yet been satiated.

Despite the assistance of the Ottoman Empire in the Second Balkan War, relations between Athens and Constantinople returned to a tense state of affairs in the year preceding the First World War. Particularly inflaming Greek nationalism was the treatment of Greek minorities under the Young Turk regime, whose "Turkification" policies seemed likely to suppress the relative cultural freedom enjoyed by Greeks within the empire for centuries. The deportation of 30,000 Greeks from Anatolia and Thrace in late 1913 particularly inflamed Greek public anger. Venizelos subsequently warned the Greek parliament in June 1914 that Greece might soon be forced to renew violence against the Porte in order to protect Greeks from further persecution (Stephens 1966: 90). Before the issue reached a head, however, the First World War broke out in August 1914.

Unlike the Balkan Wars, a venture in which "the nation had been united and had supported the government wholeheartedly in its nationalist enterprises" (Triandafyllidou and Paraskevopoulou 2002: 83), the public and its leaders became deeply divided about whether to enter the First World War, a divide that became known as "The Great Schism." Venizelos, as the voice of Greek nationalists, strongly supported joining the Entente powers as a means of furthering Greek territorial ambitions, particularly in Asia Minor. He was opposed by a loyalist camp, however, led by King Constantine I, who supported a neutralist policy and the acceptance of a "small, but honorable" Greece. After Constantine dismissed Venizelos in 1915, Venizelos established a provisional government in Thessalonica and, by 1916, full-blown civil war seemed a distinct possibility.

Allied pressure, which included an embargo and a limited invasion of parts of Greece, eventually forced the abdication of Constantine and led to the reinstatement of Venizelos as prime minister. Venizelos brought the country into war within days of his return to Athens. In the face of a silenced domestic opposition and an international climate that not only permitted Greece to enter the war against the Ottoman Empire, but ultimately demanded it, Venizelos' actions brought Greece a seat at the victory table and a share of the spoils of war.

Occupation and Defeat in Asia Minor—1919–1923

What for Greeks became the "Asia Minor Catastrophe" and for Turks a War of Independence was not so much a separate incident from the First World War as it was an extension of it. As a stipulation of the Treaty of Sevres of 1920, the Ottoman Empire was carved up among the victorious powers, including Greece, which was granted much of the coastline of Asia Minor, particularly around the heavily Greek populated port of Smyrna. Greek administration of the Smyrna region, which was to be followed by a plebiscite to determine its status, was accepted by the defeated Ottoman government of the time, and the stationing of Greek forces there could hardly be considered an invasion in any traditional sense. However, the Greek presence in Asia Minor was viewed as such by the revolutionary forces of Mustafa Kemal (later Kemal Ataturk), which posed a growing threat to the moribund Ottoman administration and the Greek position alike.

Almost immediately after the First World War ended, scattered Turkish resistance fighters began harassment of allied forces in the region. During 1919–1920, the question of resistance to allied forces led to increasing friction between the forces of the Ottoman Sultan and the growing movement of nationalists led by Kemal. By April 1920, the nationalists had established a revolutionary government in Ankara, while the Sultan ordered the deaths of Kemal and any of Kemal's followers. With the leaking of the terms of the Treaty of Sevres in May 1920, recruits flocked to Kemal's cause and Turkey became embroiled in a civil war within which the nationalists quickly gained the upper hand against the Sultan's forces.

At the same time, the growing discontent of an increasingly war-weary Greek public was manifested in elections in 1920 in which Venizelos, the face of Greek nationalist ambitions, was heavily defeated by royalists, who advocated the "small but honorable" concept of a Greek state. Nevertheless, the return of King Constantine to power did not represent a break from aggressive Greek policies in Asia Minor.

Due to the presence of the large Greek diaspora in the remaining Ottoman lands, Greece had a greater stake in the outcome of the civil war than any other state, and offered to intervene against the Kemalist forces mobilizing in the interior. With the strong encouragement of British prime minister Lloyd George, Greek divisions advanced from Smyrna, and, by the end of 1920, had moved deep into Anatolia and seemed in striking distance of Ankara itself. Time was on the side of the Turkish nationalists, however, who seemed to gain strength with every Greek advance. During 1921, Greek forces met much stiffer resistance than they had the previous year, making only limited advances. The following year in 1922, the situation turned completely around as Turkish armies managed to break through the Greek lines, leading to a chaotic retreat by Greek forces. Within a month of the breakthrough, the Turks had retaken Smyrna and completed the conquest of the entire peninsula.

The conflict took a heavy toll on the civilian populations of Asia Minor. As each side advanced, first the Greeks, and then the Turks, abuses against civilians of the other nation were commonplace, culminating in the destruction of Smyrna (renamed Izmir) at the end of the Turkish campaign. When the conflict ended, the large majority of Greeks in Asia Minor had fled or been forced to evacuate from their homes, greatly reducing the size of the Greek diaspora in the region. Rather than seeking to reverse the ethnic cleansing that had taken place, negotiations surrounding the Treaty of Lausanne, signed in 1923, not only sanctioned the population transfer, but, also, in the name of peace, sought to further diminish the presence of transborder nationalities in each state.

Normative-Demographic Implications of the Era of the Great Idea
Public support for irredentism in Greece was strong throughout much of this period, causing a series of Greek leaders to attempt to placate nationalist sentiment at home through provocative policies and rhetoric. The degree of international constraints encountered by Greek leaders varied much more widely, and helps explain quite a bit of the variation in Greek militarism during this period.

During certain periods, such as the Crimean War, the major powers that sought to dissuade Greek irredentist policies toward the Ottoman Empire, Great Britain, and France, were occupied in major warfare that hindered their ability to monitor and influence Athens' policies. During other periods, such as the Russo-Turkish War, heavy allied pressure largely succeeded in preventing meaningful Greek intervention. During yet other periods, such as the Thirty Days' War of 1897, the Great Powers actively dissuaded Greek irredentist moves, but were ultimately rebuffed as public nationalism overrode international considerations (due, in large part, to the presence of rebellion in Ottoman Crete).

For most of the period, however, Great Power support for the continued sovereignty and territorial integrity of the Ottoman Empire dampened the enthusiasm of Greek leaders for overt policies of aggression against the Porte. The role of international constraints in Europe at the time is partly reflected in the fact that, before the Balkan Wars, the only territorial gains achieved by Greece were granted by international conferences convened by the Great Powers. *The only major irredentist military actions taken by Greece were during times of diaspora rebellion or short periods during which international constraints were weak.* At the same time, the overwhelming superiority of the Ottoman military offered Greek leaders pause and represented an additional reason why policies of supporting internal subversion were generally the preferred path through which irredentism was pursued.

The Balkan Wars represented an auspicious circumstance for Greek revisionism due to the deft diplomacy of Venizelos, who allied the state with other revisionist countries in the region. While warned by the Great Powers, including Russia, against the initiation of conflict against the Ottomans, the alliance was too broad and the conflict over too quickly for outside powers to intervene. Following the wars, relations with the Ottoman Empire remained tense due to the perceived mistreatment of the remaining Greek diaspora, and war threatened again in 1914. However, the outbreak of the First World War, ironically, placed the Greek-Turkish conflict on hold for several years.

The Ottoman decision to side with the Central Powers during the First World War not only removed the traditional international constraints on a Greek attack on Turkey, but actively encouraged Greek intervention. The traditional guarantors of the Ottoman Empire, Great Britain and France, now actively sought to destroy the sovereignty of the Empire and placed heavy pressure on Greece to intervene. Only the views of "Prusso-file" royalists prevented the quick entry of Greece into the war sought by Venizelos. Eventually, the active intervention of the Entente powers in Greek politics swept away King Constantine and his supporters, opening the door for Greek intervention.

Allied pressure for Greek intervention against the Ottoman Empire continued into the postwar period. British prime minister Lloyd George pressed for the Greek occupation of Smyrna and the subsequent invasion of the interior launched under Constantine. As indicated by the defeat of Venizelos at the polls in 1920, the Greek public no longer could be viewed as an important force advocating retrieval of Greek populations abroad. In fact, in a reversal of the normal expected chain of events leading to irredentist conflict, international pressures promoting conflict were pitted against an increasingly war-weary public. Nevertheless, "at no time in Greek history had the international situation been so favorable to Hellenic aspirations" (Dakin 1972: 223), and international factors became the paramount deciding factor for Greek leaders reticent to pass up a historical opportunity. In the end, it was the unusual state of international affairs prevailing at the time surrounding the events of the First World War, whereby the traditional international order seeking to preserve state borders and state sovereignty completely broke down, that paved the way for the disastrous irredentist interventions of the Greek government during this period.

II: Lausanne and Its Aftermath: 1923–1955

The defeat of the Greek military in Asia Minor opened the way to negotiations for a new treaty intended to supersede the Allied-dictated Treaty of Sevres. Lasting over eight months, the negotiations, which began under the auspices of the League of Nations in October 1922, culminated with the signing of the Treaty of Lausanne in July 1923. The Greek delegation was led by Venizelos, who had been appointed chief negotiator in the wake of a military coup that had forced the abdication of Constantine after the Greek defeat. Ironically, the man most associated with early twentieth century Greek irredentism was to negotiate terms that largely put the Great Idea to rest.

As the last comprehensive settlement stemming from the First World War, the Treaty dealt with a variety of issues unrelated to Greece, such as the status of the Bosporus and Dardanelles, the disposition of former Ottoman territories, and a multitude of economic and property issues. In defining the borders between Turkey and Greece, the treaty stipulated that Turkey would receive all of Asia Minor and Eastern Thrace, the area of Europe directly west of Constantinople. Greece received most of the Aegean islands. Turkey agreed to abandon any future claims to Cyprus and recognize the island's annexation to the British Empire.

During the course of the Lausanne negotiations, both states agreed to a population exchange in the Convention Concerning the Exchange of Greek and Turkish Populations, which was signed by Greek and Turkish representatives in January 1923. The Convention stipulated that any *religious* minorities[2], with the exception of Muslims in Western Thrace and the Greek Orthodox population of Constantinople, were to be forcibly evicted to the opposite country if they did not voluntarily leave by May 1923. Members of each minority group who had already fled or been forced out as the result of earlier conflicts were to constitute the "first installment" of minorities transferred according to the Convention (Articles 3 and 4). A Mixed Commission of Greek, Turkish, and League of Nations representatives was formed to oversee the transfer.[3]

Devised under the leadership of the League of Nation's High Commissioner for Refugees, Fridtjof Nansen, both Greek and Turkish representatives alternately expressed support and reservations for the exchange. Ultimately, support from both sides was secured because both states perceived that the treaty was in the interest of their people. Greek officials were the first to suggest the idea as a method of preserving the lives of the approximately half million (out of a prewar population of about 1.6 million) Greeks who remained in Asia Minor when it became clear that Allied troops would not intervene to prevent continuing abuses, some would suggest "genocide,"[4] against the diaspora population (Barutciski 2003: 26). Turkish officials, on the other hand, saw the exchange as a necessary security measure that would permanently remove the casus belli that had been utilized by the Greek state against the Ottoman Empire numerous times over the past century. The deputy-head of the Turkish delegation in Lausanne is said to have declared during the negotiations that "as there would be no minorities in Anatolia, there would be no foreign intervention" (Aktar 2002: 87).

The relatively orderly population transfers under the Lausanne agreements were small compared to the forced evacuations that had taken place during hostilities (particularly for Greeks). While over a million Greeks fled during the Turkish advances of 1922, the population exchange witnessed the transfer of slightly under 200,000 (Hirschon 2003a: 14). The Muslim population transferred to Turkey after 1923 numbered about 350,000 (Hirschon 2003a: 15). Altogether, the impact on Greek society was much greater than that on Turkish society, as the population of Greece grew by about 20 percent during a very short period, while emigrants to Turkey totaled a much more manageable four percent. The total size of the Greek Muslim minority population after the transfer was about six percent while the Greek Orthodox population of Turkey was reduced to approximately two percent.[5] These small percentages gradually became much smaller during the remainder of the century due to emigration.

The impact of the population transfer on Greek-Turkish relations was not immediate, but the eventual effect was profound. Although the morality of forcibly evicting hundreds of thousands of people from their homes based on their religion is more than questionable, the effect that the elimination of large transborder minority groups was to have on interstate relations is undeniable. For several years, outstanding disputes from the settlement of the war and the population exchange kept the rival states from reconciling, but, by the end of the decade, most of these issues had been resolved. Because, "for the first time in modern Greek history the ethnological limits of the Greek people coincided, in general, with the territorial limits of the Greek state" (Psomiades 1968: 106), and because the new Turkish state recognized Greek sovereignty of Western Thrace, the uncertainty and suspicion that had characterized relations between Greece and the Ottoman Empire was replaced by a more stable relationship between Greece and Turkey. Psomiades (1968: 108) notes the impact of the events following the conflict in Asia Minor thus:

> The exchange of populations and the new boundary realignments had removed the major irritants in the long history of the two peoples and transformed the conflict between a decaying empire and one of its chief adversaries in a stable arrangement between two non-imperial, non-expansive nation states.

Relations between Greece and Turkey grew particularly warm between the period 1928 and 1955—almost 30 years of peace that would have been almost unfathomable had the presence of large transborder minority groups still existed. During this period, Greece and Turkey became "the closest partners in the Balkans" (Oran 2003: 103). While the reduction of the transborder ethnic presence enabled the development of closer ties during this period, common security concerns provided the impetus. The initiation of closer ties began with the return of Venizelos to power in 1928, who, in a set of policies reminiscent of "Nixon going to China," risked and endured a public backlash (especially among the émigrés from Asia Minor) in order to cultivate a new relationship with Ankara.

The relationship began with a series of letters between Venizelos and Prime Minister Ismet of Turkey, and resulted in a groundbreaking trip by Venizelos to Turkey in 1930, where he and his counterpart signed the Treaty of Friendship, Neutrality, Conciliation, and Arbitration, which resolved most of the outstanding issues of the previous decade. According to the treaty, any further disagreements that could not be resolved were to be submitted to the League of Nation's Permanent Court of International Justice. In 1933, the two countries signed another Friendship Pact, which guaranteed "the inviolability of their borders and committed them to consult each other on matters of common interest" (Bahcheli 1990: 14).

The growing stability of relations between Greece and Turkey allowed both states to lead the way in attempting to create a new, more stable environment in the Balkans as a whole. At the same time, the rise of Italian revisionism led both states to pursue a policy of common security, and both states, together with Romania and Yugoslavia[6], formed the Balkan Entente of 1934. The Entente failed to achieve its goals, and was destroyed with the Axis occupation of Yugoslavia and Greece in the Second World War. During this conflict, both Greece and Turkey declared neutrality, although Greece suffered the unfortunate fate of being invaded by Italy in 1940.

The end of the Second World War replaced the fascist threat with the Stalinist threat, which provided the impetus for continued warm relations between the two states. The highpoint of postwar cooperation was reached in 1952, when both states became full members of the newly formed NATO alliance. At the end of this year, official visits by the Greek king and queen to Istanbul and Ankara and the prime minister of Turkey to Athens were hailed as a continuing sign that the difficulties of the past had been finally overcome and that the cooperation between the two states that had characterized the interwar period would continue in the postwar period.

Such hopes were overly optimistic, however. As the threat from Russia receded with the death of Stalin the following year, and as the decolonization movement began to receive greater attention worldwide, the seeds for renewed tension began to germinate on the island of Cyprus. Once again, the issue of foreign Greek diaspora would become a major issue in Greco-Turkish relations. This time, however, the Turkish government was also to advocate a series of positions on behalf of its own foreign diaspora. The Cypriot situation would degenerate into a tangled diplomatic and military imbroglio based upon unification nationalism and stronger and weaker forms of irredentism, leading eventually to a de facto exchange of Greek and Turkish populations in 1974 comparable to that which had occurred in the 1920s.

Normative-Demographic Implications of the Period after Lausanne
The defeat in Asia Minor led to a mass exodus/expulsion of Greeks living in the region. The Convention Concerning the Exchange of Greek and Turkish Populations, signed by Greece and Turkey during the Lausanne negotiations, sanctified the expulsion of most of the remaining Greeks from Asia Minor and Turks from remaining Greek territories. In the end, however, the effect of the war

and the subsequent population exchanges was the "establishment of a new status quo after a decade of war," which represented the start of a new era of interstate peace between the two formal rivals (Coufoudakis 1985: 186). Barutciski (2003: 27) describes how a process that, in the contemporary world, would be viewed as a travesty of human rights abuse actually contributed to interstate peace:

> Despite the great human hardship engendered by population exchanges, the improvement in regional stability cannot be ignored. The unmixing of populations in Asia Minor helped put an end to hostilities and secure pacification of the warring parties.

After a difficult start, the following three decades represented the warmest period of Greek-Turkish relations in history. As displayed in Figure 8.1, bilateral militarized disputes came to an abrupt halt after 1925. The flight and removal of the Greek diaspora ended the irredentism that had colored Greek foreign policy since independence. The Great Idea vanished from the public imagination. At the same time, Turkish leadership under Ataturk quickly foreswore his state's Ottoman past, settling for a smaller, "Turkified," state.

III. The Return of Transborder Nationality as an Issue between Greek and Turkey

The Cyprus Question Arises: 1954–1963
On September 6, 1955 Turkish mobs in Istanbul rioted and looted homes and businesses owned by Greeks. The riots were ignited by the announcement that a bomb had exploded next to the house in which Kemal Ataturk had been born in Thessaloniki, Greece. Evidence later suggested that Turkish authorities had been behind the bombing, which represented an attempt to draw international attention to the Turkish position on Cyprus (Coufoudakis 1985: 190). The incident, fostered by recent claims made by Greece on the island, caused "a quarter-century of Greek-Turkish détente to collapse overnight" (p. 194).

The desire of Cypriot Greeks to unite with the Greek state did not suddenly develop during the mid-1950s, although the active pursuit of this goal by the Greek government represented a new policy. Ever since the transfer of the island from Ottoman to British hands in 1878, Greek representatives on the island expressed a frequent desire for *enosis*, or unification with Greece (Woodhouse 1986: 270). Shortly after Turkey renounced any claims to the island as a condition of the Treaty of Lausanne, a delegation of Cypriot representatives traveled directly to London to petition the British government for the unification of Cyprus with Greece. British officials swiftly rebuffed the notion.

Greek officials paid the Cypriot issue little attention before the postwar period. As long as the mighty British Empire controlled the island, there "could be no question of international pressure" (Tsoucalas 1969: 157) and little desire existed to alienate a powerful ally by questioning the status of the island. This changed during the 1950s as norms of decolonization in the name of "self-determination" began to take hold in international circles. Unlike the situation of other colonial territories, however, the Cyprus case was unusual in that the dominant population of Greeks (who made up approximately 80 percent of the population compared to approximately 20 percent Turks) sought the absorption of their territory by another state rather than outright independence. Necatigil (1996: 23) notes that the Cypriot case was actually more reflective of "irredentist nationalism of the nineteenth century" rather than the mid-twentieth century notion of self-determination, which emphasized an "ultimate objective of achieving independence." In a plebiscite organized by the Orthodox Church in Cyprus during 1950, voters almost unanimously supported the choice of *enosis* with the mainland.

In 1954, Greece finally decided to become involved in the Cyprus issue and assert its irredentist claims vis-à-vis the British government under the banner of "self-determination." The link with the norm of self-determination was important, as Greek officials, and the influential Archbishop Makarios, Cypriot leader of the *enosis* movement, perceived correctly that, although Greek Cypriots were primarily motivated by a desire to unite with Greece, the international community would be much more receptive if the issue were framed as one within which an occupied people sought freedom from a colonial power (Attalides 1979:34). By internationalizing the issue, the Greek government laid both the first steps to Cyprus' independence and future conflict with Turkey over the governance of the demographically heterogeneous island.

The Turkish Cypriot community reacted strongly toward the prospect of *enosis*, and antiunion pronouncements and demonstrations became widespread (Bahcheli 1990: 39). The main Turkish party of the day, KITEMP, rather than joining with the Greeks in attempting to secure a British withdrawal, demanded a continued British presence. The Turkish government, which had up to that point been "content for the British to rule the island indefinitely" (p. 31), supported the demands of Turkish Cypriot leaders until it became evident that continued British rule was no longer a possibility.

The Turkish reaction to the situation was unusual in the context of the theories of transborder nationalism presented in this work. Unlike the Greek government, the Turkish government held few designs on Cyprus, having forgone any irredentist aspirations permanently with the Treaty of Lausanne. More important than the legal arrangement, however, Turkish history played a role in creating a Turkish identity that associated the acquisition of multiethnic territories with the decay of the Ottoman Empire. Ethnic homogeneity, however, was widely viewed as a bedrock principle of the modern Turkish nation-state. The Turkish government, therefore, unlike the Greek government, did not view annexation of the entire island of Cyprus as a desirable goal.

Nevertheless, the presence of the diaspora, in the end, did become an important issue for Turkey, as the threat of Greek rule, whether based in Athens or Nicosia, over the Turkish minority was viewed much less benignly than that of British rule. Turkish leaders viewed the British authorities as neutral arbiters who had prevented the domination of the Turkish minority by Greek Cypriots.

Although relations between the Greek and Turkish governments had steadily improved over the previous decades, 25 years of intergovernmental goodwill had not been enough to heal all the wounds and suspicion that a century of Greco-Turkish enmity had created. The historical Greco-Turkish rivalry held relevance not only for the competing nationalisms of the Cypriot communities, but also for the Turkish government, which, from a strategic viewpoint, viewed the potential occupation of Cyprus by Greek forces much more ominously than the continued use of the island as a British base in the Eastern Mediterranean. As it became clearer that British rule would no longer continue over the island, the Turkish government came to support partition of the territory between Greece and Turkey—a position unacceptable to the Greek government or Greek Cypriots.

Both the Greek and Turkish governments lent support to underground paramilitary movements on the island in an effort to influence the *enosis* debate through covert violence. The Greek government provided materials for a movement known as EOKA, whose objectives were both nationalist and anticommunist.[7] Ultimately, the organization sought to promote *enosis* by fomenting instability and making continued occupation costly for British forces. Although the group utilized assassinations and bombings against British forces and officials, it focused primarily on the intimidation of Turkish Cypriot leaders and sections of the Turkish Cypriot population. The Turkish government helped create the Turkish Resistance Organization (TMT), which similarly targeted the Greek (but not British) population of the island in pursuit of its anti-*enosis* objectives.

By 1958, these two proxy insurgencies had contributed to and facilitated intercommunal strife that escalated to the point that the British government declared a state of emergency. The period 1957–1958 witnessed a series of clashes that culminated in large-scale rioting and the evacuation of ethnic minorities from several villages (Bahcheli 1990: 41). The turmoil served the goal of EOKA in that it hastened the process of British withdrawal. The Turkish government, however, refused to consider any future status for the island that might include the possibility of *enosis*. With *enosis* ruled out, the parties began negotiation on the nature of Cypriot independence and how such independence would incorporate the demands of both the Greek and Turkish governments—both of which had largely assumed the role of representative for their respective national kin on Cyprus.

In August 1958, the British announced the framework for the future governance of Cyprus. The state was to become "independent," but independence was to include a complicated set of arrangements that provided a shared role for Britain, Greece, and Turkey in the country's administration. Although reluctant to forgo the goal of *enosis*, the Greek Cypriots of the island, led by Makarios, felt compelled to participate in a process that the British made clear would have continued even in their absence (Woodhouse 1986: 278).

The negotiations yielded the Zurich-London agreements of 1959. The agreements established a corporatist-type, power-sharing government that guaranteed a large role for Turkish Cypriots in policymaking and important government posts. Furthermore, the agreements included the Treaty of Guarantee, which was included at the insistence of Turkey, in order to ensure protection of the Turkish diaspora. Article IV of the Treaty stated that

> [i]n so far as common or concerted action may prove impossible, each of the three guaranteeing Powers reserves the right to take action with the sole aim of re-establishing the state of affairs established by the present treaty.

The Zurich-London arrangements held out the possibility for a renewal of stable relations between Greece and Turkey. By providing for the ability of both the Greek and, particularly, Turkish communities to block any unwanted legislation over their respective communities, the issues that traditionally cause transborder nationality to provoke international conflict were temporarily resolved, as neither side was able to project significant political power or control over the other community. However, the inability of the state to repress the aspirations of the Turkish community was also a symptom of a state that was unable to govern, as the Turkish "veto" was used frequently, creating a state of government paralysis by 1963. The brief return to normalized relations that existed between Greece and Turkey from 1959–1963 (Coufoudakis 1985: 198) degenerated thereafter when the Cypriot leader Makarios unilaterally abrogated the Zurich-London agreements, stripping the Turkish Cypriot community of the constitutional guarantees that they had enjoyed during the first years of the Republic.

Cyprus: Two Diaspora, One State, 1963–1974
Demographically speaking, the newly independent Cyprus became part of a "majority-majority" (contending government) dyad in conjunction with Greece and a "minority-majority" (irredentist-type) dyad in conjunction with Turkey upon independence in 1960. The earlier constitutional arrangements of the Zurich-London treaties had mitigated the inflammatory influence of transborder demographics on Greece-Turkish-Cypriot relations through an intricate power-sharing arrangement that prevented any side from exercising strong control over any other.

By the end of 1963, it had become increasingly clear that the power-sharing arrangement between the two communities on Cyprus was extremely ineffective, if not unworkable.[8] Disagreements over taxation, the division of municipal borders in towns, the ethnic composition of the armed forces, and a host of smaller issues led to a breakdown in cooperation between Greek and Turkish leaders and raised again the question whether an independent Cyprus was viable. In response to the continuing governmental crisis, President Makarios proposed, in late 1963, a set of changes to the Cypriot Constitution known as the "thirteen points." This plan would have created a "integrated, unity state, where Turkish Cypriots had no veto rights" (Bahcheli 1990: 59).

The threat of Greek domination in Cyprus led to a series of events that insured such an outcome. On December 23, 1963, full-scale intercommunal conflict broke out, leading to the removal/withdrawal of Turkish politicians from the government. The intense conflict, spearheaded by paramilitary groups, lasted three months before the United Nations authorized a peacekeeping force (UNFICYP), which arrived in Cyprus in late March. While the 6,500 strong UN force helped dampen hostilities to a certain degree, fighting continued for months after the deployment, only slowing once the large majority of Turkish residents of the island had retreated into numerous "enclaves."

In the face of massive public pressures emanating from "Turkish-Cypriots, opposition parties, and public opinion," the initially reticent Turkish prime minister, Ismet Inonu, relented to domestic nationalist pressures and informed the U.S.

government on June 4, 1964, that he intended to send the state's armed forces to intervene in Cyprus (Bahcheli 1990: 63). However, nationalist pressures from below were met with even stronger pressures from above, as U.S. president Johnson warned in no uncertain terms that if Turkish actions precipitated Soviet intervention against Turkey NATO obligations would no longer be applicable. The U.S. warning had the desired effect of dissuading the Turkish government from invading, but, later in the year (August 1964), Turkish jets bombed the island in a successful effort to head off the invasion of Turkish Cypriot enclaves by Greek Cypriot paramilitary forces.

By the end of 1964, events on the island had largely calmed, as Turkish Cypriots, now separated from the Greeks of the island within protected (but still geographically interspersed) enclaves, achieved a modicum of security, despite an economic blockade put in place on the enclaves by Nicosia. The tense peace lasted from the end of 1964 until November 1967, when the Greek-Cypriot National Guard, only marginally under the control of the Makarios government, launched an offensive against two Turkish enclaves in an action which claimed over a dozen lives. Once again, the Turkish government threatened to intervene, only to turn back when the Greek government offered concessions that included the withdrawal of 12,000 Greek troops stationed on the island in violation of the Zurich-London agreements. Although the Turkish government was "widely criticized by many Turks for losing a favorable opportunity to use force," the concessions made by the Greek government allowed Turkish leaders to weather critical opinion at home (Bahcheli 1990: 75).

Altogether, the conflict between the two communities was to claim approximately a thousand lives during the period 1963–1967 (Bercovitch and Jackson: 1997). The loss of life, coupled with several regional war scares, led to renewed efforts to reach a settlement in the late 1960s and early 1970s. Partly facilitating the effort were the newly moderated views of President Makarios, who reversed himself after two decades and stated that *enosis* was no longer a possibility. The Greek government also increasingly sought accommodation with Turkey over the Cyprus issue, in part due to heavy U.S. pressures. Turkish and Turkish Cypriot officials, for their part, hoped for changes to the status quo that would alleviate the economic deprivation experienced by the "enclaved" Turkish Cypriot population (Attalides 1979: 99).

The talks that began in 1968 under auspicious circumstances, however, dragged on for five years. Despite the long time frame, however, progress seemed to be made during these "intercommunal talks" and "the gap between the two positions seemed easily within range of possible bridging" (Attalides 1979: 102). By 1973, a variety of compromises seemed within reach that would have moved Cypriot governance from the corporatist-type arrangements of the early 1960s to a more federal type arrangement, whereby Greek Cypriots would largely control the national government, but would be constrained by strong local governments, including those in Turkish Cypriot dominated areas. Although the parties involved seemed amenable to comprise on many of the large issues by the end of 1973, several issues concerning security forces and the judiciary, in particular, remained unresolved (Attalides, p. 103). At the same time, the unwillingness of Greek Cypriot leaders to formally and permanently abandon the goal of *enosis* became an important stumbling block (Bahcheli 1990: 87).

Perhaps the most important overarching factor that eventually signaled the end of the talks, however, was the growth of a heated rivalry between Makarios and the military government in Athens. The junta viewed Makarios as becoming dangerously independent, and warned the leader in 1972 that he was "breaking the common front" and that the "center of Hellenism" lay in Athens (Bahcheli 1990: 79). Furthermore, the strongly anticommunist regime in Athens viewed Makarios' views as dangerously leftist, referring to him from within as the "red priest."

While Makarios attempted to placate different segments of the Greek Cypriot community by claiming support for *enosis* while, at the same time, stressing that it was not feasible, the junta in Athens steadily increased its support for *enosis*—even if *enosis* meant heavy concessions to Turkey, including the possibility of partition. Thus, Makarios, the original leader of the modern *enosis* movement, became the voice of an independent Cyprus, while the military government increasingly sought to bring Cyprus under its control. The Athens' junta was also suspected of supporting EOKA B, a resurrected form of the underground extremist paramilitary group, in order to undermine Makarios and derail the intercommunal talks. Support for EOKA B became much more blatant in 1974, when, after the death of EOKA's notorious leader, General Grivas, Athens assumed more direct control of the group (Attalides 1979: 163).

The newly aggressive stance of the Greek government derived in large part from a coup that replaced the moderately nationalist junta leader, Georgios Papadopoulos, with the extreme nationalist, Dimitrios Ioannides, in late 1973. In comparing the two leaders, Hitchens (1983: 77) suggests: "If Papadopoulos was a Fascist in the Mussolini mould, Ioannides was more like an authentic Nazi . . . a believer in military cultism." While disputes between Athens and Nicosia had simmered under the previous military government, they came to a quick boil under the new junta. In an act of defiance, Makarios sent the Greek junta a letter in early July, 1974, which demanded the withdrawal of officers of the Greek military from Cyprus and accused the Greek government of "following a policy calculated to abolish the Cyprus State" (Necatigil 1993: 89). Makarios' letter turned out to be both provocative and prescient, as Greek officers on the island led a successful coup against him shortly thereafter, on July 15, installing a extremely nationalist, pro-*enosis* president, Nicos Sampson, in his place.

The Turkish government was clearly alarmed by the turn of events on the island, and preparations for intervention, justified according to Turkish authorities under the Treaty of Guarantee, began to take place. Turkish prime minister, Bulent Ecevit, came under intense pressure to act to protect the Turkish minority in Cyprus from the new threat. Strong pressures emanated specifically from the military, which had acted three years ago to remove a civilian leader from power, According to Hitchens (1983:141), the military played a key role in pressing for swift action, suggesting that

> [t]he written record of 1974 shows that it was the armed forces which pushed, at every stage, for a policy of force . . . It was the Turkish Security Council and not the cabinet or the parliament, which took the major decisions and which issued the crucial orders.

On July 20, the Turkish military landed on Cyprus, and met intense resistance from the Cypriot National Guard and EOKA B fighters. The much stronger Turkish forces, however, overwhelmed the local forces, and eventually went on to secure almost 40 percent of the island. In the wake of the invasion, a massive population transfer occurred, as Greek Cypriots fled south from the invaders, while Turkish Cypriots moved north into areas controlled by their would-be protectors. When the fighting ceased, the formerly ethnically heterogeneous island was divided into two territories populated by largely demographically homogeneous populations of Turks in the north and Greeks in the south.

Normative-Demographic Implications of the Troubles in Cyprus
As Figure 8.1 indicates, bilateral disputes became frequent once again around 1960, when Cyprus was granted independence. This unusual situation yielded a unique irredentism by proxy state of affairs, whereby Greek governments sought to reduce the influence of Turkey over Greek Cypriots, while Turkey attempted to do the same for Turkish Cypriots vis-à-vis Greece. Although Cyprus became an internationally recognized state, the Cypriot government retained only partial sovereignty, as reflected in the Treaty of Guarantee and other stipulations of the Zurich-London agreements, which gave Britain, Greece, and Turkey the legal right to intervene in the island state's affairs. Most citizens of Cyprus itself regarded the state as an artificial creation, and identified more with their "homelands" than with any greater Cypriot identity. According to Turkish Cypriot leader Rauf Denktash, writing in 1972: "Cypriots are (and continue to be) the extension of Greece in Cyprus through Greek Cypriots, and the extension of Turkey in Cyprus through Turkish Cypriots" (quoted in Attalides 1979: 102).

The interstate rivalry that was rekindled over Cyprus was, thus, intricately related to the presence of Greek and Turkish transborder groups on the island. Although these groups had been present when Great Britain controlled the island, the lack of any armed rebellion against the colonial occupants coupled with the sheer military infeasibility and undesirability of challenging one of the most powerful states on earth, essentially rendered Cyprus a nonissue until Greece questioned Cyprus' status before the United Nations. After that point, the main goals of Greece, Turkey, and the two rival communities of the island involved mitigating the power of the "other" nationality over their own national group. Intercommunal fighting on the island, in particular, aroused public nationalism in Greece and Turkey, leading to a series of near conflicts that were avoided, in large part, due to the perceived heavy constraints posed by the international community—particularly the United States.

The invasion of Cyprus by Turkey in 1974 led to ethnic cleansing and population transfers reminiscent of the events in Asia Minor during the 1920s. The de facto partition of Cyprus, however, also eliminated the intercommunal warfare that had threatened to drag Greece and Turkey into armed conflict on several occasions. Cyprus no longer poses the same problems arising from transborder nationality that it did during the 1960s, as the Cypriot Greek and Turkish communities now live in largely homogeneous territories that are effectively under the control of separate governments.

IV. Greece and Turkey as Strategic Rivals: 1975–Present?

The de facto partition and population transfer on Cyprus eliminated the last major outstanding "nationalist" issue between Greece and Turkey. While the Cyprus issue continued to play a role in souring relations between the two countries, it no longer contributed to interstate instability in the same manner as it had in the past. This is due to the fact that, with the populations of the island separated, neither community possessed the interest or ability to forcibly exercise political control over the other. Rather, the Turkish north of the island, which declared itself the Turkish Republic of Northern Cyprus in 1983, was subsumed under the direct protection of the Turkish military. At the same time, the internationally recognized Republic of Cyprus, composed almost entirely of Greek Cypriots, became far less likely to witness future Turkish intervention. As Greek Cypriot leaders had never accepted the idea of a "double *enosis*," whereby part of the island would be annexed to Greece and part to Turkey, the established Turkish presence in Northern Cyprus contributed to the dissolution of public preferences for unification with Greece. At the same time, the Turkish display of resolve headed off any future calls for *enosis* from future leaders in Athens, who adopted a "Cyprus decides, Greece supports" (Coufoudakis 1985: 206) policy during the coming years. Thus, after 1974, both the irredentist and contending government angles of the conflict largely drew to a close.

Nevertheless, the strategic importance of Cyprus, which lies only 40 miles off the Turkish coast, continued to make the region an important element of Turkish-Greek relations. However, Cyprus was only one of several strategic areas of contention between the two states, and several issues continued to cause friction over the coming decades. Demands by Turkey to revisit its rights to the Aegean continental shelf and the control of air transit over the Aegean became increasingly central to the strained relations of the two rivals.

As defenders of a status quo that favored the interests of their state, Greek leaders sought throughout the 1970s and 1980s to convey an impression of peaceful intentions in the face of Turkish revisionism. Shortly after the forced "resolution" of the Cyprus issue, Greek prime minister Konstantinos Karamanlis suggested, in a speech given in April 1976, the conclusion of a mutual nonaggression pact with the Turkish government. Not surprisingly, leaders of Turkey, the stronger and more revisionist power at this point, saw little to gain from such an agreement and declined. Shortly afterward, Greece and Turkey nearly became involved in armed conflict during the summer of 1976 over the conduct of oceanographic research by a Turkish vessel in a region of the Aegean continental shelf claimed by Greece as its own.

Ongoing negotiations over strategic-economic issues surrounding the Aegean took place throughout the late 1970s and 1980s, interrupted several times by events such as the Turkish recognition of the independence of Northern Cyprus. Once again in 1987, the two countries approached the brink of conflict over an oil-drilling dispute. Later, in 1996, conflict again threatened to break out over the control of a small, uninhabited Aegean island. In January 1998, the decision of the Cypriot government to purchase Russian antiaircraft missiles brought about threats of a blockade by Turkish leaders who saw the delivery and installment of such missiles as a serious strategic threat. While all of these crises were resolved peacefully, the underlying issues that fostered them remained a hindrance to improved relations between Greece and Turkey.

Nevertheless, these strategic-economic issues did not and do not represent the same type of underlying problem that issues surrounding transborder nationality have presented. Neither economic nor strategic issues prevent the type of indivisible, largely zero-sum type of conflict that surround problems involving conational diaspora. Strategic issues, in particular, often arise as a reflection of underlying suspicion and distrust between states—a state of affairs brought about by the preexistence of rivalries often associated with transborder nationality. It is no accident that the first challenges to the status quo in the Aegean were made by Turkey in 1973,[9] just as events unraveling in Cyprus bred increasingly intense ill will between the two states.

In the absence of underlying revisionist fears surrounding other issues, however, strategic issues affecting the balance of power between two states become less salient. Mutual suspicions between Greece and Turkey represented a legacy of the Cyprus dispute, and, to a lesser degree, the historical record of conflict stretching back to Greek independence. Even when transborder issues are mitigated or resolved, it takes time for the mutual enmity which they engender to dissipate. During this period of "dissipation," other issues between the states remain magnified in their importance, and public pressures on politicians make compromises with national rivals difficult. However, as has been the case with India and China as described in the previous chapter, the salience of strategic issues, even unresolved ones, tends to diminish as memories of conflict fade and the perception of mutual threat subsides.

Disagreements over territories based solely on economic or strategic considerations do not represent the permanent underlying baseline of hostility engendered by transborder nationality. With the elimination of the transborder issue following the separation of the two communities of Cyprus, Greece and Turkey became freer to pursue closer relations once more, hindered only by the politics of historical memory that sometimes animate public pressure groups.

By the late 1980s, there were signs that the disputes of the past would no longer present an insurmountable obstacle to contemporary comprises and warmer relations. At the end of January 1988, the prime ministers of each state met in Davos, Switzerland, initiating a series of negotiations that became known as the Davos Process. The talks produced two key committees, the "Joint Committee on Cooperation," which oversaw a variety of cultural exchanges and pursued advances in economic cooperation, and a "Greek-Turkish Political Committee," which sought to advance political dialogue on the strategic issues dividing the two states. A former Turkish ambassador to Greece (Akiman 2000) notes that the talks represented "[the first time] since the Venizelos-Ataturk era . . . that the two countries seriously laid down their mutual problems before them in full recognition that it was to their benefit to work together and cooperate." Although no bold resolution of any of the more serious bilateral problems was achieved through the Davos Process, the "spirit of Davos" became the cornerstone of a new attitude of rapprochement adopted by both sides during the late 1990s.

A clear attempt to break from the past began in 1999, when a new Greek foreign minister, Georgios Papandreou, took office in the wake of revelations concerning Greek support for the recently apprehended Turkish separatist leader, Abdullah Ocalan. Papandreou worked closely with the Turkish government in managing events surrounding the NATO bombing of Kosovo during that year. In August and September, two serious earthquakes inflicted heavy damage and loss of life in each country. The quick response of each in providing aid to the other in the wake of the catastrophes helped mitigate nationalist sentiment among the respective publics. At the end of the year, in December 1999, it became clear that Greece would no longer pose the barrier to Turkey's membership in the EU, as it had in the past, when it offered support for Turkey's candidacy at the European Council's conference in Helsinki. Greek leaders became active supporters of Turkey's accession to the EU in coming years, especially during the Copenhagen Conference of 2002 and the more recent EU summit of December 2004, which confirmed the initiation of negotiations for Turkey's accession.

Greek-Turkish relations are perhaps closer today than they have ever been—which is not to say that important obstacles in their relationship do not still exist. Aside from the strategic issues described, there also remains a small, but important transborder ethnic presence in each country as a legacy of the Treaty of Lausanne. A small minority of Greeks, numbering in the tens of thousands, remains in Istanbul. This group has largely been hostage to the rise and decline of relations between the two states, and has suffered harassment and expulsion during periods of conflict. As long as Turkey continues to take steps to improve its human rights record, it is unlikely that Istanbul's Greek community will become an issue in interstate relations—but a shift in the direction of Turkey's internal politics could bring about renewed concern, and renewed tension, if the status of this group is threatened.

Similarly, Muslims, approximately half Turkish, make up about 1 percent of the Greek population, and are concentrated in the border region of Western Thrace (Dokos and Tsakonas: 2003: 12). Once again, the group's small size means that it is unlikely to become a vocal minority, but the potential that Turkey would eventually use the treatment of this group as a pretext for an attack on the strategically important region remains a worry for some analysts. Although perhaps exaggerating the threat, Dokos and Tsakonas (p. 15) reflect the lingering suspicions of many Greeks toward the intentions of their group neighbors when they claim "Turkish territorial aspirations vis-à-vis Greek Thrace could eventually become the most important challenge to Greek security." In this sense, the presence of even a small transborder group can be seen as elevating the baseline of hostility between Greece and Turkey—if only to a small extent and with the expectation that a variety of other factors will likely mitigate the influence of this factor.

Normative-Demographic Implications of the Post Cyprus-Partition Era
Even if the role of transborder nationality as a factor in interstate relations subsides, lingering interstate distrust associated with public remembrance of past conflict may linger on and influence the salience that suspicious neighbors accord to their strategic territorial interests. Only a short distance from the Turkish coast, Cyprus

represents an extremely important strategic territory. Although transborder issues involving the island are less volatile than in the best, no better example of the strategic rivalry surrounding Cyprus exists than the crises of the late 1990s precipitated by the Cypriot purchase of antiaircraft missiles from Russia.

At the same time, a myriad of issues surrounding economic and strategic claims in the Aegean arose almost simultaneously with the Turkish invasion of the island. Rivalries over strategic territory generally require the perception of a present or potential threat among the states engaged in the rivalry. Given that only a small transborder presence exists in each country today, however, the underlying source of conflict, instability, and mistrust has been reduced. This suggests that, as memories of past nationalist-based international conflict recede, the strategic issues between the two states will similarly diminish in importance. Although there remains a strong economic component to the disputes as well, agreements over economically valuable land and sea territories exist between many democracies, and rarely lead to armed conflict.

The recent détente between Greece and Turkey illustrates the potential for a new era of warmer relations that is likely to become more robust as long as neither state is allowed to exercise strong influence over large numbers of the other's dominant nationality. Thus, the most stable scenario for future interstate relations between Greece and Turkey would involve the continued demographic and de facto political separation of the two nations of Cyprus. Otherwise, the international repercussions arising from the presence of transborder demographics might arise once more.

Domestic Influences on Greek and Turkish Dispute Initiation

Military Influence

One of the chief assertions of this work has been that governments heavily influenced by state militaries behave more aggressively when an irredentist-type situation exists. The twentieth century history of relations between Greece and Turkey seem to reflect a similar tendency whereby military intervention in politics leads to higher levels of conflict initiation when irredentism was an issue. Furthermore, the Greek junta during the early 1970s, when faced with a heated "contending government" situation with Makarios' Cyprus, pursued an "overthrow-merger" strategy similar to the "secession-merger" strategy often associated with irredentist disputes.

Table 8.1 lists the direct military interventions taking place in Greek and Turkish politics during the twentieth century and whether those interventions took place during a period characterized by transborder nationalist disputes. Furthermore, the table summarizes the nature of policies initiated by the military-influenced state either during or within five years following the intervention of the military in politics.

In terms of the Greek government, the intervention of the Military League in 1909 led to the installment of Venizelos, who became one of the most notable nationalist leaders in Greek history. The nationalist preferences of the military,

Table 8.1 Military Interventions and Subsequent Greek and Turkish Foreign Policies

Year	Event	Transborder Issue	Foreign Policy Outcome
Greece			
1909	Goudhi coup	Large diaspora	Installment of Venizelos; Balkan Wars 1912–1913
1916	"National Defence" Revolt	Large diaspora	Support from Entente powers; Constantine forced to resign; Venizelos assumes power; Entry into First World War
1922	"Venizelist" coup	Small diaspora[1]	Negotiations at Lausanne
1925	Pangalos coup	Small diaspora	Little Aggression (although Pangalos launched a small invasion of Bulgaria in 1925, ostensibly to protect mistreated Greek diaspora)
1936	Mextaxas dictatorship	Small diaspora	No aggression
1967	Military junta under Papadopoulos	Cyprus question	Some aggression—some negotiations
1974	Military junta under Ioannides	Cyprus question	Overthrow of Mikarios provokes Turkish intervention
Turkey			
1960	Gursel coup	Cyprus question	Long period of military influence in Turkish politics initiated—invasion plans initiated in 1963 and 1967, but called off under heavy international pressure
1971	Military forces Demirel Resignation	Cyprus question	Ecevit gains power as first post-coup civilian leader in 1974; orders invasion of Cyprus soon thereafter
1980	Military overthrows Demirel	Small diaspora	Frequent conflicts over the strategic Aegean issues
1997	Intervention against Islamists	Small diaspora	1998 dispute over Cyprus missiles; followed by contemporary detente

Note:
1. As has been explained, British rule over Cyprus was hardly considered an issue worth raising at this point in history, and played no role in Greek policy. Although other factors played a role, one could argue that the question of 'military feasibility' (namely, an extreme lack thereof) is the theoretical element of this work that best explains why Greece did not challenge Great Britain on the issue.

therefore, paved the way for future irredentist endeavors initiated by Venizelos, including the Balkan Wars and Greek intervention in the First World War and the subsequent Asia Minor debacle.

Although the Greek military largely withdrew from politics following the rise of Venizelos, the "Great Schism" that developed during World War I led to renewed political action by the military. After the removal of Venizelos by

Constantine, segments of the Greek military revolted during August 1916, forming the "National Defence" movement that supported Venizelos' return to power. Supported by these elements of the armed forces, Venizelos was able to establish a provisional government in September 1916, which subsequently declared war against the Central Powers in November 1916. With the intervention of Entente forces against Constantine the following year, Venizelos' military-influenced provisional government took power and quickly made Greek entry into the conflict official. According to Veremis (2003: 69), the intervention of the military into Greek politics in 1916 opened a "Pandora's Box" that "mark[ed] the beginning of systematic military involvement in Greek politics." Although the implications of high levels of military influence over domestic policymaking were not to (temporarily) subside until the 1950s, the importance of military influence over foreign policy changed dramatically after 1922.

With the reduction of the Greek diaspora following 1922, military interventions in politics affected foreign policies toward Turkey to a much lesser degree. When the Greek military again assumed power in 1967, however, the Cyprus issue was at the forefront of the foreign policy agenda. While the nationalist instincts of military leadership during this period were initially restrained by a desire for close relations with the United States, the desire for a decisive reckoning of the Cyprus situation led to the ill-fated overthrow of the Cypriot government by the military junta. Although certainly not the only reason for periods of Greek aggression in the twentieth century, the desire of Greek military leadership to pursue nationalist goals contributed to prominent instances of Greek intervention abroad.

The high point of Turkish military intervention in politics came at a time when relations between the two states were already facing a period of instability due to the Cyprus situation. After 1960, the influence of the Turkish military on Turkish domestic and foreign policies has been strong, if not always overt. During one of the "highpoints" of Turkish military influence over civilian leadership during the 1960s and early 1970s, the Turkish government initiated plans to invade Cyprus during at least three separate years: 1963, 1967, and 1974. As has been noted, this period also represented peaks in intercommunal violence, which one would have expected to trigger military threats by the Turkish government even in the absence of military influence over policy. Nevertheless, it has been argued in previous case studies that the presence of military influence over policy not only seems to foster aggressive foreign policy behavior in irredentist situations, but also the escalation of disputes into full-scale warfare—as was the case for Somalia in 1977–1978; and for Pakistan in 1965 and 1997. In the case of Turkey, only strong American warnings and certain logistical weaknesses kept Turkey from invading Cyprus during the 1960s. During 1974, however, no such factors were important enough to dissuade the Turkish state from invasion—an invasion, prompted in part, by strong pressures on Prime Minister Ecevit emanating from Turkish military circles.

Turkish governments during the 1980s and 1990s were also influenced by a weak (and nonexistent between 1981 and 1983) civil-military divide. However, with the de facto partition of Cyprus after 1974, the source of friction between Greece and Turkey shifted to more strategic-oriented differences. The intervention of the Turkish military in domestic politics as late as 1997 indicates, at least until recently, that foreign policy decision makers must at least take into considerations the preferences of military leaders. Nevertheless, with issues of transborder nationality largely resolved, it is unlikely that policies that take into account the influence of the military would be any more systematically aggressive than civilian policies. Therefore, despite the last half-century of Greco-Turkish rivalry, there is little reason to believe that a reassertion of the Turkish military's influence over civilian leadership, which is becoming increasingly unlikely as Turkey seeks entry into the EU, would necessarily initiate a more aggressive Turkish foreign policy and represent an end to the recent period of détente enjoyed between the two states.

Diaspora Discontent

The connection between military influence over policy and irredentist-type aggression is most clear when diaspora groups can be described as discontented. Within the context of each of the irredentist-type situation examined in this study, there is reasonable evidence to suggest that diaspora groups were highly discontent with their foreign rulers—with the exception of the Turkish diaspora of Cyprus under British rule. The degree of discontent within Greek-inhabited areas of the Ottoman Empire is difficult to assess empirically, but it is clear that such discontent existed. It seems fair to surmise that, based on the relatively frequent uprisings by Greeks within the Empire and the assistance provided by resident Greeks to the Greek army in Asia Minor during the postwar intervention, Greek citizens of the Ottoman Empire looked favorably upon the idea of incorporation into a politically democratic and relatively economically prosperous Greek state as opposed to minority status in a decaying Sultanate. At the very least, there was a perception among Greek leaders and publics that the redemption of Greek areas was a goal desired by its inhabitants—which is the main point of including this concept in the analysis. During the strongly-military influenced tenure of Prime Minister Venizelos, efforts to retrieve the perceived oppressed diaspora of the Ottoman Empire led to the Balkan Wars, the First World War, and the ensuing Asia Minor intervention.

As evidenced by the overwhelming support of *enosis* offered in the 1950 referendum, it is clear that Greeks within Cyprus were similarly discontent with their status as citizens of a foreign empire. However, because that empire was the British Empire rather than the Ottoman Empire, Greek governments, including military governments, steered clear of confronting London until the diplomatic situation became favorable with the spread of the decolonization movement. Clearly, the overwhelming military superiority of the British Empire, combined with the longstanding entente that existed between the two countries, both contributed to the silence of Greek leaders on the Cyprus issue during the interwar period.

The Turkish case is slightly more varied. As described earlier, Turkish Cypriots actively fought to retain British rule on the island and clearly accepted that the island would not revert to Turkish rule. The discontent of this group following independence, however, was clearly evident. Especially after being shut out of politics and economically blockaded after 1963, it is no surprise that Turkish residents of the island welcomed Turkish intervention on their behalf when it arrived. Although the data used in analyzing this case would suggest that Cyprus was relatively more prosperous than Turkey (with a GDP approximately 25 percent higher through most of the period 1960–1990), the average level of income of Turkish Cypriots was substantially lower than that of the Greek population of the island. Thus on multiple grounds—economic, political, and in terms of physical security—the Turkish diaspora on Cyprus clearly represented a discontented nationality. During the 1960s and 1970s, when the involvement of the Turkish military in politics was strong, the perceived desire of Turkish Cypriots for liberation led to near wars on numerous occasions and culminated in the invasion of 1974.

Military Feasibility

As indicated in the figures 8.2 and 8.3 below, Greek aggression against the Ottoman Empire was not feasible until after the First World War. The point at

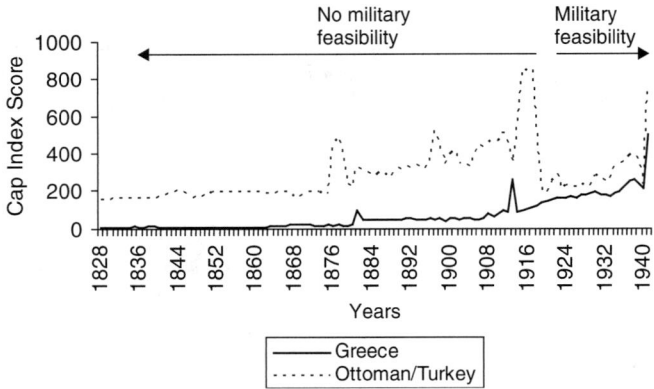

Figure 8.2 Capability Index Scores (pre-World War II)

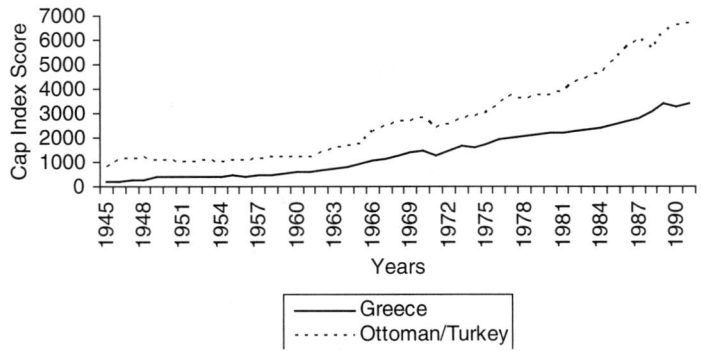

Figure 8.3 Capability Index Scores, 1945–1991

which Greek capabilities finally became "feasible" came about after the Empire's collapse following the First World War and its subsequent reduction to the rump state of Turkey. Very similar to the balance of power existing between Pakistan and India, Greece possessed approximately 25–40% of the capabilities of Turkey throughout the twentieth century (according to the capabilities index utilized in this study). Unlike the nineteenth century, however, the primary revisionist power in the late 20th century Greek-Turkish rivalry was Turkey. Thus, despite the certain level of deterrence presented by the Greek military, Turkey still possessed the ability to credibly threaten military action against the Greek state over Cyprus and later strategic disputes.

Thus, the real period of interest as far as the question of military feasibility is concerned is the nineteenth and early twentieth century. Contrary to the expectation that realist considerations would play a systematic role in restraining aggressive behavior when a putatively revisionist state faced an overwhelmingly stronger adversary, Greece adopted fairly consistent hostile policies toward the Ottoman Empire—even though those policies tended more toward the subversive than overtly aggressive. Clearly, the military might of the Ottoman Empire strongly outweighed that of the Greek military, which largely relied on irregular forces until the late nineteenth century (the data utilized in this work suggest a ten-to-one advantage in manpower for the Ottoman Empire in 1875, for instance). Nevertheless, at certain junctures, Greek actions in the nineteenth and early twentieth century, particularly the ill-conceived invasion of the Empire launched in 1897, seemed to defy any realist considerations and attest to the strength that public nationalism sometimes places on foreign policy decision making.

Greek aggression during this period partly bespeaks the faith of Greek leaders that the Great Powers would continue to guarantee Greek sovereignty were the Ottoman Empire to retaliate against their state—faith that seems justified based upon the reticence of the Ottoman Empire to initiate disputes against Greece during the 1800s. However, it was also an impressive indication of the strength of Greek irredentist preferences that the Greek government adopted a consistently hostile stance toward the much more powerful Ottomans from Greek independence until the First World War. As was the case with Somalia and Pakistan, the willingness of Greece to maintain hostile policies against the Empire attests to the willingness of smaller states to confront larger states over nationalist issues that are central to those states' foreign policies and very national identities.

Conclusion

More than perhaps any other single factor, the presence of transborder national groups has conditioned the nature of relations between Greece and Turkey/Ottoman Empire. When these groups were large and politically active, relations between the two states were characterized by high levels of interstate conflict. When transborder groups were small and politically dormant, relations between the two states improved.

Due to mutually agreed upon and forced population exchanges, these states experienced four distinct eras related to the presence or relative absence of the transborder question. The first era existed before the population exchanges and expulsions related to the conflict in Asia Minor and subsequent Treaty of Lausanne negotiations. Between independence and 1923, Greek leaders pursued rather constant policies of subversion and outright military aggression against the Ottoman Empire. While public nationalist sympathies and pressures were widespread and strong through much of this era, two factors in particular sparked the pursuance of overt aggression by Greek governments. The first was the presence of diaspora rebellion, with the most noteworthy example of the uprising in Crete during the 1890s that sparked the Thirty Days' War of 1897. The second factor was the relative weakening or "inversion" of international constraints presented by the Great Powers. Greek leaders took advantage of the preoccupation of Great Britain and France during the Crimean War, for example, while, during the Russo-Turkish War, Great Britain restrained Greek action by initiating a naval blockade. Eventually, during the First World War and its aftermath, international pressure was "inverted" such that the Great Powers actually intervened in Greek affairs to ensure that policies of irredentist aggression were initiated against the Ottoman Empire.

The second era occurred between the population exchanges of 1923 and the emergence of the Cyprus issue during the mid-1950s. During this period, relations between Greece and Turkey grew increasingly warm as the memories of their past rivalry faded. The relative absence of the transborder nationality issue paved the way for this détente by removing the source of instability and friction that had earlier led to a century of instability and distrust between the Ottoman Empire and Greece.

The third era involved the emergence of the Cyprus issue that occurred after Greece openly challenged Great Britain's claim to the island before the United Nations. During earlier decades, the Cyprus question had failed to capture the imagination of Greek and Turkish leaders and publics due to the shear military infeasibility of challenging Great Britain on the matter. However, with the strengthening of norms of self-determination that occurred on the international level during the 1950s, Greece was able to challenge Britain on the diplomatic level. Once this occurred, it led Cyprus on the path to independence, but also raised questions concerning the power structures under which Greek and Turkish Cypriots were to be governed. Initially, these power structures were shared between Turkey, Greece, Britain, and the Cypriot government, which, in turn, was constituted in a corporatist manner that provided veto "protection" for both communities. Once this arrangement broke down, however, rivalry between Greece and Turkey intensified greatly because of the newfound vulnerability of the islands distinct communities, and both states repeatedly threatened one another militarily on behalf of their national kin on the island. Only the separation of the islands' nationalities, resulting from the de facto partition of the island following Turkish invasion in 1974, ended this era of instability.

The last era is the current era, within which, once again, the issue of transborder nationality has not been particularly salient. Although, since 1974, Greece and Turkey have clashed on multiple occasions, these clashes were primarily a result of conflicting strategic and economic claims rather than issues of transborder nationality. As such, the issues involved are more amenable to compromise, and more likely to decrease in salience as the nationalist rivalries of the past fade from public memory. The recent period of rapprochement between the two states is evidence that, without the presence of underlying issues of transborder nationality, leadership in both states are much freer to pursue peaceful policies without having to deal with strong nationalist pressures from below.

Finally, this chapter addressed the issues of domestic-type political factors and their role in promoting state aggression within already unstable situations involving transborder nationality. Coupled with diaspora content, which was evident in each of the irredentist situations described (with the exception of the Turkish diaspora on Cyprus during British rule), military influence served to encourage aggressive foreign policy strategies. During the twentieth century periods when transborder issues were at stake and a military government (or, more commonly, a civilian government strongly influenced by military leadership) was in power, strongly aggressive policies were adopted by states with revisionist goals or were only deterred by strong international constraints.

The military-installed Greek leader, Venizelos, led the state into the Balkan and First World Wars. The Greek military leadership of the late 1960s and early 1970s, after a period of attempted negotiations, helped spark the Turkish invasion by overthrowing the Cypriot government in a policy that appeared designed to lead to *enosis*. Greek military influence or control over policy during the interwar period when transborder issues had largely disappeared, however, did not noticeably affect Greek relations toward Turkey.

Turkish military influence over policy was strong during the period after 1960. On multiple occasions during the 1960s, Turkish leadership decided to invade Cyprus and risk war with Greece only to be dissuaded by international actors, particularly the United States. Eventually, it was a civilian leader in Turkey, Prime Minister Ecevit, who actually invaded the island. However, as the first civilian prime minister following a period of direct military intervention in politics, Ecevit relied heavily on the preferences of military leaders when executing foreign policy decisions.

Key factors hypothesized in this work to affect interstate relations influenced relations between Greece and Turkey. The interplay of public nationalist pressures and international constraints explain much concerning the general state of bilateral relations during the various eras mentioned. At the same time, military influence over policy correlates well with the initiation of particularly aggressive policies by one side or the other during periods when transborder nationality was a salient issue.

At present, the future of relations between Greece and Turkey looks particularly promising. The main danger to future relations ironically lies with the potential for peace and communal reintegration in Cyprus. Were these to occur, however, it is particularly important that the outcome include the presence of commonly acceptable political structures that are both workable and mitigate the threat perceptions of the two communities. At the same time, it is important that an integrated government promote a common Cypriot identity that loosens the ties binding the two communities to their respective motherlands. Only such a fundamental shift in identity would assure that a reintegrated Cyprus would cease to be a future threat to relations between Greece and Turkey.

CHAPTER 9

CONCLUSIONS AND IMPLICATIONS

This work has argued that in order to understand the frequency of conflict between many states in the international system one must begin by understanding the destabilizing role of nationalism. While the relations between all states are, to some degree, influenced by liberal and realist-type considerations, an important, and often highly violence prone, subset of states in the international system faces challenges associated with the issue of transborder nationality. Leaders within these states are confronted with normative pressures emanating from the international community, which tend to favor the preservation of state sovereignty as a primary constituent norm of the state system, and from domestic constituents, who often favor the pursuance of nationalist policies in an effort to "protect" national kin abroad by minimizing or eliminating the influence of a foreign government's policies over the group.

Three major situations exist when assessing normative causality—with each related to the presence or absence of transborder demographics and the existence or absence of violent resistance on the part of national kin in states outside of the homeland state. In the first instance, international pressures supporting international sovereignty affect the decision-making process of homeland state leadership more than nationalist pressures from below. This is generally the case when no significant transborder presence exists, as is the case among the majority of state pairings in the international system. These dyads will tend to be more systematically peaceful than dyads in which a transborder presence exists.

A second possibility is that international pressures proscribing the transgression of another state's sovereignty will exist at roughly the same level as nationalist pressures from within society that demand the elevation of national kin self-determination abroad. This may result because nationalism in society is elevated within society, as is often the case in irredentist-type situations, or because international norms supporting sovereignty and territorial integrity are weaker than usual, as is often the case in contending government dyads. In situations within which international and societal normative pressures approach parity, a state of foreign policy "indeterminacy" is realized. When this state of affairs is brought about, it is unclear how potentially revisionist states will behave—creating an almost Hobbesian-type environment within which it is unclear whether international norms will be respected or not. The difficulty inherent in predicting the actions of such states lends itself further to bilateral instability as the potential targets of aggression will, in turn, pursue their own policies of "defensive revisionism" in an effort to counter future threats to their own state sovereignty and security. These dyads will, thus, tend to be more systematically conflictual than dyads lacking a transborder nationality.

Last, it is possible for a situation to exist when domestic nationalism reaches such a point that the imperative of domestic political survival is clearly contingent on the willingness of a state leader to pursue nationalist goals almost regardless of international prescriptions and consequences. This occurs most frequently when conationals abroad rebel against their government—whether that government is actively controlled by a foreign nationality or, in rarer cases, perceived as beholden to a foreign occupier or possessing a political system viewed as foreign and oppressive. The presence of conational rebellion abroad can be expected to result in decision making that largely disregards respect for norms of state sovereignty, thereby fostering the most systematically conflictual subset of bilateral relations.

Against this normative backdrop, this work also examines several other factors associated with the initiation of disputes in potentially irredentist situations. These factors are particularly relevant in cases of "foreign policy indeterminacy" (i.e., irredentist situations lacking diaspora rebellion), when it is unclear upon what bases a leader will choose a course of action. Leaders are faced with several key considerations, including: the degree of military influence over policy; the level of nationalist preferences among diaspora groups; and relative military balances of power vis-à-vis other states.

Military influence over policy was shown to frequently tip the balance toward aggressive policymaking within irredentist-type situations. Decision making under military regimes (or civilian regimes likely to be beholden to strong military influence) often results in the pursuance of subversive or overtly militaristic nationalist policies designed to support the self-determination of diaspora groups abroad. Such policies are particularly frequent when it is clearer that a diaspora group is desirous of self-determination. Furthermore, realist-type considerations play a certain role in determining whether or not aggressive actions are actually "feasible"—with feasibility defined as the ability to mount a stiff enough defensive effort to make retaliation by states targeted by aggressive or subversive policies highly costly.

The next section reexamines the quantitative and qualitative evidence underlying the findings of this work. I will also discuss the implications of studying transborder nationality for international relations theory and future research directions. After examining the implications for political science scholarship, a further section will examine the implications for international policymaking. Based upon the findings of this work, I present several possible prescriptions for dealing with situations involving transborder nationality and the subsequent interjection of nationalist preferences into international relations.

Generalized Findings—The Quantitative Analysis

The quantitative analysis discussed in chapter 5 showed that dyads that share a national group tend to have more militarized interstate disputes than dyads lacking such a group if that national group makes up the majority of the population of at least one state. This includes minority-majority dyads, which are associated with the rise of irredentist-type nationalism, and majority-majority dyads associated with contending government conflicts. Dyads within which a significant same-national minority exists in both states were not found to be more systematically conflictual than other dyads.

The existence of militant diaspora rebellion was shown to be particularly inflammatory for interstate relations in minority-majority dyads. Majority-majority dyads did not display any increase in intradyadic hostility given the occurrence of nationalist rebellion.

The analysis further explored the role of demographic variables in three specific types of disputes. The first type involved territorial disputes. Here it was found that demographic variables played a particularly important role, as the characterization of a dyad as minority-majority or majority-majority provided the only systematic link out of all the variables, with the exception of relative capabilities, in relation to disputes over territory. Particularly striking in this instance was the weakness of joint democracy in predicting territorial disputes.

I also examined disputes involving the destruction and replacement of one state's government by another state. These "regime change" disputes were most associated with the presence of majority-majority demographics and a lack of joint democracy. In other words, the expected rise of contending government nationalism may lead to the attempted destruction of one state by another. At the same time, this phenomenon is less associated with states that are jointly democratic as such states pose less of a threat to the legitimacy of one another (and, if they are characterized by majority-majority demographics, may choose peaceful merger over conflict).

My analysis also revealed the types of disputes that are unlikely to involve transborder dyads any more often than nontransborder dyads—namely, policy-based disputes. Militarized disputes involving issues not related to territory or governance are best explained by liberal democratic peace variables. Peaceful resolution of potential policy disputes, which tend to present more room for negotiations than territorial or regime change disputes, is most closely associated with the presence of jointly democratic states, which offer structural and normative incentives for compromise.

Finally, the quantitative analysis examined the role of specific factors affecting the foreign policy formulation of decision makers in potentially revisionist homeland states within minority-majority (irredentist-type) dyads. I utilized two different models in assessing these factors. The first was a standard regression model that assessed the individual variables while controlling for the other variables. This model revealed a strong role for military influence over foreign policy and diaspora uprisings in promoting the unilateral aggression of irredentist state leaders. The presence of military feasibility was also found to influence the initiation of disputes, although, curiously, not in cases of dispute initiation involving fatalities.

The second model sought to establish patterns emerging from the interaction of key factors involved in foreign policy formulation. Within this analysis, diaspora uprisings were found to affect dispute initiation largely independently of other factors. Other domestic factors (in combination) primarily influence conflicts under conditions of expected "foreign policy indeterminacy"—whereby transborder nationality exists, but diaspora groups remained military passive. Given the absence of diaspora rebellion, it was shown that the combination of (1) military influence over policy, coupled with (2) the presence of a diaspora group residing in a state with relatively poor political or economic conditions as well as (3) the presence of military feasibility, best explains why conflictual policies are initiated by homeland states.

Case Study Findings and Corroborative Evidence—Normative-Demographic Aspects

The case studies found in chapters 6–8 focus primarily on irredentist-type nationalist situations that have arisen when minority-majority demographics have existed between states. These cases provided a variety of corroborative evidence suggesting that the theoretical underpinnings and findings of the quantitative research provided a great deal of explanatory power in understanding the interactions among the states examined.

The case studies provided evidence suggesting that public pressure on executives to act aggressively was higher in homeland irredentist states than within states lacking a foreign transborder group. When comparing bilateral state relations of within transborder dyads compared to nontransborder dyads, the studies clearly bears out the assertion that interstate relations suffered greatly due to outstanding nationalist issues. The plight of diaspora groups left outside the homeland due to the perceived misalignment of postindependence borders captured public imaginations and was manifested as Greater Somalism, Islamic jihadism, and the Great Idea. Leaders of states that were home to such diaspora, facing uncertain threats emanating from homeland states, often pursued aggressive policies of their own. While stressing the importance of state sovereignty and territorial integrity through diplomatic channels, states targeted by irredentist neighbors often took aggressive measures with the intention of increasing their own security at the expense of their neighbor's, such as the limited Ethiopian invasion of Somalia during the 1980s and India's invasion of Bangladesh during the early 1970s.

Throughout the case studies, I also noted the rise and decline of international normative constraints. While international constraints on Somali behavior were fairly strong throughout, shifting superpower alliances and international sanction of territorial annexations in the Western Sahara and East Timor fed the perception of Somali decision makers that they might weather the diplomatic storm resulting from the Ogaden invasion. In the case of Pakistan and India, the ability of Pakistan to appeal to UN resolutions in support of a Kashmiri plebiscite as well as Kashmir's continued status as a disputed territory lessened international opposition to Pakistani intrigues in a region divided not by state borders, but, rather, lines of control. The Greek case leading up until 1923 most poignantly displays the role played by international normative constraints, as the presence or absence of Great Power pressure for and against Greek irredentist policies represented the decisive factor, in most cases, concerning whether or not overtly militant policies were pursued against the Ottoman Empire.

Homeland states displayed a consistent willingness to transgress international norms throughout the case studies when diaspora rebellion erupted in foreign states. In the Somali case, diaspora rebellion in Ethiopia helped draw Somalia into war during the 1970s. Diaspora rebellion in Kenya led to the pursuance of subversive policies in support of *shifta* rebel groups by Somalia, but public support for such policies began to wane in response to reports of rebel excesses, contributing to a diminished level of aggression toward Kenya. Kashmir was an interesting case in that diaspora (i.e., Islamic Kashmiri) rebellion was noticeably absent until the late 1980s. However, once the insurgency began, Pakistani and Indian relations suffered accordingly, resulting in the Kargil Gap conflict of 1999, as well as a variety of more limited military incursions by each state into the other's region of control. Last, the presence of diaspora rebellion was a main causal factor in influencing Greek irredentist policies during the nineteenth century. When coupled with favorable international circumstances for intervention, such as the Crimean and Russo-Turkish War, diaspora rebellion in regions such as Thessalonica and Crete roused public opinion and subsequently pressured executives to pursue aggressive policies on numerous occasions. Most noteworthy was the Thirty Days' War of 1897, when public nationalist pressures in response to the rebellion of Greek diaspora became so manifest that Greek decision makers launched an invasion of the much more powerful Ottoman Empire in the face of Great Power opposition and witnessed the swift defeat of a Greek army that was doomed from the outset. The fact that leaders have continued to pursue aggressive irredentist-type policies throughout the Cold War, despite the very fact that no successful irredentist annexations have occurred since the Second World War, attests to the power of public nationalism in forcing decision makers into risky foreign endeavors despite the likelihood of defeat.

In contrast to bilateral relations between states sharing a diaspora group, bilateral relations between other state pairings tended to be less conflictual. Despite severe ideological differences and different superpower alliances through much of the period studied, Kenya and Ethiopia enjoyed warm relations in comparison to the relations of either state with Somalia. The fact that the warmth of this relationship was partly attributable to the mutual Somali threat each state faced does not detract from the fact that it was the question of transborder nationality, not questions of Cold War ideology, which represented the defining issue within the Horn of Africa.

Similarly, relations between China and Pakistan were extremely close throughout the period studied. This was despite the fact that each state, once again, possessed a radically different ideological view and, before the advent of Sino-American détente, represented natural geopolitical adversaries. Clearly, the presence or lack of a significant transborder nationality largely defined the state of relations among three of Asia's largest states.

The example of Greece and Turkey is useful because two periods have existed when the transborder question was largely absent. The first period, which existed after the 1923 Treaty of Lausanne and before the Cyprus issue arose, was characterized by continually warming relations between the two states. However, in the wake of the Turkish invasion of Cyprus and the de facto partition of the island after which the transborder question once again was rendered largely mute, relations between the two states remained tense as a consequence of numerous quarrels over strategic and economic land and sea territories that had arisen during the years of conflict over the Cyprus question. As a point of comparison, India and China, states for which transborder nationality is not a salient issue (with one another), went to war over strategic territorial issues in the early 1960s and experienced several decades of tense relations thereafter. Unlike relations between India and Pakistan, however, the Sino-Indian relationship has gradually improved throughout the years and strategic territorial issues, while still outstanding, have become less salient. The same might be expected in the future for Greece and Turkey. Given the relative absence of transborder ethnicity as a salient issue, as collective recollections of past conflict fade, one might expect the saliency of strategic and economic disagreements to decline—or at the very least, be addressed by more diplomatic, and less militaristic, interstate policies.

Case Study Findings and Corroborative Evidence—Foreign Policy Formulation

The main findings of the statistical analysis suggest that military influence over government decision making within potentially irredentist homeland states tends to increase the propensity for the initiation of aggressive policies toward states that are home to national diaspora. This trend was evident most clearly in the case of Pakistan, which witnessed much more aggressive policies during periods when military influence over policy was strongest. In particular, the civilian Bhutto administration, which took power during the 1970s, pursued policies of active détente toward India, while civilian administrations in the early 1990s seemed to restrain the potential for Pakistani aggression when insurgency erupted in Kashmir. Similarly, civilian governments in Somalia acted with greater restraint toward Kenya and Ethiopia during the 1960s, despite the presence of Somali insurgent activity, than the military government of Siad Barre during the 1970s. In the twentieth century history of Greek-Turkish relations, the influence of military leaders over policy was strong much of the time that irredentist issues were present, and seemingly contributed to the aggressive policies pursued by each state. At the same time, military governments that came to power during periods when transborder nationality did not represent a significant issue were no more likely to pursue aggressive policies than their civilian counterparts.

An interesting pattern that emerged from the case studies involved the willingness of military-influenced homeland state governments not simply to initiate aggressive policies with a higher frequency, but also to escalate disputes to a higher level than their civilian counterparts. In each of the case studies, there was evidence that the presence of military influence in decision making influenced the initiation of major wars. The Somali invasion of Ethiopia in 1977 and the Pakistani invasions of Kashmir in 1965 occurred under military governments, while the Turkish invasion of Cyprus in 1974 and the Kargil Gap invasion by Pakistan in 1999 occurred during periods when military leaders held sway over civilian authorities. The high point of Greek irredentist militarism, which occurred in the period during the First World War, occurred as the result of policies pursued by Eleftherious Venizelos, who, despite receiving a democratic mandate, maintained close ties with military leaders.

When strongly military-influenced governments perceived a desire for liberation among "discontent diaspora" group, aggression was most likely to occur. The Pakistani government launched an invasion of Kashmir in 1965, for example, partly in response to perceptions that civil unrest indicated antigovernment sentiment in the region. Along the same lines, but with the opposite outcome, the growing acceptance of Kenyan rule displayed by Somalis of that state after the 1960s served to mute aggressive policies pursued by Mogadishu under Barre's military government.

Although the revisionist states examined in the case studies were all militarily inferior to those states upon which they had territorial designs, during most periods they were not so inferior as to completely discourage the pursuance of subversive or overtly militarist policies. Throughout most of the periods covered within the case studies, homeland states saw greater or lesser levels of militant behavior as militarily feasible. However, the states analyzed were only willing to risk large-scale invasion of diaspora-inhabited lands when unusual constellations of international events made it possible or the possibility of assistance from militant members of the diaspora was thought to make such aggression more likely to succeed. However, small-scale attacks and subversive policies, which are less likely to provoke a costly retaliation, were common. The major exception to the expected constraining influence of military feasibility concerns Greek policies toward the Ottoman Empire during the nineteenth century, which were rather consistently aggressive despite the massive imbalance of power. Although these policies rested largely on the expectation that Great Power influence would restrain Ottoman retaliation, the presence of such risk-acceptant policies over such a long period attests to the strength of Greek irredentist preferences during this era.

The Implications of Transborder Nationality for International Relations Theory

Over the past several decades, international relations scholarship has been largely built around variations in four major approaches. The first approach focuses upon realist-type considerations, which stress the relative capabilities of states and assume that the common desire of states and foreign policy decision makers lies in increasing state power and/or security. The second approach focuses upon liberal-type factors, which stress the role of transnational interest group linkages, state structures, and domestic normative preferences in influencing state preferences. Liberal scholars are most associated with democratic peace theory, which suggests that joint democratic governance plays a key role in mitigating international disputes. A third approach focuses on international institutions as organizations that convey information, aid interstate coordination of policies through reduced transaction costs, and establish rules of the game through repeated state interactions that make transgression of these rules (some would say norms) more costly. The fourth, and most recent, approach to international relations found in constructivist literature focuses primarily on the role that normative considerations play in decision making—and views normative considerations derived from "intersubjective understandings" as key causal influences on actor behavior. This work has drawn from each of these paradigms, while, at the same time, revealing the limitations of each approach.

The realist-type concept of "military feasibility" was utilized in the domestic foreign policy model in order to control situations when relative military weakness presented a clear constraint on executive decision making. The concept rested on the realist notion that a state with revisionist goals could only rationally and credibly pursue those goals if there existed a balance of military capabilities that would render potential military reprisals costly. In a sense, this turns realist theory on its head by suggesting that balance of power situations are often more conflictual because it provides revisionist states greater latitude in pursuing various levels of aggression. Similarly, in the case of the bilateral normative-demographic model, the control variable indicating relative capabilities showed that *increasing* levels of power *disparity* promoted peace. Thus, while capabilities seem to matter, as suggested by realist theory, the nature of balance of power considerations operate much more closely to that suggested by "power transition theory," which takes into account how state capabilities and state preferences (i.e., revisionist-seeking or status quo-oriented) are related.

The models incorporate much of the spirit of liberal scholarship, if not necessarily confirming all of the findings. The focus of liberal scholarship on domestic politics and foreign policy preference formation is key to the two major models employed in this study. However, this study also found that the central liberal tenet regarding the relationship between peaceful interstate relations and joint democracy may operate less systematically when issues of transborder nationality arise. The relative importance of national group linkages, for example, was found to provide a better explanation for international disputes based on territorial considerations than democratic peace theory. In addition, the presence or absence of an oppressive government beholden only to a "narrow selectorate" did not seem to affect the initiation of disputes in irredentist situations.[1] Nevertheless, in the case of most types of disputes, the presence or absence of joint democracy was found to be important, and thus, its role in mitigating conflict in general should not be ignored.[2]

Chapter 2 examined the role of international institutions in the development of international norms of self-determination and sovereignty. As was emphasized, the international community has never arrived at a simple and parsimonious formula for determining when the more generalizable emphasis on international respect for sovereignty should yield to more specific considerations of self-determination for national groups. In respect to the ability of the international community and associated interstate organization's ability to transmit appropriate rules of the game to state actors in situations involving transborder national ties, the "neo-institutional" approach to international relations "assumes too much" (Saideman 2001: 217). However, the fault of over-assumption lies not in the fact that the creation of international norms lacks a causal impact on state behavior, but, rather, that other factors arising from domestic political imperatives may override abstract international proscriptions. In this sense, Ambrosio (2001) is correct in associating the presence or absence of irredentist aggression with the selective application of international normative pressures—but this fact only captures part of the picture.

Constructivist scholarship benefits from its ability to generalize the processes leading to the formulation of actor preferences, but often suffers from the lack of specificity concerning the nature of causal inference. The work draws upon constructivist literature to explain the development of domestic nationalism and how it often places decision makers in a difficult position by forcing them to reconcile the political demands of constituents for whom nationalism is an important element of political culture and international institutions and actors, who tend to favor the preservation of norms of state sovereignty. Unfortunately, constructivist theories are often difficult to measure empirically, and thus, serve as underlying theoretical constructs that help explain the connection between more tangible factors and conflict. In this case, the tangible phenomenon is the presence of transborder demographics. However, due to the intangibility of the normative aspect of the theory, the linkage with demographics remains speculative—despite compelling evidence presented in the case studies attesting to the causal impact of such norms.

Central Asia—Flashpoint of the Future?

Although this work has focused on the role of transborder nationality in sparking past conflict, the consistency of such conflict over long periods between states sharing national groups suggests that many of the findings may apply to the future of interstate relations. Although periods of bilateral enmity may wax and wane, the usual flashpoints of international crisis continue to revolve around situations characterized by transborder nationality, including relations between countries such as India and Pakistan, Taiwan and China, Israel and its Arab neighbors, and North Korean and South Korea. These traditionally dangerous dyads have been joined by more recent rivalries involving transborder nationality in areas such as the former Soviet Union (in Moldova, for instance) and Central Africa (Rwanda's involvement in the Democratic Republic of the Congo).

The findings of this work suggest that one of the most likely regions to experience nationalist-driven conflict in the future is Central Asia. Since independence, the former Soviet republics of Central Asia have maintained a close eye on potential Russian revisionism in light of the large Russian diaspora groups still scattered throughout the region. At the same time, former Soviet Central Asian states have all experienced unstable relations with Afghanistan, a state sharing significant transborder national ties with most of the former Soviet Republics. In total, the former Republics of Central Asia experienced 13 militarized disputes with Afghanistan during the (pre-9/11) period 1992–2000 alone.

Relations among the former Central Asian republics have been surprisingly peaceful, perhaps in part to the common threats that Soviet revanchism and Islamic militancy have posed to all governments in the region. Nevertheless, this work has suggested that common security interests often fail to supersede nationalist considerations in defining the course of bilateral relations. Although militant conflict has thus far not erupted, experts on Central Asia have focused upon the future threat posed by transborder nationality in the region since the dissolution of the Soviet Union (see, for instance, *Central* Asia 2002; Raman 1999; and Fuller 1994). Analyzing recent data (2001–2003) with the normative-demographic model employed in chapter 5 results in predictions of near-future militarized interstate disputes that range from approximately 10 percent annually between Uzbekistan-Kazakhstan and Uzbekistan-Turkmenistan to approximately 35 percent annually between Uzbekistan-Tajikistan and Uzbekistan-Kyrgyzstan.[3] Significantly, most of the transborder demographics in the region include Uzbekistan—as either a homeland or kin state. According to Raman (1999), the "politics of Central Asia is . . . always marked by a subterranean fear of Uzbek hegemony and irredentism." While it is possible that the states of Central Asia will continue to coexist in the relative harmony that has characterized the past decade, the history of relations among transborder states suggests that policy makers ought to pay close attention to this region in the future.

Implications for Policymaking—Some Suggestions

The findings of this study suggest several policies that can mitigate the destabilizing influence of transborder nationality on international relations. The following policy suggestions imply that the mitigation of interstate disputes is desirable, although one could argue that, in some cases, interstate conflict might actually be preferable to other alternatives. Unfortunately, the difficulty in making such a distinction brings me to the first point:

1. Work toward strengthening international normative constraints supporting state sovereignty and noninterference.

This first suggestion is the most difficult and potentially treacherous in its implications for international peace. The difficulty inherent in this suggestion lies in the fact that few states would readily accept an international system based solely on the inviolability of state sovereignty. The desire of state leaders, often prodded by public interest groups, to seek the protection of human rights and group interests at the cost of traditional considerations of state sovereignty will continue to encourage particularistic transgression of traditional international norms. This is particularly true with the growth of telecommunications that facilitate the conveyance of images of "oppressed" peoples abroad. More than pure sensationalism, however, it is difficult to argue, for instance, that the preservation of Cambodia's territorial integrity under the Khmer Rouge should have represented an inviolable deterrent to a Vietnamese invasion that halted a genocide that claimed millions, including many within the Vietnamese diaspora.

State interests and biases further prevent the adoption of absolute norms proscribing interventions abroad. The interest of the United States, for instance, in maintaining close ties with Indonesia during the Cold War led to the sanctioning of Indonesia's invasion of East Timor. The limited support offered by Iran and Egypt for Somalia aggression provided the Somali state with a small measure of diplomatic cover for undertaking the Ethiopian invasion. Similarly, the support of many Islamic nations for Pakistani designs on Kashmir encouraged the continuation of a militant approach.

Perhaps the most one can ask in terms of the international community is for the development of a common normative consensus under circumstances that represent a particular threat to international peace and stability. The international community led by the United States conveyed a strong message during the Gulf War that the invasion of one Arab state by another would not be condoned internationally (the perceived weakness of international norms by Saddam Hussein, not coincidentally, contributed to the original invasion of Kuwait). On the other hand, the lack of international response to Armenia's invasion of Azerbaijan sent the opposite message. If international pressures are to be effective, they must be expressed firmly and clearly in anticipation of possible interstate aggression and involve a united resolve on the part of the international community to condemn, sanction, or even respond militarily to aggression. The alignment of such factors, however, tends to be rare.

2. Promote economic development and inclusive democratic processes in "kin" states

One of the better long-term strategies for mitigating irredentist conflict may lie in elevating the economic and political status of diaspora groups. The implication for international conflict lies in the idea that a diaspora that is increasingly content with its political status will be less likely to seek secession or incorporation by a homeland state. At the same time, nationalism among domestic audiences in homeland states can be expected to wane as material conditions improve for diaspora groups—placing less pressure on executives to take foreign policy stances. At the very least, scholars of domestic conflict have suggested that states that are more economically developed are less likely to experience domestic rebellion, while states that are more democratic are more likely to contain ethnic-type rebellion. As has been shown, the prevention of nationalist rebellion by diaspora groups is perhaps the single biggest step that can be taken to avoid high levels of interstate conflict. Unfortunately, there is strong disagreement among scholars as to the appropriate form that democratization efforts should take when the goal is to minimize the alienation common among diaspora groups. Nevertheless, this should not detract from the willingness of the international community to promote democratic governance in kin states. Although democratization carries risks for domestic stability, government repression of diaspora groups presents almost certain negative implications for international stability when a homeland state lies near.

3. Negotiate solutions to such disputes on an international, not intercommunal level

This work has argued that diaspora groups play a strong role in influencing the level of nationalism displayed among the polity of homeland states. This in turn influences the preferences of foreign policy makers toward states in which diaspora reside. While the second policy suggestion advocates paying close attention to the social and economic conditions of diaspora groups, it is the international community, not a state with national ties to the diaspora, should spearhead efforts to improve conditions for diaspora groups. All too often, such pressure applied by conational states spills over to increasing demands and threatening behavior that leads to bilateral distrust and instability.

The leadership of states that are home to transborder groups can best improve bilateral relations by seeking to reduce the political influence of local communal groups on policy. Rather than fan the flames of nationalism at home, homeland state leaders, in particular, should seek to cultivate loyalty to state institutions while downplaying imagery of a greater national community. The first step that an executive can take to improve bilateral relations is to refrain from intentionally inflaming domestic nationalism, which can be expected to "blowback" and create a stronger domestic political impetus for interstate aggression.

Rhetorically distancing the interests of the state from the interests of the nation helps alleviate domestic nationalism, and may create enough policy space for a leader to pursue more productive relations with another state that is home to a conational group. Reducing the influence of diaspora groups on domestic policy helps promote negotiated solutions not only by reducing the degree of nationalist pressures on an executive, but also by reducing the number of key actors involved in negotiation. Negotiating compromises in nationalistically charged situations is extremely difficult between two parties—adding additional local parties, who are possibly even more extreme in their nationalist preferences, makes negotiation exponentially more difficult.

While bypassing local diaspora groups in the negotiation processes may result in such groups rejecting the legitimacy of the negotiations altogether, such an outcome becomes less likely the more clearly a homeland state leadership signals its intentions to revoke its support for such groups were they to act in an intransigent manner. Recent examples of negotiations in which local parties were bypassed include the Dayton Accord negotiations, which were only successful due to the willingness of Slobodan Milosevic to overlook Bosnian Serb objections, and the Northern Ireland peace process, which occurred mainly as a joint United Kingdom-Ireland initiative, with local Protestant and Catholic parties largely excluded (Woodwell 2005). Similarly, as I described in chapter 8, the willingness of Greece, Turkey, and Great Britain to bypass local leaders in the late 1950s allowed for the finalization of political arrangements. The subsequent breakdown of the Zurich-London agreements in 1963, however, points to the importance of continued cooperation among international actors when inevitable setbacks to regional peace agreements are encountered.

4. Encourage Civilian Control over the Military

After the fall of Communism in Eastern Europe, some of the earliest initiatives taken by Western Powers involved efforts to promote a stricter divide between civilian and military authority in the region. The findings of this work suggest the wisdom of such a strategy, particularly in a region with numerous potential irredentist conflicts. While stronger civilian control over policymaking is not likely to end outstanding nationalist grievances, the reduction of military authority over policymaking diminishes the influence of a strong, frequently militantly nationalist domestic lobby. When military leadership within a homeland state holds strong influence over government policy, one would expect that nationalistically oriented foreign policies will intensify and quite potentially escalate to war.

5. Do not encourage the military buildup of revisionist states

This suggestion might seem obvious, but third parties have nevertheless ignored nationalism as a factor in deciding whom to sell arms. A large Soviet-supplied military buildup and modernization effort preceded Somalia's invasion of Ethiopia. Similarly, American efforts to modernize and assist the reorganization and growth of the Pakistani military preceded the 1965 invasion of Indian-controlled Kashmir. The targets of nationalist revisionism rarely have cause to adopt aggressive policies against revisionist states except in their own defense. Thus, the main consequence of enhancing the military capabilities of states desiring to pursue irredentist-type policies is to provide such states with a credible military apparatus that helps shield them from potentially retaliatory consequences of more limited aggression or enables them to conduct their own large-scale military operations abroad. Neither potentiality has positive consequences for interstate stability.

6. Carefully weigh the consequences of demographic integration versus separation

The findings of this work inevitably raise the question of whether the international community should consider supporting partitions and population transfers when faced with intractably conflictual situations involving transborder nationality. Kaufmann (1996 and 1998), for instance, argues that the alteration of state borders and transfer of national populations has historically lent itself to the reduction of both interstate and intrastate violence.

The findings of this work in many ways might seem to support the contention of Kaufmann's thesis—at least as it relates to interstate relations. At the same time, there are many problems with the international validation of ethnic cleansing. First, it is clear that population transfers that occur during the course of interstate conflict will likely involve a high degree of brutality and violence in an attempt to eliminate or coerce civilian populations into fleeing a particular region—as was the case with Greek citizens inhabiting Asia Minor in 1923 or those inhabiting Northern Cyprus in 1974. Kaufmann himself recognizes that "outside powers or institutions" must offer "protection, transport, subsistence, and resettlement" as an alternative to allowing forced resettlement of civilians "at the mercy of their ethnic enemies and of bandits" (1998: 124).

However, the involvement of the international community in partitions and population transfers presents an important problem aside from the obvious difficulty of mustering international will to partake in an endeavor that represents an infringement of traditional human rights norms. As this work has argued, the presence of international norms supporting the maintenance of state sovereignty and territorial integrity represent a constraint on executives within potentially revisionist transborder states. International sanctioning of border alterations or population transfers might, in the long term, alleviate interstate tensions in a particular situation, but at the cost of weakening international norms that serve to dampen international aggression in other cases. Perhaps Kaufmann is correct in suggesting "when all else fails" that partition and population transfer might merit consideration in a dire situation involving the potential for extreme destruction or genocide. The threshold of potential violence must clearly be set very high, however, in order to justify weakening future international normative constraints on interstate aggression.

At the same time, it is unwise in many cases to risk future intercommunal and interstate stability in the name of idealism. If ethnic cleansing has resulted in a new de facto political order, as has been the case in Cyprus, the reintegration of geographically separated national communities runs the risk of reigniting the same violence that led to the forced separation of those communities in the first place. Under some circumstances, the rectification of past injustices might demand that such a reintegration process take place, but well-intentioned policy makers should at least recognize the domestic and international risks involved.

Final Word

Although I have stressed the difficulties posed to interstate relations when states share national groups, the establishment of relatively peaceful relations between transborder states is possible even when political, economic, and institutional factors seem unfavorable. Exceptions exist to even the most determinate patterns and human agency often fosters outlying outcomes. This work presents few answers, for example, for the historical pattern of peaceful relations between Thailand and Malaysia, two states with a major transborder presence (Malays and Muslims in southern Thailand, some of whom committed acts of violence over recent years). At the same time, while I have suggested that the influence of military influence over policy is a powerful correlate of aggressive nationalist behavior, the olive branch extended to Israel by Anwar Sadat, who rose from a military background and remained strongly influenced by military leadership, remains one of the genuinely courageous examples of peacemaking within a nationalistically charged situation.

Although fortunate exceptions to the general state of conflict existing between states sharing national groups exist, the path to managing problems of interstate nationalist conflict will need to focus more upon the prospect of conflict mitigation rather than often overly optimistic hopes for the rapid elimination of interstate and international suspicion. The role of outside actors in promoting political inclusiveness, economic growth, the weakening of military control over policy, and other measures designed to reduce levels of bilateral enmity between transborder may serve to reduce the incidence of conflict to some degree. However, the single best manner of mitigating the influence of nationalism in international relations is for the international community to send the clearest signals possible that the forcible attempt to actualize a reorganization of state borders represents an unacceptable threat to international peace that will be met with strong international condemnation and resistance. At the same time, it may be necessary under situations of ethnonational oppression for the international community to realize that inaction cannot necessarily always be justified in the name of interstate peace. Unfortunately, there is no magical philosophical formulation to resolve the tension inherent between the search for international peace and the need to protect those threatened upon the basis of their nationality.

NOTES

1 Introduction

1. I frequently use the term diaspora as shorthand for a conational group that resides in a different state than the state being referenced. Although primarily used here to refer to "irredenta" groups, the term encompasses any conational group abroad, regardless of its size or political status.
2. The term kin state will be used to refer to states that are the target of irredentist or contending government nationalist aspirations. The term implies the presence of a state that is home to a national group with "kinship" ties to a homeland state, which is presumed to be susceptible to transborder nationalist preferences. The national "kin" themselves may represent a majority or minority of the "kin state's" population, and the two terms should not be confused.
3. Throughout this work I refer to "irredentist-type" circumstances, "transborder nationalist" situations, or other similar terminologies to indicate demographic patterns amenable to nationalism. The actual degree of nationalist sentiment driving potentially destabilizing policies naturally varies from case to case. One key to understanding the role that certain demographic patterns contribute to bilateral instability lies in the fact that states that are home to diaspora often interpret even mild manifestations of support by homeland states for those diaspora groups as potential signals of future (and more escalatory) interference., For instance, a homeland state may express rhetorical support for expanded group rights on behalf of national kin in another state; offer financial aid to political parties supporting greater autonomy; or even support an insurgent movement with secessionist goals. Each of these may be perceived by the foreign state as an infringement of its sovereignty and pose a future threat to its territorial integrity, even if none of these actions represents the most extreme examples of "irredentism" per se.
4. I discuss the parameters of a "politically relevant" minority in chapter 5. The term is used here to emphasize the fact that minor groups with little hope of influencing state policy domestically or abroad provide little theoretical leverage when analyzing transborder relationships.
5. A single dyad cannot usually be represented as both an irredentist-type (MINMAJ) and contending government-type (MAJMAJ). Such dyads often, however, share a minority group (MINMIN) in addition to the MINMAJ or MAJMAJ classification. In total, MINMAJ and MAJMAJ dyad-years each represent approximately 15 percent of the total dyad-years, while MINMIN dyad-years represent approximately 19 percent of the total.

6. I code the transborder relationships—the remainder of the information is from the Correlates of War project.

2   Nationality, Nation, and Ethnicity

1. Good examples include Gurr (2000: 4): "The 'constructivist' view, which underlies the Minorities at Risk project, is that national identities are enduring constructions . . . The criteria by which people are judged to be group members also can change but usually around the margins" or Saideman (2001: 23): "There is a long-running debate about whether national identity is a given in society (primordial) or created by politicians as they see fit. I follow the moderate position: multiple national identities frequently co-exist, and the political context determines the salience of particular identities."
2. While the Hechter (2000) example is fundamentally individualist and rational, his work as a whole contains a great deal of leeway for group identity and loyalties.
3. While the subjective-objective debate involving ethnicity can be applied to nationality to some degree, the widespread recognition of the political nature of nationalism necessarily skews most arguments toward the subjective-instrumental paradigms. The fact that nationality is a more subjective concept than ethnicity is actually crucial to understanding the nature of nationalism—as will be described in greater depth later.
4. Miller (1995: 77–80) makes the argument that the reciprocal obligation among conations to preserve one another's basic rights is an important ethical foundation of nationalism. Here, I argue that it is precisely the norm of reciprocal obligation that pervades national communities that can be seen as fundamental preferences underlying collective action.
5. Sovereignty, as utilized in this work, refers to the internationally recognized norm that allows a state government to exercise control over a given territory in a matter that is free from outside interference. Sovereignty, in this sense, is broken down into two major elements—one stressing the importance of territorial integrity, the other the importance of noninterference. Norms of self-determination are suggested in this work to pose a threat to both elements of sovereignty.
6. Examples include the 1960 UN Declaration on the Independence of Colonial Peoples and the 1970 Declaration on Friendly Relations.

3   Sovereignty and Self-Determination: Conflicting Norms as the Basis for International Conflict

1. This work adopts the common political science assumption that leaders are primarily motivated by a desire to retain office—thereby requiring leadership to respect both the demands of state constituents as well as avoid censure by the international community, which is likely to yield negative consequences to the domestic political position of the executive due to his or her association with the diminished international status of the state (or as a consequence of punitive measures such as sanctions that the international community might consciously adopt with the aim of undermining the position of state leadership).
2. To expand on the tension between normative and interest-based causality further, it may be most appropriate to say that causality is unclear when tension exists between these two influences *within a particular case*. In other words, when norms

suggest a certain course of state action and "traditional" conceptions of state interest (land, wealth, strategic interest, and so on) suggest a similar course of action, it is impossible to establish conclusively that either factor played a definitive role in influencing decision making—although further "thick" research might reasonably point the body of evidence in one direction or another (or, most likely, that both factors serve to reinforce one another).

If one examines a large number of cases, however, one can establish a role for norms if a *systematic* association between norms and behavior occurs in the absence of any systematically similar association between the presence of state interests (defined narrowly) and state behavior. Similarly, even in the presence of a systematic role for interest-based behavior, one can statistically control for the role of particular interests over a larger number of cases in order to determine whether normative causality operates independently. Later in this work, the role of economic and strategic interests in promoting state aggression is assessed alongside other factors in order to ensure that the key theoretical constructs are not simply masking concrete, "instrumental," state interests. The results indicate that strategic and economic interests promote foreign policy aggression—but no more so in irredentist cases than in nontransborder dyads.

3. Durability, a measure of the persistence of a norm within international law/society, is also a common indicator utilized to assess normative strength. Since the two primary norms discussed here, self-determination and territorial integrity have both been invoked throughout much of the twentieth century, it is safe to assume that each can be considered durable.
4. Within contending government situations, however, the effect on public nationalism of a domestic uprising among conationals against the "alien" government is less clear, as the benefits of liberating conationals must be weighed against the harm that conflict would inflict upon the group.
5. This is not to say that the role of international constraints does not vary within irredentist-type disputes. Chapter 7 describes, for instance, the key role played by varying levels of international constraints on Greek foreign policy and how different irredentist conflicts occurred or were deterred in part because of these constraints. Ambrosio (2001), as mentioned earlier, views international constraints as the primary variable affecting levels of irredentist aggression. His argument applies better to contending government dyads, however, within which public nationalist pressures are more muted, and thus are less likely to challenge international normative constraints as a causal factor. In irredentist-type situations, international constraints might be high, but domestic pressures might nevertheless overwhelm these constraints in the calculations of a leader wishing to remain in power.
6. Even if differences in state size and material capabilities indicate that one state is better able to threaten the security of a conational state more than another, such factors have to do with opportunity structures more than underlying preferences. Furthermore, on a *systemic* level, such imbalances of power are equally likely across all dyads, thus not biasing patterns of behavior in one direction or another.
7. One could apply similar logic to any domestic rebellion—whether ethnic-based or not. Due to the suggested theoretical interaction between ethnic demographics and ethnic-based rebels, this paper focuses on ethnic-based rebellions. Nevertheless, general rebellion was also tested with the analysis, and the effects of a noninteracted general rebellion variable were found to be quite similar to those of the ethnic-based rebellion variable—in large part due to the fact that so many civil conflicts involve a strong ethnic component.

4 The Determinants of Aggressive Behavior in Irredentist-Type Situations

1. Admittedly, national kin could also exist in a poverty stricken area of an otherwise wealthy state or live under conditions of generalized economic discrimination. Unfortunately, no data exists to measure the relative wealth of different ethnonational groups within states on a global basis over an extended time frame.
2. The assumption of this section is that almost, if not all, states have an single executive at the head of government with final responsibility on questions of foreign policy—particularly questions of war and peace. While this executive might at times be heavily constrained and have to share authority on matters, such as spending, that might be related to foreign policy, final decisions on foreign policy is considered to be driven primarily by a single individual.
3. Fearon (1994) examines audience costs during crises, but his model only assumes a nebulous audience cost of some kind, without specifying any particular sources of these costs. He concludes that democracies are likely to have the highest audience costs, although he also briefly mentions military generals in autocracies and the role of the Politburo in the Soviet Union (p. 583) as potential alternate audiences. In their empirical examination of his findings, Partell and Palmer (1999) suggest that Fearon's focus on democracies may be overstated, and that the potential for strong audience costs may exist in autocracies as well.
4. Bueno de Mesquita et al. consider not only "selectorate" size, but the size of "winning coalitions" within the selectorate. The authors would likely argue that autocracies are better described as having small winning coalitions rather than small selectorates—with the sizes of selectorates varying more widely within both autocracies and democracies. However, this work takes a somewhat less dogmatic approach, and assumes a strong correlation between both selectorate and the basic characterization of a state's polity with the understanding that the word selectorate generally assumes a small winning coalition.
5. The fact that strong nationalism exists within most armed forces does not imply that one could liberally apply the term "fascism" to such sentiment. Huntington (1957: 91) provides a good contrast between what he considers the model of the military mind and how it differs greatly from typical fascist ideals.
6. When speaking of the military in general, it is implied that we are primarily concerned with those in the officer corps most capable of directing collective military action. As Huntington (1957: 3) notes, the appropriate focus on civil-military relations involves the relation of military officers to the state.

5 Empirical Assessment

1. For an extended exposition on the difficulties of coding ethnicity (including some remarks on the sources used herein), see Fearon (2002).
2. One of many more recent discussions about narrow versus broader ethnic criteria can be found in Varshney (2001). Many would argue that an ethnic group that expresses territorial claims is no longer simply an ethnic group, but a "national" group (for instance, Brass 1991). I use the terms ethnic, national, and ethnonational interchangeably when referring to a group itself—but utilize the term nationalist when referring to the political goals of ethnic group leaders that emphasize state control of territory. Thus, while a group must at least have a potential role in

politics to be included in the study as a politically relevant ethnicity, not all such groups are necessarily represented by expressly nationalist leaders.
3. The dataset labels minorities according to a number of ethnic, linguistic, religious, or identity-based cleavages. In order to maintain consistency, I alter/eliminate two of the codings. The data treats Palestinians and Arabs separately, I consider them one group. The coding of Southerners in Chad is also eliminated as an overly broad coding.

   In addition, a small number of majority groups exist in the Minorities at Risk dataset. These cases are easily identified by cross-checking other data sources, and are coded appropriately in the dataset utilized for this study.
4. A minority fits the four "at risk" criteria if that minority is (1) currently subject to discrimination; (2) disadvantaged from past discrimination; (3) challenging an advantaged ethnic group; or (4) supports a political organization that advocates expanded group rights.
5. Linguistic criteria, when conflicting with other criteria, are given weaker status. For example, the Ireland-Great Britain dyad is coded as minority-majority, due to the Catholic/Irish minority in Northern Ireland, rather than majority-majority because of linguistic commonality.
6. Three percent is, admittedly, an arbitrary cutoff. This decision implies that about 3 percent of a population is enough for a minority's presence to be a factor in political life, even if that minority is not considered "at risk."
7. A short discussion describing the criteria defining "contiguous" dyads is given in appendix 5.2.
8. In rare cases in which it is questionable whether a group represents a minority or majority of population, a consensus of the four sources is considered. Fortunately, there were no cases in which at least three of the four sources were not in agreement.
9. Only two cases receive a "2"—Sweden-Finland and India-Pakistan. Both states in each dyad have an ethnic majority, while both states are also home to a significant ethnic minority of the other state. Recoding this variable as a 1 in these cases increases the coefficient and significance of the key transborder explanatory variables to a small degree while decreasing the coefficients and significance of the control variables indicating joint democracy and capability-ratios (in both the MID and FATAL models). Because the resulting estimates are more conservative, I retain the original coding as the primary coding.
10. The coding of the italicized-boldfaced variables indicated in the following sections is explained in greater detail in appendix 5.1.
11. Endogeneity note: The presence of *kin uprising* in the regression model poses a potential problem for analysis because government material support of rebels may affect both the existence of bilateral conflict (left side of the regression equation) as well as the existence of rebellion in kin states (right side variable). This seems unlikely, however, given the nature of the coding of the dependent kin uprising variable, as described in appendix 5.1. This variable codes "uprisings" that may consist of as few as 25 deaths during a year. Such a rebellion could easily be sustained in the absence of homeland government support, which should be more associated with the *intensity or level* of rebellion, rather than the *presence* thereof. However, the variable only indicates the latter, rather than the former.

    However, in order to verify that the results of this section are valid, several measures are taken to ensure that endogeneity does not fundamentally affect the results. Woodwell (2004) conducts tests using similarly coded variables in order to show that the initiation of homeland state aggression (MIDs and fatal MIDs) does not affect the onset of diaspora rebellion. In order to assess whether the *continuation* of rebellion is affected by the model used, I conduct an analysis that drops all "rebellious" dyad-years subsequent to the first year of rebellion in a dyad.

The results are very similar to the original results in the FATAL model, except that the coefficient of the kin uprising variable actually increases greatly in strength (the MINMAJ remains very close to the value displayed in the results). In the MID model, the results for kin uprising largely remain the same, but the coefficient for MINMAJ increases from .44 to .85. Thus, when eliminating the possibility of endogeneity, the results of the key variables are actually more prone to strengthening, rather than weakening. The results presents herein therefore represent the more "conservative" findings.

12. The theoretical reasons underlying the inclusion of these variables, as well as more specific coding information, are provided in appendix 5.1A.
13. If the variable indicating minority rebellion in MINMAJ dyads is eliminated, the coefficient of the MINMAJ variable rises to roughly the same level as that of the MAJMAJ variable in most tests.
14. This statement should not be misinterpreted to mean that policy disputes are uncommon in transborder dyads. Policy disputes are actually more common than "territorial disputes" in transborder dyads. However, policy disputes are not systematically more common in transborder dyads than in dyads that do not share ethnonational groups.
15. The marginal effect of diaspora uprisings within irredentist dyads is extremely large due to the consistently conflictual relationships between states within a relatively small number of dyads-years. Altogether, dyad-years witnessing diaspora uprisings in irredentist contexts represent about 2.6 percent of the dyad-years in the sample, or about 19 percent of the total minority-majority dyad-years.
16. The classification tree is presented in appendix 5.4. Terminal nodes in table 5.7 that are associated with significant positive, significant negative, and "No MIDs" outcomes are indicated.
17. Due to the similarity of the MID and FATAL models displayed in earlier regression, the tree modeling concept is only used in order to test for nonfatal MIDs.
18. I will continue, at points, to utilize the term "nation" in this discussion with the understanding that, more specifically, it was "politicized ethnicity" that was tested.
19. Generally speaking, any armed ethnic group has likely drawn enough attention to itself to merit inclusion in the MAR dataset.
20. Many of these groups might not be considered in the current "winning coalition," a term described by Bueno de Mesquita et al (2003) as an important determinant of political behavior alongside selectorate size. The restriction of the variable to very low polity values should help ensure that both selectorate size and winning coalition sizes are small.
21. In most cases in political science when such a capability index is used, military expenditures play a role in the construction of the index. Unfortunately, due to the imprecise reporting of, or lack of data concerning such expenditures, I feel that inclusion of military spending in a capability index adds additional measurement error to an already imprecise concept.
22. In order to avoid a "dummy variable trap" whereby perfect multicollinearity exists among a series of dichotomous variables, one such variable must be dropped and used a benchmark against which the others may be measured.

NOTES   207

23. Although this represents a bit of a sloppy fix, the effect on the data and results turns out to be minimal. The only variable significantly affected by the process of filling in the missing dyad-years is the trade variable itself, which shifts from insignificance to weak significance in several equations. A similar process is utilized with the IGO variable, which remains equally insignificant after missing dyad-years are added.
24. My appreciation goes out to Todd Allee for providing me with this data.
25. Hazlewood (1975) suggests that non-violent domestic strife is associated with diversion, whereas violent domestic strife is associated with encapsulation.
26. When no further conditions are stipulated, the GEE approach achieves the same results as a population-averaged logit regression. Utilizing GEE, however, has the advantage of facilitating, through *Stata 7.0*, the use of robust standard errors.
27. For further information about the technical aspects of General Estimating Equations, their applications, and suggested utilization vis-à-vis conditional models, I highly recommended Zorn's (2001) very concise and readable article.
28. See *Stata 7.0* reference manual for a full explanation of Stata's *xtgee* command.
29. There are rare circumstances when this is obviously not the case—for instance, when a small power is part of a grand alliance (such as Iraq's participation in wars against Israel or the participation of numerous small nations in the Gulf War). Still, noncontiguous confrontations must generally involve an unusual set of circumstances.
30. Without, once again, stretching the term diaspora too far, the Soviet Union only had small, contiguous diaspora populations. While China has several noncontiguous diaspora groups, its lack of a blue-water navy has largely rendered it unable to project military power overseas.
31. Unlike many tree diagrams associated with game theory, there is no sequential organization to such a tree.

6   Somalia, Ethiopia, and Kenya

1. Another important, and recent exception, has been the imbroglio in the Democratic Republic of the Congo—sparked, in large part, by the transborder presence of Hutu and Tutsi diaspora in the Congo.
2. The regression used to calculate these figures is slightly different than that found in table 5.1 due to the fact that the results reflect out of sample predictions (i.e., the relevant dyads are removed when calculating the regression used to make predictions).
3. Debate still exists as to whether the Somalis should be considered one or many ethnic groups. Somalia is one of the rare cases in which ethnicity is more difficult to pin down than nationality. It is clear that most Somalis, with the possible exception of the Isaaq people, regard themselves as part of a common nation, despite the ascribed differences between them linked to family lineage.
4. The three main imperialist powers were Britain, Italy, and Ethiopia—which steadily expanded its frontiers under the reign of Menelik II (1889–1913). The roots of the 1977–1978 Somali-Ethiopia war lay in the recognition by colonial powers of Ethiopian sovereignty in the Somali-inhabited Ogaden region during the 1890s.

5. The Ogaden is a geographic, rather than administrative, region. It encompasses the entire lowland of the Harar and Bale provinces of Ethiopia (Hoskyns 1985: 28).
6. Multiple spellings exist in the Latin alphabet for most of the proper Somali names. I tend toward using the most Anglicized version.
7. A plebiscite was conducted in French Somalia in 1977 leading to the colony's independence as the state of Djibouti. The Somali government, largely satisfied that "self-determination" had indeed been exercised by the people of the region, dropped all further claims to the colony's territory and Somali population.
8. The preponderance of sources suggest that Somali resistance in Ethiopia during this period was quite limited, although the scope of both rebel activity and Somali aid remains in dispute. According to Leis (1980: 232), any scattered resistance that existed in the early 1960s, was forced underground as a result of Ethiopian successes in the clashes of 1964. Henze (1985: 31), however, paints an entirely different picture when he suggests that Ethiopian insurgents numbered as many as 15,000 in 1969, and were supplied "liberally" with weapons by the Republic. Part of the discrepancy in the accounts is likely due to the fact that rebels in the Ogaden were not organized under any central group, and *many were not ethnic Somalis*. For this reason, the subversive activities of the Somali government in the region may have represented more of an instrumental policy of destabilization than a nationalistically-driven policy of ethnonational "rescue."
9. My research has shown that the largest transborder group shared between Ethiopia and Kenya is the Oromo. While the Oromo are the largest single ethnic group in Ethiopia, they only represent a very small percentage of the Kenyan population (approximately numbering 55,000). Information available at http://www.ethnonet-africa.org/data/kenya/genpop.htm (retrieved October 2004).
10. Because it was kept secret until 1979 (Sauldie 1987: 27), the mutual defense treaty was clearly not meant to deter Somalia from aggression—and thus has not been addressed as a potential factor affecting the degree of Somali revisionism.
11. Part of the reason that Kenyan and Ethiopian diplomacy was so much more successful than that of Somalia undoubtedly involved the fact that its leaders during the 1960s, Jomo Kenyatta and Haile Selassie, were among the most respected members of the African community. At the same time, Somali leaders had risen from relative obscurity.
12. In part due to instability in the region, the presence of widespread oil and gas deposits have, to this day, not been verified or developed. Nevertheless, exploration of the region for fossil fuels has accelerated over the recent decade.

7 India, Pakistan, and China

1. According to the rules used to code transborder ethnicity for use in the econometric testing in chapter 5, India and Pakistan represent one of the few cases which qualify as a double irredentist situation. Not only is India home to a significant Muslim minority (about 12 percent of the population), but Pakistan is also home to a Hindu population that numbers in the millions and is considered "at risk" by the Minorities at Risk project. Neither the territories of non-Kashmiri Muslims in India nor the territories inhabited by the Hindu population of Pakistan, however, have been the subject of significant irredentist politicking. This, in part, is likely a consequence of the fact that the groups are relatively dispersed geographically,

despite the fact that most tend to live near the Pakistani-Indian border. The only majority Muslim state in India is the province of Jammu and Kashmir.
2. Strangely, the model actually suggests a slightly higher percent of fatal MIDs than it suggests for all MIDs. This statistical quirk is largely a result of the fact that the peace-years control variable for fatal MIDs yields a much lower coefficient than that for MIDs. Because there are relatively so few years without fatal MIDs relative to other dyads, the baseline value resulting from the combination of other variables, which starts from a very high value, carries almost the entire load in determining the average yearly fatal MID probability without mitigation by the peace-years variable.
3. The Muslim majority region of Kalat, in Muslim Baluchistan, located in western Pakistan, also declared independence and was invaded and annexed by Pakistan in 1948.
4. The Pathan ethnic group is also referred to, more commonly today, as Pashtun.
5. Although the full story will never be known, it is unlikely that Pakistani officials deliberately organized and initiated the incursion of Pathan raiders into Kashmir. However, once the movement had taken shape, Pakistani security forces clearly acquiesced in their transborder movements and almost certainly provided some level of material support, particularly at the local level.
6. The division of Kashmir in 1948 was originally along a "ceasefire line." Two decades later the "ceasefire line" became known as the "Line of Control."
7. The plebiscite was to determine accession to India or Pakistan. Curiously, the UN never entertained the idea of maintaining an independent Kashmir.
8. At the time of this writing, the text of the Simla Accord was available at http://www.jang.com.pk/thenews/spedition/pak-india/accord3.htm.
9. Closely tied to the military, and composed largely of military officers, ISI cultivated an increasing degree of autonomy from the military during the 1980s and 19990s. The responsibilities of the ISI include military intelligence, similar to the American Defense Intelligence Agency (DIA), but also international and domestic surveillance (like the CIA and FBI combined).
10. One such exaggeration concerns the development of a hypothetical situation known as Operation Topac by a group of retired military officers that was first published in the *Indian Defence Review* in 1989. Although admittedly "part fact, part fiction," the existence of an Operation Topac continues to be propagated as reality by many Indian writers and the Indian government itself (see, for instance, http://www.indianembassy.org/new/NewDelhiPressFile/Kargil_July_1999/Fundamentalist_Challenge_July_16_1999.html). Retrieved November 2004.
11. The main thesis presented by Schofield is that the military actually acts as a restraining force when civilian leadership is present, but acts aggressively when assuming an unfettered degree of foreign policy authority.

8 Greece and Turkey

1. Koliopoulos makes this point based on review of transcripts of Greek National Assemblies during the 1920s. Of particular importance was the Third National Assembly held at Epidaurus, which set the conditions by which Greek representatives desired the British ambassador of the time to open negotiation with the Porte. Foreshadowing the ethnic cleansing and transfers that would eventually take place, the same assembly stressed their wish that "the Greeks and the Turks would no longer live together."

2. The use of religion as the primary determinant of nationality was unfortunate for many on both sides. Turkish-speaking Christians in Anatolia and the Greek-speaking Muslim of Crete were particularly reluctant to leave.
3. An example of the role of the Mixed Commission occurred when a dispute arose concerning which Greeks in Constantinople were to be considered "established," and thus excluded from the population exchange. The issue caused a rupture in Greek-Turkish relations, which were not fully restored until 1925.
4. Many historians and scholars have come to refer to the ethnic cleansing of Greeks in 1922 as the "Pontian genocide." Not surprisingly, many in Turkey object to the use of this term.
5. Bahcheli (1990: 12) notes that even these small minorities, and their subsequently treatment at the hands of Greek and Turkish authorities, "did cause irritations in the future"—a subject that will be addressed later in this chapter.
6. Known as the Kingdom of Serbs, Croats, and Slovenes at the time.
7. Unlike in Greece, where, in the wake of the civil war, Communist sympathizers were largely suppressed, the Communist Party remained an influential political force on Cyprus.
8. Whether the Zurich-London agreements provided a workable framework for governance is a debatable issue. Bahcheli (1990: 59) argues that "not withstanding its complexity and its limited amending power, the Constitution was as workable as Greek and Turkish-Cypriots wanted it to be" and further notes, placing the blame on Greek Cypriot leaders who sought to undermine the legitimacy of the accords, that "some Greek-Cypriot leaders have publicly acknowledged that the Accords could have been made to work."
9. Of particular note during this year were decisions by the Turkish government to grant licenses to the Turkey's national petroleum company (TRAO) for research in the Aegean and the sending of the research vessel Cardali into the area.

9 Conclusions and Implications

1. The relevance of the democratic peace theory for the unilateral initiation of conflict has, however, not received the same degree of theoretical or empirical support as "joint democracy" mechanisms.
2. The role of democratic peace theory was found to be related to contending governments dyads, for example, due to the more central role played by conflicting state ideology in these cases. Furthermore, intradyadic conflict among transborder dyads is not merely restricted to questions of territory and governance. Like other dyads, interstate relations can be expected to improve in these situations given the presence of joint democracy due to its strong association with conflict resolution in policy-related disputes.
3. The major difference in dispute rates between these dyads involves the role of the peace-years control variable. The last two dyads have a markedly higher prediction of conflict than the first two in large part due to MIDs that occurred between Uzbekistan and Tajikistan and Kyrgyzstan during 1999.

BIBLIOGRAPHY

Adar, Korwa (1994) *Kenyan Foreign Policy Behavior towards Somalia, 1963–1983*. Lanham, MD: University Press of America.
Afzal, M Rafique (2001) *Pakistan: History & Politics: 1947–1971*. Oxford: Oxford University Press.
Akbar, M. K. (1997) *Pakistan: From Jinnah to Sharif*. New Dehli: Mittal Publications.
Akiman, Nazmi (2000) Turkish Policy towards Greece: From the Brink of War to a Diplomatic Breakthrough: Five Eventful Years in Athens. Retrieved August 2005 from the Center for European Studies, Harvard. http://www.ksg.harvard.edu/kokkalis/leaders_akiman.html
Aktar, Ayhan (2002) "Homogenising the Nation, Turkifying the Economy: The Turkish Experience of Population Exchange Reconsidered." In *Crossing the Aegean: An Appraisal of the 1923 Compulsory Population Exchange Between Greece and Turkey*, edited by Renee Hirschon. New York: Berghahn Publications. 79–95.
Ambrosio, Thomas (2001) *Irredentism: Ethnic Conflict and International Politics*. Westport, CT: Praeger.
Anderson, Benedict (1983) *Imagined Communities*. London: Verso.
Armed Conflict Dataset. Version 1.0. Department of Peace and Conflict Research. Uppsala University. September 2002.
Attalides, Michael (1979) *Cyprus: Nationalism and International Politics*. New York: St. Martin's Press.
Bahcheli, Tozun (1990) *Greek-Turkish Relations since 1955*. Boulder, CO. Westview Press.
Banks, Arthur (2002) Cross-National Data Series. Center for Comparative Political Research. State University of New York-Binghamton.
Barre, Siad (1971). *My Country and My People; The Collected Speeches of Major-General Mohamed Siad Barre, President, the Supreme Revolutionary Council, Somali Democratic Republic, 1969–1970*. Mogadishu: Ministry of Information and National Guidance.
Barutciski, Michael (2003) "Lausanne Revisited: Population Exchanges in International Law and Policy." In *Crossing the Aegean: An Appraisal of the 1923 Compulsory Population Exchange between Greece and Turkey*, edited by Renee Hirschon. New York: Berghahn Books. 23–39.
Beck, Nathaniel, Katz, Jonathan N., and Richard Tucker (1998) Taking Time Seriously in Binary Time-Series–Cross-Section Analysis. *American Journal of Political Science* 42 (4). 1260–1288.
Bercovitch, Jacob and Richard Jackson (1997) *International Conflict Management: 1945–1995*. Washington, DC: Congressional Quarterly.
Boekle, Henning, Volker Rittberger, and Wolfgang Wagner (1999) "Norms and Foreign Policy: Constructivist Foreign Policy Theory." Working paper for the Tuebingen Center for International Relations/Peace and Conflict Studies. 34a.

Brass, Paul (1991) *Ethnicity and Nationalism: Theory and Comparison*. New Delhi: Sage.
Brecher, Michael, and Jonathan Wilkenfeld (1997) "The Ethnic Dimension of International Crises." In *Wars in the Midst of Peace*, edited by D. Carment and P. James, pp. 164–193. Pittsburgh, PA: University of Pittsburgh Press.
Breton, Albert and Margot Breton (1995) "Nationalism revisited." In *Nationalism and Rationality*, edited by A. Breton, G. Galeotti, P. Salmon and R. Wintrobe. Cambridge: Cambridge University Press. 98–115.
Breuilly, John (1982) *Nationalism and the State*. Manchester, UK: Manchester University Press.
Brines, Russell (1968) *The Indo-Pakistani Conflict*. London: Pall Mall Publishing.
Brooks, Stephen (1997) Dueling Realisms. *International Organization* 53 (3). 445–477.
Buchheit, Lee (1978) *Secession: The Legitimacy of Self-determination*. New Haven: Yale University Press.
Bueno de Mesquita, Bruce, Alastair Smith, Randolph M. Siverson, and James D. Morrow (2003) *The Logic of Political Survival*. Cambridge, MA: MIT Press.
Carment, David and Patrick James (1998) Escalation of Ethnic Conflict. *International Politics* 35 (1998). 62–82.
——— (1995) International Constraints and Interstate Ethnic Conflict. *Journal of Conflict Resolution* 39: 82–109.
Cassese, Antonio (1995) *Self-determination of Peoples: A Legal Appraisal*. Cambridge: Cambridge University Press.
Castagno, A. A. (1964) The Somali-Kenyan Controversy: Implications for the Future. *The Journal of Modern African Studies* 2 (2). 165–188.
Central Asia (2002): Border Disputes and Conflict Potential. ICG Asia Report Number 33. Retrieved February 1, 2005 from International Crisis Group.: http://www.icg.org//library/documents/report_archive/A400606_04042002.pdf, last accessed on May 23, 2007.
Choudhury, Golam (1988) *Pakistan: Transition from Military to Civilian Rule*. Scorpion Publishing: Essex, UK.
——— (1971) *Pakistan's Relations with India*. Meenakshi Prakashan: Meerut, India.
CIA World Factbook (2001) Retrieved July 2001 from the Central Intelligence Agency. Online version at: http://www.cia.gov/cia/publications/factbook/index.html.
Connor, Walker (1993) *Ethnonationalism: The Quest for Understanding*. Princeton: Princeton University Press.
Coser, Lewis (1956) *The Functions of Social Conflict*. Glencoe, Illinois: Free Press.
Coufoudakis, Van (1985) Greek-Turkish Relations, 1973–1983: The View from Athens. *International Security* 9 (4). 185–217.
Dakin, Douglas (1972) *Unification of Greece: 1770–1923*. New York: St. Martin's Press.
Diggle, Peter, Kung-Lee Liang, and Scott Zeger (1994) *Analysis of Longitudinal Data*. New York: Oxford University Press.
Dixit, J. N. (2002) India-Pakistan in War and Peace. New Dehli: Books Today.
Documents on the Foreign Relations of Pakistan: China, India and Pakistan (1966) edited by K. Sarwar Hasan. Pakistan Institute of International Affairs: Karachi.
Dokos, Thanos and Panayotis Tsakonas (2003) "Greek-Turkish Relations in the Post–Cold War Era." In *Greece and Turkey in the 21st Century: Conflict or Cooperation: A Political Economy Perspective*, edited by Christos Kollias and Gulay Gunluk-Senesen. New York: Nova Science Publishers, Inc. Section 1.1.
Dualeh, Hussein Ali (1994) *From Barre to Aideed: Somalia: The Agony of a Nation*. Nairobi. Stellagraphics, Ltd.
Ethnologue: Languages of the World, 14th Edition (2000), edited by Barbara Grimes. Dallas: SIL International.

Elkin, Jerrold and Brian Fredericks (1983) Sino-Indian Border Talks: The View from New Dehli. *Asian Survey* 23 (10). 1128–1139.

Farer, Tom (1979) *War Clouds on the Horn of Africa: The Widening Storm*. Carnegie Endowment for International Peace: New York.

Fearon, James (1994) Domestic Political Audiences and the Escalation of Political Disputes. *The American Political Science Review* 88. 236–269.

——— (2002) Ethnic Structure and Cultural Diversity around the World: A Cross-National Data Set on Ethnic Groups. Paper presented at the Annual Meeting of the American Political Science Association, September, Boston.

Feldman, Herbert (1972) *From Crisis to Crisis: Pakistan 1962–1969*. Oxford University Press: London.

Finer, S. E. (1962) *The Man on Horseback; The Role of the Military in Politics*. Praeger: New York.

Fuller, Graham (1994) Central Asia's Geopolitical Future. *Post Soviet Prospects* 2 (8).

Ganguly, Sumit and Kanti Bajpai (1994) India and the Crisis in Kashmir. *Asia Survey* 34 (5). 401–416.

Ganguly, Sumit (1996) Explaining the Kashmir Insurgency: Political Mobilization and Institutional Decay. *International Security* 21 (2). 76–107.

Garver, John (1996) Sino-Indian Rapprochement and the Sino-Pakistan Entente. *Political Science Quarterly* 111 (2). 323–347.

Gelpi, Christopher (1997) Democratic Diversions: Governmental Structure and the Externalization of Domestic Conflict. *The Journal of Conflict Resolution* 41 (2). 255–282.

Gleditsch, K. S. (2002) Expanded Trade and GDP Data Version 1. Journal of Conflict Resolution 46.

Goertz, Gary and Paul Diehl (1992) Toward a Theory of International Norms: Some Conceptual and Measurement Issues. *Journal of Conflict Resolution* 36 (4). 634–664.

Guelke, Adrian (1996) The United States, Irish Americans, and the Northern Ireland Peace Process. *International Affairs* 72. 521–536.

Gurr, Ted Robert (2000) *People versus States: Minorities at Risk in the New Century*. Washington DC: United States Institute of Peace Press.

Hasan, Khalid (1998) Kashmir Freedom Struggle: A Chronology 1924–1998. Retrieved November 2004. Found at: http://www.infopak.gov.pk/public/kashmir/kashmir-chronology.htm.

Hasan, Mushirul (2002) The Partition Debate—II. Retrieved November 2004 from *The Hindu*. January 3, 2002. Found at: http://www.hinduonnet.com/thehindu/2002/01/03/stories/2002010301241000.htm

Hayes, Louis (1984) *Politics in Pakistan*. Boulder, CO: Westview Press.

Hazlewood, Leo (1975) "Diversion Mechanisms and Encapsulation Processes: The Domestic Conflict-Foreign Conflict Hypothesis Reconsidered." In *Yearbook of International Studies*, edited by Patrick McGowan. Beverly Hills, CA: Sage.

Healy, Sally (1983) "The Changing Idiom of Self-determination in the Horn of Africa." In *Nationalism and Self-determination in the Horn of Africa*, edited by. I. M. Lewis. London: Ithaca Press.

Hechter, Michael (2000) *Containing Nationalism*. Oxford: Oxford University Press.

Hegre, Håvard, Tanja Ellingsen, Scott Gates and Nils Petter Gleditsch. Toward A Democratic Civil Peace? Democracy, Political Change, and Civil War 1812–1992. *American Political Science Review* 95 (1). 16–33.

Heldt, Birgir (1999) Domestic Politics, Absolute Deprivation, and the Use of Armed Force in Interstate Territorial Disputes, 1950–1990. *Journal of Peace Research* 31 (4). 451–478.

Henze, Paul (1985) *Rebels and Separatists in Ethiopia: Regional Resistance to a Marxist Regime*. Santa Monica, CA: Rand Corporation.

Hirschon, Renee (2003a) "'Unmixing Peoples' in the Aegean Region." In *Crossing the Aegean: An Appraisal of the 1923 Compulsory Population Exchange between Greece and Turkey*, edited by Renee Hirschon. New York: Berghahn Books. 3–12.

——— (2003b) "Consequences of the Lausanne Convention: An Overview." In *Crossing the Aegean: An Appraisal of the 1923 Compulsory Population Exchange Between Greece and Turkey*, edited by Renee Hirschon. New York: Berghahn Books. 13–20.

Hitchens, Christopher (1983) *Hostage to History: Cyprus from the Ottomans to Kissinger*. New York: Verso.

Horowitz, Donald (1985) *Ethnic Groups in Conflict*. Berkley, CA: University of California Press.

Hoskyns, Catherine (1969) *Case Studies in African Diplomacy*. Dar-es-Salaam: Oxford University Press.

Huntington, Samuel (1957) *Soldier and the State; The theory and Politics of Civil-Military relations*. Cambridge: Belknap Press of Harvard University Press.

Huth, Paul (1996) *Standing Your Ground: Territorial Disputes and International Conflicts*. Ann Arbor, MI: University of Michigan Press.

Huth, Paul and Todd Allee (2002) *Democratic Peace and Territorial Conflict in the 20th Century*. Cambridge University Press: Cambridge.

India and Pakistan (1951). *The Economist* 161 (5630). July 21, 1951. 139–140.

The Indian Express, January 22, 2002. Retrieved November 2004 at: http://www.indiaexpress.com/

Jalalzai, Musa Khan (2000) *The Foreign Policy of Pakistan: Sectarian Impacts on Diplomacy*. Lahore, Pakistan: Dua Publications.

Janowitz, Morris (1977) *Military Institutions and Coercion in the Developing Nations*. Chicago: University of Chicago Press.

Kacowicz, Arie (1994) The Problem of Peaceful Territorial Change. *International Studies Quarterly*, 38 (2). 219–254.

Kaufmann, Chaim (1998) When All Else Fails: Ethnic Population Transfers and Partitions in the Twentieth Century. *International Security* 23 (2). 120–156.

——— (1996) Possible and Impossible Solutions to Ethnic Civil Wars. *International Security* 20 (4). 136–175.

Kohn, Hans (1944) *The Idea of Nationalism*. New York: The Macmillan Company.

Koliopoulos, John (1987) *Brigands with a Cause: Brigandage and Irredentism in Modern Greece, 1821–1912*. New York: Oxford University Press.

Laitin, David and Said Samatar (1987). *Somalia: Nation in Search of a State*. Boulder, Colorado: Westview Press.

Lefebvre, Jeffrey (1991) *Arms for the Horn*. Pittsburgh: University of Pittsburgh Press.

Legro, Jeffrey (1997) Which Norms Matter? *International Organization* 51 (1). 31–63.

Legum, Colin and Bill Lee (1979) *The Horn of Africa in Continuing Crisis*. New York: Africana Publishing Company.

Lewis, I. M. (1980) *A Modern History of Somalia*. New York: Longman Group Ltd.

——— (1963) Pan-Africanism and Pan-Somalism. *The Journal of Modern African Studies* 1 (2). 147–161.

——— (1961) *A Pastoral Democracy*. London: Oxford University Press.

Mann, Michael (1995) A Political Theory of Nationalism and Its Excesses. In *Notions of Nationalism*, edited by Sukumar Periwal. Budapest: Central European University Press.

Marshall, Monty and Keith Jaggers (2000) *Polity IV Codebook*. Retrieved July 2001 from the Polity IV website at: http://www.cidcm.umd.edu/inscr/polity/index.htm#data

Marshall, Monte (1997) "Systems at Risk: Violence, Diffusion and Disintegration in the Middle East." In *Wars in the Midst of Peace*, edited by D. Carment and P. James, pp. 82–115. Pittsburgh, PA: University of Pittsburgh Press.

Mearsheimer, John (2001) *Tragedy of Great Power politics*. New York: Norton.
Miller, David (1995) *On Nationalism*. Oxford: Clarendon Press.
Minorities at Risk Project (1999) Minorities at Risk Dataset, version MARv899. College Park, MD: Center for International Development and Conflict Management, University of Maryland.
Morgenthau, Hans (1948) *Politics among nations; The Struggle for Power and Peace*. New York: AA Knopf.
Mousseau, Michael (2000) Market Prosperity, Democratic Consolidation, and Democratic Peace. *Journal of Conflict Resolution* 44 (4). 472–507.
My Country and My People: Selected Speeches of Jaalle Major-General Mohamed Siyad Barre President of the Supreme Revolutionary Council (1974) Mogadishu: Ministry of Information and National Guidance. Vol. 1–2.
Necatigil, Zaim (1993) *The Cyprus Question and the Turkish Position in International Law*. Oxford: Oxford University Press.
Neuberger, Benyamin (1986) *National Self-Determination in Postcolonial Africa*. Boulder, CO: Lynne Rienner Publishers.
Oran, Baskin (2003) "The Story of Those Who Stayed: Lessons From Articles 1 and 2 of the 1923 Convention." In *Crossing the Aegean: An Appraisal of the 1923 Compulsory Population Exchange Between Greece and Turkey*, edited by Renee Hirschon. pp. 97–116. New York: Berghahn Books.
Organski, A. F. K. and Jacek Kugler (1980) *The War Ledger*. Chicago: University of Chicago Press.
Park, Richard Leonard (1952) India Argues with Kashmir. *Far Eastern Survey* 21 (11). 113–116.
Partell, Peter and Glenn Palmer (1999). Audience Costs and Interstate Crises: An Empirical Assessment of Fearon's Model of Dispute Outcomes. *International Studies Quarterly* 43. 389–405.
Peckham, Robert Shannon (2000) Map Mania: Nationalism and the Politics of Place in Greece, 1870–1922. *Political Geography* 19. 77–95.
Perlmutter, Amos (1969) The Praetorian State and the Praetorian Army: Toward a Taxonomy of Civil-Military Relations in Developing Polities. *Comparative Politics* 1 (3). 382–404.
Polity IV Project (2000) Polity IV Dataset. [Computer file; version p4v2000] College Park, MD: Center for International Development and Conflict Management, University of Maryland.
Posen, Barry (1993) Nationalism, the Mass Army, and Military Power. *International Security* 18 (2). 80–124.
Psomiades, Harry (1968) *The Eastern Question: The Last Phase*. Thessaloniki: Institute for Balkan Studies.
Purvis, Andrew (2000) Détente in the Aegean. *Time* [Europe] February 7, 2000.
Raman, B. (1999) Explosions in Tashkent: The Background. Retrieved February 20005 from the Security and Political Risk Analysis (SAPRA) web page, found at: http://www.subcontinent.com/sapra/terrorism/tr_1999_03_001.html
Razvi, Mujtaba (1971) *The frontiers of Pakistan; A tudy of Frontier Problems in Pakistan's Foreign Policy*. Karachi: National Publishing House.
Rinehart, Robert (1982). "Historical Setting." In *Somalia: A Country Study*, edited by Harold Nelson. Washington DC: US Army.
Russett, Bruce and John Oneal (2001). *Triangulating Peace: Democracy, Interdependence and International Organizations*. New York: Norton.
Saideman, Stephen (2001) *The Ties that Divide: Ethnic Politics, Foreign Policy & International Conflict*. New York: Columbia University Press.

Salmore, Barbara and Steven Salmore (1973) "Political Regimes and Foreign Policy." in *Why Nations Act*, edited by Morris A East, Steven A Salmore, and Chris F. Hermann, pp. 103–123. Sage: London.

Samatar, Ahmed (1988) *Socialist Somalia: Rhetoric and Reality*. London: Zed Books, Ltd.

Sambanis, Nicholas (2001) Do Ethnic and Non-Ethnic Wars have the same Causes? *Journal of Conflict Resolution* 45 (3).

Sauldie, Madan (1987) *Super Powers in the Horn of Africa*. New Dehli: Sterling Publishers Private Ltd.

Schofield, Julian (2000) Militarized Decision-Making for War in Pakistan: 1947–1971. *Armed Forces and Society* 27 (1). 131–148.

Selassie, Bereket Habte (1980) *Conflict and Intervention in the Horn of Africa*. New York: Monthly Review Press.

Shah, Mehtab Ali (1997) *The Foreign Policy of Pakistan: Ethnic Impacts on Diplomacy*. London: I. B. Taurus.

Simmel, Georg (1955) The Web of Group Affiliations. *Conflict and the Web of Group Affiliations*. New York: The Free Press. 128–195.

Simon, Sheldon (1967) The Kashmir Dispute in Sino-Soviet Perspective. *Asia Survey* 7 (3). 176–187.

Singer, J. David, and Melvin Small. Correlates of War Project: International and Civil War Data, 1816–1992. Ann Arbor, MI: J. David Singer and Melvin Small [producers], 1993. Ann Arbor, MI: Inter-university Consortium for Political and Social Research [distributor], 1994.

Smith, Anthony (2001) *Nationalism*. Cambridge: Polity Press.

——— (1991) *National Identity*. London: Penguin.

Smith, Michael L. (1973) *Ionian Vision; Greece in Asia Minor, 1919–1922*. New York: St. Martin's Press.

S-PLUS Version 6.2. Insightful Corp., Seattle, WA.

StataCorp (2001) Statistical Software: Release 7.0. College Station, TX: Stata Corporation.

Stephens, Robert (1966) *Cyprus: A Place of Arms*. New York: Praeger.

Syed, Anwar (1974) *China and Pakistan: Diplomacy of an Entente Cordiale*. Amherst, MA: University of Massachusetts.

Tilly, Charles (1975) *The Formation of National States in Western Europe*. Princeton: Princeton University Press.

Tilly, Virginia (1997) Untangling Language about Ethnicity. *Ethnic and Racial Studies* 20 (30). 497–522.

Triandafyllidou, Anna and Anna Paraskevopoulou (2002) When is the Greek Nation? The Role of Enemies and Minorities. *Geopolitics* 7 (2). 75–98.

Tsoucalas, Constantine (1969). *The Greek Tragedy*. Harmondsworth, UK: Penguin Publications.

Turton, E. R. (1972) Somali Resistance to Colonial Rule and the Development of Somali Political Activity in Kenya 1893–1960. *The Journal of African History* 13 (1). 119–143.

Vanhanen, Tatu (1999) Domestic Ethnic Conflict and Ethnic Nepotism. *Journal of Peace Research* 36: 55–73. Retrieved July 2001 from the online dataset at www.prio.no\jpr\main.htm.

Varshney, Ashutosh (2001) Ethnic Conflict and Civil Society: India and Beyond. *World Politics* 53. 362–398.

——— (1991) India, Pakistan, and Kashmir: Antinomies of Nationalism. *Asian Survey* 31 (11). 997–1019.

Vasquez, John (1993) *The War Puzzle*. New York: Cambridge University Press.

Veremis, Thanos (2003) "1922: Political Continuations and Realignments in the Greek State." In *Crossing the Aegean: An Appraisal of the 1923 Compulsory Population Exchange Between Greece and Turkey*, edited by Renee Hirschon. New York: Berghahn Books.
Walt, Stephen (1987) *The Origin of Alliances*. Cornell: Cornell University Press.
Walter, Barbara (2002) *Committing to Peace: The Successful Settlement of Civil Wars*. Princeton: Princeton University Press.
Waltz, Kenneth (1979) *A Theory of International Politics*. Reading, MA: Addison-Wesley Publishing.
Weber, Max (1968) *Max Weber, Economy and Society: An Outline of Interpretive Sociology*. New York: Bedminster Press.
Wendt, Alexander (1999) *A Social Theory of International Politics*. Cambridge: Cambridge University Press.
Widmalm, Sten (1997) The Rise and Fall of Democracy in Jammu and Kashmir. *Asian Survey* 37 (11). 1005–1030.
Woodhouse, C. M. (1986) Modern Greece: A Short History. London: Faber and Faber.
Woodward, Peter (1996) *The Horn of Africa: State Politics and International Relations*. London: Tauris Academic Studies.
Woodwell, Douglas (2005) The "Troubles" of Northern Ireland: Civil Conflict in an Economically Well-Developed State. In *Understanding Civil War: Evidence and Analysis (Volume 2)*, edited by Paul Collier and Nicholas Sambanis, Eds. 2005. Washington: The World Bank. 161–190.
——— (2004) Unwelcome Neighbors: Shared Ethnicity and International Conflict During the Cold War. *International Studies Quarterly* 48 (1). 197–223.
Zorn, Christopher (2001) Generalized Estimating Equation Models for Correlated Data. *American Journal of Political Science* 45. 470–490.

INDEX

Please note that page numbers followed by the letter "f" are located in a Figure; "t" are located in a Table; and "n" are located in a Note.

Abdullah, Sheikh Mohammed, 136, 150, 154
affective motivations in foreign policy, 41–5
Afghanistan
   irredentist dispute with Pakistan, 21
   recent disputes with other Central Asian States, 195
   Soviet intervention, 153
African demographics, 99
Aksai Chin, 142
Armenia, 30, 197
Arusha Memorandum of Understanding, 107, 108
Asia Minor "catastrophe" (1920s ethnic cleansing of Greeks), 162–3, 166
Ataturk, Kemal, 162
audience costs, 45, 46, 52, 59, 67, 76, 119, 127, 204n
Awami League, 138, 152
Azad Kashmir, 135, 136, 138
Azerbaijan, 30, 197

Balkan Entente, 167
Balkan Wars, 161–2, 164, 179
Bangladeshi secession, *see* Indo-Pakistani War of 1971
Barre, Siad, 107, 108, 109, 110, 114, 115, 116, 117, 118, 120, 123, 124, 125, 126, 149, 192, 193
Bhutto, Benazir, 151, 154, 155
Bhutto, Zulfikar Ali, 137, 139, 140, 151, 152, 153, 156

Cardali, 210n
Central Asia, prospects for irredentism, 195–6
Chile, and economic self-determination, 21
China-Pakistan "entente", 144, 145
Christianity in Ethiopia, 111
civic nationalism, 16, 20
classification tree, 71, 72t, 87, 94f, 206n, 207n
collective action, 6, 15, 17, 18, 23, 47, 77, 202n
Constantine I, 162, 163, 164, 165, 180
constructivism, 13, 14–15, 27, 31–2, 193–4, 195, 202n
contending government nationalism, 4, 6, 9, 23, 24, 29, 29t, 31, 34, 35, 36, 37, 38, 39, 58, 60, 61, 62t, 63, 65, 74t, 75, 78, 201n, 203n, 210n
   definition, 2–3, 36–7
   Greece and Cyprus, 157, 171, 175, 178, 187, 189
   relation to demographics, 2t
Convention Concerning the Exchange of Greek and Turkish Populations, 167
Copenhagen Conference (2002), 177
Cyprus, 165, 177–86, 191, 192, 199–200

Davos negotiations (Greece-Turkey), 176
Dayton Accords, 198
democratic peace theory, 37, 38, 60, 76, 82, 189, 193, 194, 210n. *See also* liberalism.
Democratic Republic of the Congo, 195, 207n

Denktash, Rauf, 174
diaspora discontent, 42, 43, 44, 50, 51, 60, 67, 68, 71, 72t, 73, 74t, 76, 77, 79, 80, 84, 87, 88, 94f, 95, 96t, 120, 127, 137, 146, 150–1, 158, 181, 182, 193
diaspora uprising, see ethno-national rebellion
Direct Action Day, 133
diversionary theory, 61, 68, 84
Djibouti, see French Somalia

"Eastern" nationalism, see ethnic nationalism
Ecevit, Bulent, 173, 180, 185
economically important resources (and interstate disputes), 61, 83–4, 122–3, 147
economic openness, 61
Egal, Ibrahim, 107, 108, 110, 114, 117, 118, 123, 125
encapsulation theory, 68, 84, 207n
Enlai, Zhou, 142, 144
enosis, 168, 169, 170, 172, 173, 175, 181, 185
EOKA, 170
EOKA B, 173, 174
Eritrea, 111, 112
Ethiopian-Kenyan mutual defense pact, 117–8
ethnic identity, 13–16, 17, 20, 23
ethnic nationalism, 15, 16, 20, 87
Ethniki Etairia, 161 see National Society
ethno-national rebellion, 4, 6, 30, 33, 34, 35, 36, 42–5, 48, 49, 50, 51, 52, 59, 60, 61, 62t, 63, 64, 64t, 65t, 66t, 67, 68t, 69t, 71, 72t, 74t, 75t, 76, 77t, 78, 79, 82, 95, 96, 188, 189, 190, 191, 197, 203n, 205n, 206n
  of Greeks in the Ottoman Empire, 159, 160, 161, 164, 184
  of Muslims in Kashmir, 130, 134, 137, 139, 140, 151, 154, 155
  of Somali groups, 104, 104t, 105, 113t, 114, 116, 117, 119, 120, 124, 126, 127, 128
European Union, Turkish entry, 157, 177, 181

fatal militarized interstate dispute (FATAL), defined, 56

feasibility of military aggression, defined, 47–8
First World War, 30, 161, 162, 163, 164, 165, 179, 181, 182, 183, 184, 185, 192–3
foreign policy formulation model,
  defined, 5, 6, 42f
  econometric results, 67, 68t
French Somalia, 102, 108, 208n

Gandhi, Indira, 138, 139, 154
Gandhi, Mahatma, 131
Gandhi, Rajiv, 143
general estimating equation (GEE), 85–6, 207n
George, Lloyd, 163, 164
Golan Heights, 22
governmental disputes (GOVMID), 37, 38, 56, 62, 63, 63t, 78, 189. *See also* "regime change".
Great Idea, 159, 160, 163, 165, 168, 190
Greek-Turkish Political Committee, 176
Greek War of Independence, 159

hair of the Prophet Mohammed, 150
hill tribes of Burma and Thailand, 58
"Hobbesian" type disputes, 32, 36
homeland state, definition of, 2, 201n
"hot pursuits", 59
Hussein, Abdirizaj Haji, 106, 107
Hussein, Saddam, 197
Hyderabad, 131, 134

"indeterminacy" of foreign policy, 4, 27, 27t, 29, 30, 33, 34, 38, 41, 42, 104n, 108, 110, 187, 188, 190
Indo-Pakistani War of 1947, 134–5, 137
Indo-Pakistani War of 1965, 44, 137, 141, 145, 146, 147, 148, 151, 153, 156, 180, 192, 199
Indo-Pakistani War of 1971, 139, 145, 147, 152, 190
Inonu, Ismet, 171–2
Inter-Service Intelligence (ISI), 140, 209n
Ioannides, Dimitrious, 173
Iraq, invasion of Kuwait, 34, 197
irredentist-type nationalism, 3, 4, 5t, 6, 7, 9, 19, 22–3, 25, 29–39, 41–53, 55, 58, 59, 60, 62t, 63, 65, 68t, 69, 70, 70t, 71, 73, 74t, 75, 76, 77t, 78, 79, 84, 85, 87, 95, 188, 189, 190, 191, 192,

193, 194, 195, 197, 198, 199, 201n, 203n, 206n, 208n
  definition, 2
  Greece and Turkey, 157–65, 169, 171, 175, 178, 179, 180, 181, 183, 184, 185, 187
  Pakistani claims on Kashmir, 129, 130, 131, 141, 145, 148, 149, 155
  relation to demographics, 2t
  Somalia, 99, 100, 101, 104t, 105, 106, 108, 110, 113t, 116, 117, 119, 120, 121, 124, 125, 128

Janagarh, 131
Jinnah, Mohammed Ali, 131, 133
Joint Committee on Cooperation, 176

Kalat, 209n
Karamanlis, Konstantinos, 175
Kargil Gap conflict, 154–5, 191, 193
Kemal, Mustafa, *see* Kemal Ataturk, 162, 163, 168
Kenyatta, Jomo, 105, 107, 208n
Khan, Ayub, 137, 144, 149, 150, 151, 153, 154
Khan, Liaquat Ali, 148
Khan, Yahya, 138–9, 151, 152
Khmer Rouge, 196
kin state, definition of, 2, 201n
KITEMP, 169
Korean War, 8, 34
Kuwait, invasion by Iraq, 34, 197

League of Nations, 7, 165, 167
Lenin, V.I., 20
liberal international relations theory, 36, 60, 63, 64, 82, 84, 187, 189, 193, 194. *See also* democratic peace theory.
Line of Control, Kashmir, 135, 138, 140, 141

majority-majority, definition of, 1. *See also* contending government nationalism.
Makarios III, Archbishop, 169, 170, 171, 172, 173, 178
McMahon Line, 142
Menelik II, 207n
militarized interstate dispute (MID), defined, 56

military feasibility, 42, 47, 48, 49, 50, 51, 52, 60, 67, 68t, 69, 70t, 71, 72, 73, 74t, 75t, 76, 77t, 78, 79, 81, 82, 88, 95, 96t, 119, 121, 122, 147, 150, 159, 174, 179n, 182, 183, 184, 188, 189, 190, 193, 194,
military influence over foreign policy, 5, 6, 42f, 46, 47, 49, 59, 67, 68t, 69–70, 69t, 71, 72t, 73, 74, 76, 77, 79, 87, 88, 94, 95, 96, 119, 120, 125, 126, 128, 130, 145, 146, 149, 154, 155, 156, 158, 178, 179t, 180, 181, 185, 188, 89, 190, 192, 193, 200
Military League, 161, 178
Milosevic, Slobodan, 198
minority-majority, definition of, 1. *See also* irredentist-type nationalism.
minority-minority nationalism, definition of, 2–3
Mirza, Iskandar, 149
Moi, Daniel Arap, 109, 118
Musharraf, Pervez, 140, 155
Muslim League, 133

Nansen, Fridtjof, 165
nationalism, defined. *See also* national identity.
national identity, 13, 15–20, 23
National Society, 161
NATO, accession of Greece and Turkey, 167
Nehru, Jawaharlal, 131, 135, 136, 142, 149
neorealism, 31. *See also* realism.
normative-demographic model, 5, 5f, 6, 26, 59, 62, 63, 73, 74t, 85, 148, 156, 163, 167, 174, 177, 190, 194, 196
norms, 4, 5, 5t, 6, 16, 18, 19, 20, 22, 24–36, 38, 39, 41, 76, 78, 95, 187, 188, 191, 193, 194, 195, 196, 197, 199, 202n, 203n, 211n
  commonality, 27
  definition, 26
  Greco-Turkish normative conflict, 163–4, 168, 184
  Indian-Pakistani normative conflict, 130–2, 135, 138, 156
  predictive capability, 27–8

norms—*continued*
  Somali normative conflict with neighboring states, 99, 100, 101, 103, 104, 105, 106, 110, 111, 112, 118, 126, 130
  specificity, 27
  Also see reciprocal obligation, norms of.
North Eastern Province (NEP), 102, 106, 107, 109, 110, 114, 118, 119, 122
Northern Frontier District (NFD), *see* North Eastern Province
Northern Ireland, 198, 205n
Northwest Frontier Province (Pakistan), 134

Ocalan, Abdullah, 177
Ogaden region of Ethiopia, 102, 111, 112, 113, 114, 122
Operation Gibraltar, 137
Operation Grand Slam, 137
Organization of African Unity (OAU), 103, 114
Oromo, 118, 208n
Osman, Aden Abdullah, 103, 105
"overthrow-merger", 31

Pakistan, irredentist dispute with Afghanistan, 21
Pakistan-U.S. defense pact (1953), 136
Papadopoulos, Georgios, 173
Papandreou, Georgios, 177
partition of India and Pakistan, 131, 132, 133, 134
Pashtuns, *see* Pathans
Pathans, 134, 209n
plebiscite, status of Kashmir, 132, 135, 136, 137, 141, 144, 148, 150
policy disputes (POLMID), 37, 56, 62t, 63, 64, 65, 74t, 76, 78

Rann of Kutch, 137, 147
rational-choice approaches to ethnicity, 15
realism, 31, 32, 36, 47–8, 60, 63, 82, 83, 141, 142, 144, 183, 187, 188, 193, 194
reciprocal obligation, norms of, 18, 23, 32, 43, 202n

"regime change", 3, 32, 34, 37, 38, 56, 63, 78, 117, 189. *See also* governmental disputes.
Russo-Turkish War, 160, 164, 184, 191

Sadat, Anwar, 200
Sampson, Nicos, 173
"secessionist-merger", 31
Second World War, 103, 133, 167
secular nationalism, 132
"seismic détente", 157
Selassie, Haile, 111, 116, 208n
selectorate model, 45–6, 204n
self-determination, 19–22
Sharif, Nawaz, 155
Shermarke, Abdul Rashid Ali, 103, 107
shifta rebellion, 106, 127
Shuria, Omar, 107
Simla Accord (1971), 139, 141, 152, 209n
Simla Conference (1914), 142
Sino-Indian War (1962), 142, 143, 144, 150, 153
Somali-Ethiopian War (1977–78), 8t, 109, 114–15, 120, 121, 123–4, 125, 128, 180, 192, 207n
Somalia Salvation Democratic Front, 115
Somaliland, 102, 113
Somali National Movement, 115–16
Somali Youth Club, *see* Somali Youth League
Somali Youth League, 102
Spanish Civil War, 17
strategically important territory, 37, 61, 68t, 69t, 83–4, 96t, 122, 142, 147, 177

Tashkent Declaration, 138–9, 151, 152
Tenneco Oil Company, 122–3
territorial disputes (TERRMID), 36–7, 38, 56, 63, 64, 65, 74t, 75, 78
Thailand, Muslim unrest in south, 200
Thirty Days' War, 161, 164, 183, 184
trade, role in mitigating conflict, 60, 61, 62t, 63, 64t, 68, 68t, 69t, 70, 70t, 77t, 82t, 84, 207a
TRAO, 210n
Treaty of Constantinople (1832), 159

Treaty of Friendship and Cooperation (Somali-U.S.S.R., 1971), 115
Treaty of Friendship, Neutrality, Conciliation, and Arbitration (1930), 167
Treaty of Guarantee, 170, 173
Treaty of Lausanne, 163, 165, 168, 169
Treaty of Peace, Friendship, and Cooperation (India-U.S.S.R., 1971), 139
Treaty of Sevres, 162, 163, 165
Turkish Resistance Organization (TMT), 170

United Liberation Front of Western Somalia, 114
U Thant, 113
UN Charter, articles dealing with self-determination, 20
UN Commission on India and Pakistan, 136
UN Covenant on Civil and Political Rights, 21
UN Covenant on Human Rights, 21
UNFICYP, 171

Venizelos, Eleftherious, 161, 162, 163, 164, 165, 167, 176, 178, 179, 179t, 180, 181, 185, 192–3
Vietnam War, 8t, 23, 34
Vietnamese invasion of Cambodia, 196

"War scare" of 1951, 148
"Western" nationalism, *see* civic nationalism
Western Somali Liberation Front (WSLF), 114, 116, 124
Wilson, Woodrow, 20
World War I, *see* First World War
World War II, *see* Second World War

Young Turks, 162

Zia ul-Haq, Muhammed, 140, 146, 152–5
Zurich-London agreements (1959), 170–1, 172, 174, 198, 210n